Ecocities:
Building Cities in Balance with Nature

Also by Richard Register:

Another Beginning

Ecocity Berkeley: Building Cities for a Healthy Future

Village Wisdom/Future Cities (Editor)

ECOCITIES

BUILDING CITIES IN BALANCE WITH NATURE

Richard Register

Illustrated by the Author

BERKELEY HILLS BOOKS
BERKELEY, CALIFORNIA

Published by
Berkeley Hills Books
P. O. Box 9877
Berkeley, California 94709
www.berkeleyhills.com
(888) 848-7303

Comments on this book may also be addressed to: jpstroh@berkeleyhills.com

Cover design by Elysium, San Francisco.
Drawings on pages 70, 113 and 250 from *Ecocity Berkeley: Building Cities for a Healthy Future* by Richard Register. Copyright 1987. Published by NORTH ATLANTIC BOOKS. Reprinted by permission of the Publisher.

Manufactured in the United States of America.
Distributed by Publishers Group West.
ISBN: 1-893163-37-7

Library of Congress Cataloging-in-Publication Data

(Available from the Publisher)

To Nancy and the ten years of shared
adventures while writing this book.

Ecocities Become Us

It's a secret now, but it can't be for long.
We are of three bodies:
One created for us, given at birth;
One created by us, labored through life;
One created with us, eternity's rebirth.
One the individual, of flesh, blood and soul;
One the community, of wood, stone and fire;
One the universe of stuff, time and changing.
This is who we are, where we are from, are, and going.
The secret is out. We are building ourselves.
We are the universe: painful, joyous work unfolding.

Contents

Acknowledgements

Without the financial and material assistance of the following people this book either would not have been completed or would have taken much longer: Charlotte Rieger, Ron Chilcote and the Foundation for Sustainability and Innovation, Marci Riseman, Walt Christiansen, Ross Jackson, Hamish Stewart and the Gaia Trust, Jerry Mander, Doug Tompkins, the Foundation for Deep Ecology, Patrick Kennedy, Sylvia McLaughlin, Dianna Barbari, Bonnie Hughes, Pat and Graeme Welch and Mal Warwick. For a big and ever-so-thorough job of editing — indispensable when an artist/activist writes a book that's not necessarily natural to his inclinations and skills — thanks to Barbara Metzger. Thanks, also, to Kirstin Miller for many good suggestions and observations.

For the moral support, encouragement, and clear reflection over the years on ideas and issues that make up so much of this book, I must give considerable credit to Nancy Lieblich, Bill Mastin, Susan Felter, Sylvia McLaughlin, Tim Hansen, Dianne Ayres, Arthur Monroe, Huey Johnson, Karl Linn and Fritjof Capra. For particularly important help with the Ecocity Builders, Urban Ecology and Arcology Circle projects and conferences that provided grist for this book's mill, my great appreciation to Russ Adams, Ray Bruman, Jim Caid, Paul Downton, Cherie Hoyle, Joan Bokaer, Serigne Mbaye Diene, Rusong Wang, Brady Peeks, Dixie LaGrande, Linda Levitsky, Mark Baldridge, Roger Pritchard, Sue Labouvie, Max Heim, Lisa Hasselbrock, Paul Revier and Michael Warburton. My ecocity debate team members were mainly Ken Schneider, Thomas Berry, Brian Swimme, E. F. Schumacher, Hazel Henderson, Jerry Brown, Ernest Callenbach, Walt Anderson, David Suzuki, Elyce Judith, Carole Schemmerling, Gary Mason, Lynne Elizabeth, Joseph Epes Brown, and, at a more remote distance for crucial ideas and inspiration, Jane Jacobs, Ian McHarg and E. O. Wilson. I am indebted — for the ecocity is the city to make peace on Earth and with Earth — to Mohandas Gandhi, whose work is at the foundation of my own. Special thanks to Paolo Soleri for his pivotal insights, his willingness to share them with me, and his courage to build. And finally — the key link in getting any book out from the struggling writer's brain to the world at large — thanks so much to my publisher, John Strohmeier, and his fine company, Berkeley Hills Books.

Foreword

By Hazel Henderson

As Richard Register says, "The quality of life depends largely on how we build our cities. The higher the density and diversity of a city, the less dependent on motorized transport, and the less resources it requires, the less the impact it has on nature."

This book is a treasure trove of such insights summarizing the role of cities in human evolution. Register reminds us that our cities are living systems that we shape, and which then shape us, our lives, and even our evolutionary possibilities. As someone who has pondered the role of cities, as an environmentalist and a futurist, I must say that *Ecocities* is the most satisfying and comprehensive new volume on the subject. Register embraces every aspect of cities and the urban experience — advocating and showcasing the best visions, concepts, designs and working solutions from all over the world.

As I read this deeply engrossing book, I thought of my childhood. I grew up in the seaside town of Clevedon, on the Bristol Channel in the west of England, in the 1940s. Nestled into limestone cliffs, most of its houses and public buildings were constructed of this same gray stone. Like most European towns, Clevedon was compact, with a density that allowed its some 4,000 inhabitants to walk and bicycle everywhere. There were few cars, plentiful and frequent bus services, and a rail line connecting Clevedon to Bristol, the nearest city, fifteen miles away. The air was clean because not only were cars unnecessary, but also gasoline was rationed during World War II. Food was also rationed, so most people grew vegetables and kept hens in their gardens or on their "victory plots."

We walked or cycled to the pier and bought the day's fresh catch from the regular fishers. We also cycled to nearby farms on the town's edge to buy our milk, butter and produce. The High Street shops were stocked with local meats, including wild rabbit — a delicacy — and a wide array of local, seasonal fruits and vegetables. People shopped every day because most had no refrigerators. Like most children, we walked to our schools and ran errands for our parents and helped with the chores and gardening. My biggest thrills were going down into the basement room where we grew our mushrooms, marveling at how they appeared almost magically, and collecting the still-warm eggs from under the sitting hens. My mother grew our food without pesticides and volunteered at the local "cottage hospital" and its well-baby clinic. My three siblings and I were born at home with a midwife in attendance. I also experienced the air raids and bombs, the loss of friends, seeing the night skies ablaze as the city of Bristol was bombarded. Yet, my overall experience of life in Clevedon was richly tactile, with close relationships and a cohesive community.

It is hard to believe that all this was only fifty years ago. I believe, along with many other systems thinkers like Richard Register, that industrial societies are in a classic "overshoot." We have overshot the optimum in cars, suburbs, sprawl and its attendant patterns of energy waste, pollution and environmental destruction. We have overshot the mark in losing community and identity among thousands of acres of huge tract homes in former family farms — with even more demand for more roads, concrete, parking lots and strip malls.

Fast-forward to the 1960s. I found myself living in a high-rise apartment in midtown Manhattan. I did not see, but rather studied these overshoots already in progress, hollowing out the city's residential boroughs and businesses. New York is one of the most complex and challenging cities in the world. I was excited by the constant activity, the contrasts. The density allowed one to live car-less, but the acres of squalid housing, the noise and the polluted air appalled me. My response was civic engagement and environmental activism in co-founding Citizens for Clean Air in 1964. This accelerated my education and led me to the works of Lewis Mumford, Buckminster Fuller, Ian McHarg and Jane Jacobs, and to my association with E. F. Schumacher, who wrote the Foreword to my first book, *Creating Alternative Futures*. I became associated with Fritjof Capra in contributing to his book, *The Turning Point*, my ideas about how faulty economics was causing many of these "overshoots" now leading to global climate change. I joined the Lindisfarne Fellowship founded by meta-historian William Irwin Thompson, together with Paul Hawken, Amory and Hunter Lovins, Stewart Brand, Lynn Margolis, James Lovelock and John and Nancy Todd.

Many years later, I visited Paulo Soleri's Arcosanti, which is described in *Ecocities*. I absorbed Soleri's philosophy and experienced his vision of ecologies as an expression of humanity evolving consciously toward Pierre Teilhard de Chardin's "noosphere." Yet, as Register points out, we humans are slow learners. Soleri's Arcosanti, a brave and important experiment in urban design costing a fraction of the price of an aircraft carrier, has never received any funding from business, government or foundations — and survives by selling its cast bronze bells and wind chimes.

I ponder that we humans have spent 98 percent of our collective history together as gatherer-hunters in roving bands. Yet we now comprise a six billion-person human family, living largely in huge mega-cities like Sao Paulo, Mexico City, Shanghai and Tokyo, with very little experience of managing our affairs at such a scale. We are consuming some 40 percent of the entire planet's primary biomass production. This is accelerating the rate of extinction of our fellow species on which we are dependent, as we have migrated to the ends of this Earth.

No one has been tracking all these dilemmas as they relate to cities better than Richard Register. *Ecocities* recognizes all these dilemmas and opportunities and the new realities of the twenty-first century, from rising atmospheric carbon dioxide, shrinking water tables, loss of agricultural land to sprawl — and the energy-wasting dead end of the automobile/ highway/fossil-fueled industrial complex. Yet signs of the transition to sustainable communities and cities, which we must make if we humans are to survive, are richly-described and brilliantly advocated. I will enjoy and learn from this passionate book for years to come.

St. Augustine, Florida
August 2001

Introduction

Cities are by far the largest creations of humanity. Designing, building and operating them have the greatest destructive impact on nature of any human activity. As we construct them today, cities also do little for social justice, not to mention for the grace and subtlety of human intercourse. Yet our built communities, from village and town to city and megalopolis, also shelter and launch many of our most creative collaborations and cultural adventures and artifacts. As we build automobile/sprawl infrastructures, we create a radically different social and ecological reality than if we build closely-knit communities for pedestrians. Contrast American sprawl with European traditional cities. We will go way beyond that comparison soon enough — far enough, in fact, to demonstrate that cities can actually build soils, cultivate biodiversity, restore lands and waters, and make a net gain for the ecological health of the Earth.

Ecocities proposes a fundamentally new approach to building and living in cities, towns and villages, an approach based on solid principles from deep history and an honest assessment of a troubled future. Our prescription will be replete with examples of wonderful architecture, transit solutions and new approaches to public and natural open spaces. We'll explore dozens of practical tools for healthy urban transformation, and invent a few.

Given that cities are so large, damaging and yet potentially beneficial, you'd think we would have long ago devised the science, study, discipline and art of ecologically-healthy city building. Why aren't people trying to systematically think through and develop it? Well, they are — it's you and I right here in these pages. Welcome to the new frontier in home building.

Philip Shabekoff, long time environmental writer for the *New York Times*, interviewed hundreds of environmentalists and one of their most common themes, he reports,[1] was this: How is it that we can win so many battles, yet regarding the really big things, we are losing the war? Species extinctions, global warming, climate change, soil loss, the collapse of ocean ecologies, and on and on — all are getting worse every day.

It's no mystery to me. We've never engaged the biggest battles. We try to make cars better rather than to greatly reduce their numbers. We try to slow sprawling development rather than to reverse its growth and shrink its footprint. We keep making freeways wider and longer, dreaming of "intelligent highways," rather than removing lanes and replacing them with rails, small country roads and bicycle paths. We continue to provide virtually every subsidy and support policy that oil companies want. It's no wonder that we're not winning the war. The objective of this book is to lay out an evolving strategy that faces the big problems head on and gives us at least *a chance* of winning.

OF CARS AND DINOSAURS

I'll start my story in the age of dinosaurs when our ancestors, the first mammals, were darting about between thundering footfalls trying to avoid the fangs and claws of those gigantic monsters, the thought of which takes our breath away even at the safe distance of 65 million years. Those furry, warm-blooded creatures managed to survive by staying just below the size of the smallest dinosaur *hors d'oeuvre,* and there they waited, frozen for millions of years in their diminutive forms. Then, in an instant — wham! — the world was slammed into another reality, and a new stage of evolution burst forth in a swirl of asteroid or comet dust. Mammals were given the opportunity to grow, diversify, learn, build, think and think collectively, here on the Sun's third planet. The oppressor was gone and freedom burst upon the evolution of consciousness like a sunrise. Cars are the dinosaurs of our time. They are destroying the reasonable and happy structure of cities, towns and villages. Once communities have been shaped for cars they remain dependent upon them. Sprawled communities can't function without their speed. Their addiction is a structural addiction, built into the physical structure of the city. Cars are preventing the next step in our now-cultural evolution, the step in which we build as if we knew we were evolving.

For the past thirty-five years I have been an activist, trying to persuade people to add some sane features to their houses, neighborhoods and cities, to change larger policies, and adopt tools and techniques for making cities more ecologically-healthy. It has been so difficult that I sometimes think it will take another truly colossal disaster to wake us up. And I think that disaster is likely to be the same one that banished the dinosaurs: climate change. This time the cause won't be a wandering asteroid with instant concussion and fire followed by a dark "nuclear winter." This time it's going to be the human-created heating of the planet. The evolutionary leap 65 million years ago was the bursting forth of the mammals. The next could be humanity collectively learning how to build a healthy future. Inescapably, that means building ecologically-healthy cities — ecocities. The difference between doing it now and doing it later is the difference between saving most of what's left of biodiversity — that is, life on Earth and our collective souls — and losing both, leaving to our descendants a deeply impoverished world.

I see this book as a kind of overview of something that exists, so far, only in small pieces scattered here and there around the world, throughout history, and in the imaginations of creative thinkers. Some people, probably numbering in the hundreds now, are becoming very sophisticated about the principles of ecocity building, and I want you to meet them and see what they've been doing. Many more people are building new systems that can fit elegantly into the ecocity, though they may not yet be aware of the potential of that larger context, and I want to suggest how we might tap that potential.

We'll start off by looking briefly at cities in their most basic form, with some attention to the rich detail that can confound and contribute to a healthy relationship with nature. Then we'll consider where the city fits into the largest of all contexts, the evolution of matter, life and consciousness in the universe. Next we will look at the city in nature and in history, and finally the city as it seems to be functioning and malfunctioning right now. After that we will explore direct approaches to building ecocities, beginning with basic principles and going on to examine dozens of ideas and projects that have great promise for the task. Throughout, doggedly adhering to the old saw that a picture is worth a thousand words, I'll make sure that you have enough imagery before you that you can't possibly digest it in one sitting. I want you to come away from the experience saying, "Wow, can we really build something like that?" or "I hadn't thought of that before!" or "That's a place I could enjoy living in!" or "Where did all that life come swarming in from? Does life just appear when you build to make room for it?" That it does.

1

As We Build So Shall We Live

As we build so shall we live. The city, town or village — this arrangement of buildings, streets, vehicles and planned landscapes that serves as home — organizes our resources and technologies, and shapes our forms of expression. It is the key to the future healthy evolution of our species and will determine the fate of countless other species as well. The city, in fact, is the cornerstone of the civilization that currently embraces the entire planet. Insofar as our civilization has gone awry, especially in regard to its impact on the environment, a very large share of the problem can be traced to its physical foundations. Considering the crisis state of life systems on Earth — the collapse of whole habitats and the increasing rates of extinction of species — it follows then that cities need to be radically reshaped. Cities need to be rebuilt from their roots in the soil, from their concrete and steel foundations on up. They need to be reorganized and rebuilt upon ecological principles.

Most people believe instead that fine-tuning the same old civilization will be enough, that there is no real need for fundamental change in the way we build and live. But simply failing to notice the crisis in the built environment won't make it go away. Only rebuilding will. Building the ecocity will create a new cultural and economic life in which we can tackle the problems of healthy evolution rather than fighting a rear-guard action aimed at repairing damage. While it probably won't rid the world of greed, ethnocentrism, and violence, building a nonviolent city that respects other life forms and celebrates human creativity and diversity is consistent with solving those problems.

What we build creates possibilities for, and limits on, the way we live. What we build teaches those who live in the city, town and village about our values and concerns. It says, "This is the way it should be," or at least, "This is the best we could do." The edifice edifies. Children in today's typical car-dominated cities learn that cars are valued so highly that it is worth risking human life and enduring high costs and serious pollution to make way for them. They also learn that people don't care much for public life or nature. In Berkeley, California, where I live, there are no public plazas or pedestrian streets, though you can be sure there are plenty of parking lots taking up hundreds of acres and cars on every road. Creeks are buried for miles, and the ridge lines from which we could once enjoy the sunset and a view of San Francisco Bay are increasingly filled with private houses that banish public access. In ways like this each city tends to reproduce in its children the values embodied in its form and expressed in its function.

More to the point, if our cities are built for cars, one sixth of us will find jobs in the automobile industry and its support systems, and another sixth will be building and fixing the buildings and infrastructure that go along with the layout automobiles require. But if we build the ecocity, larger numbers of people will find jobs involving its building and operation. By shifting steadily toward an ecocity infrastructure we could soon train people to be streetcar and bicycle builders and mechanics, organic gardeners, restorationists, naturalists, "green" designers and builders and pedal-powered delivery people, all with a minimal impact on nature. As we build, so shall we live.

Even more, as we live so shall we become. And not only in attitudes, skills and habits, but also, eventually, in physical form. As Americans spend more and more time sitting motionless before television and computer screens and in ever fatter SUVs, they are becoming increasingly overweight and unhealthy. Another way of looking at this is to see that we build environments that help build us. We indirectly self-design in a very significant way, turning ourselves into a species that reinforces its own design by building its environment in particular ways. In ecology and evolution biology, we have learned that species shape one another physi-

Small town for about 200 people on a coastal bay and mouth of a creek with fishing, vineyards and sustainable forestry as main economy.

cally and behaviorally. Pollinating insects and birds adjusted their proboscises and beaks to their task, and flowers shaped themselves to cooperate with them, feeding themselves while accomplishing the work of pollination efficiently. Some bird's nests have evolved over thousands of years, affecting the bird's behavior and even body shape. All creatures respond to and change their habitats, climate and even atmospheric and soil chemistry, altering them over the years. If we want to live an ecologically-healthy and responsible life we need to build so that we can do so.

WHAT WE SEEM TO BE BUILDING

Since 1991 I have traveled to every continent but Antarctica talking about ecocities. I am one of several dozen people on this loosely-linked lecture circuit who are thinking about redesigning and building whole cities on ecological principles. My experience suggests that a meaningful and growing number of people around the world is beginning to take a strong interest in urban form and dysfunction, and in the ecologically-healthy alternatives that ecocities offer. Cities such as Vancouver, British Colum-

21

bia; Portland, Oregon; Curitiba, Brazil, and Waitakere, New Zealand are making ecological progress on a number of fronts, and the international ecovillage movement is steadily growing. We are seeing good works, and that is significant and heartening. But society is still moving overwhelmingly in the opposite direction.

For more than twenty-five years, for example, I've been trying to help reshape the city of Berkeley. With others I've co-founded two non-profit organizations — Urban Ecology, in 1975, and Ecocity Builders, in 1992 — and these groups have managed to open portions of creeks that had been buried for decades, to redesign a street as our "Slow Street," to establish a bus line, to write an ordinance making attached solar greenhouses legal in front yards, to build a few of these greenhouses, to plant and harvest street fruit trees, to develop energy-saving ordinances, to delay freeway construction, to tear up parking lots to plant gardens and urban orchards, and to affect the course of particular development projects by pointing out their impacts on the city's ecological health. These and other projects have not only created physical features and functions and established laws, but also stimulated discussion of these issues as well.

It has gradually become clear, however, that few people notice. New single-story buildings are being built in Berkeley's downtown, where taller buildings would place transit and passengers in mutually supportive proximity. Transit service itself is being cut and fares are rising. The neighborhood around one of the major transit stations has been rezoned for reduced development, when a higher-density "transit village" would have helped housing, transit, energy conservation, pollution abatement and the economy. Large freeway-oriented projects and big parking lots have been built as an outcome of a planning process with considerable public support and input — many people wanted it that way. These projects and parking lots have required the widening of Interstate-80 from eight to ten crowded and inadequate lanes. The University of California has built several very large buildings and parking lots in that period with little regard to their surrounding urban and natural environment.

At the national level, despite ever more intense verbal attacks on sprawl, the big news going into the third millennium is bigger sport utility vehicles and capitulations to more highways, parking spaces, bridges and other car infrastructure. For example, in 1960 one-third of the citizens of the United States lived in cities, one-third in suburbs, and one-

City for 200,000 with three high-density centers linked by light rail and all other transportation by foot and bicycle. Cars, trucks and wagons travel to the country, trains to other cities.

third in rural locations. By 1990 well over half lived in suburbs. Between 1970 and 1990 the population of California increased approximately 40 percent while the land area of cities and suburbs went up 100 percent. Between those years the country witnessed what has sometimes been called "the second suburbanization of America," in which, instead of commuting daily from suburb to city center, tens of millions of people began traveling from suburban house to suburban workplace. It's not uncommon for spouses to work thirty to sixty miles apart while their children attend school at the third corner of a geographical triangle encompassing hundreds of square miles.

Since 1970 giant suburban developments have popped up on a scale and in numbers barely imaginable before. Industrial and "back office" business parks have appeared on farm, range, forest and filled marsh lands miles from any other development. These office and commercial zones are surrounded by acres of land converted to dead-level asphalt and concrete slabs, sweltering in the summer, pouring car-contaminated waters into the creeks, rivers and bays when it rains, and draining oily, salty, rubber dust and sooty snow melt in winter. Privately-owned malls, accessible only by car, have largely replaced town and neighborhood centers, shifting social spaces from public to private control. New communities of hundreds, even thousands of families are hiding behind walls and guard posts, abandoning the inner cities and physically distancing themselves from social accountability. They are doing this for the sake of a security based on financial credit and the physical isolation created by cars, asphalt, gasoline and concrete block walls. Only expected guests and the electromagnetic waves and wires of radio, television, computers and telephones dare enter.

In 1972, before the Oil Embargo and the subsequent energy crisis, cars consumed on the average of about 30 percent more energy per mile than they did fifteen years later. About a third of the United States' oil was coming from the Middle East. By 1992, after a new wave of suburbanization, the United States was getting approximately 60 percent from the Middle East. The less fuel it takes to drive about and the cheaper per mile, the farther people are willing to drive. The better the gas mileage, the more the suburbs sprawl out over vast landscapes, the more demand there is for cars and freeways, and the more cars are needed to service the expanding suburbia. Ultimately and ironically, the more gasoline is needed. Thus the energy-efficient car helps create the energy-inefficient city. The car is part of a whole system of complex, necessarily interconnecting parts existing in an interdependent relationship with the total environment it helps create.

The bigger picture — represented by total commuting time for large populations, world use of fossil fuels, ocean tanker oil spills, war for oil in the Middle East, waste of investment capital in building infrastructure that will go on damaging the world for many decades, and so on — is far from encouraging. China started closing Beijing's streets to bicycles to make way for cars in 1998, and it is currently engaged in a massive highway-building program. It plans enormous shifts of population from rural areas and farming to cities and manufacturing and business, and shifts from rail, bicycle and pedestrian cities to cities for motor vehicles on rubber tires — a colossal transformation in the wrong direction. In Brazil, Turkey, India, Africa and Australia, large highway projects are being built as they emulate America's destructive example. People in these places say quite directly and, from their point of view completely reasonably, "You Americans have cars. Who are you to say we shouldn't? Now it's our turn."

GETTING DOWN TO BASICS

To move forward from this point it is helpful to look at the whole system we are part of rather than one small part at a time. Theologian Thomas Berry gets us off on the right track.

> Unaware of what we have done or its order of magnitude, we seek to remedy the situation by altering our ways of acting on some minor scale, by recycling, by diminishing our use of energy, by limiting our use of automobiles, by fewer development projects. The difficulty is that we do these things, not primarily to cease our plundering of the Earth in its basic resources, but to make possible continuation of our plundering industrial life patterns by mitigating the consequences. We mistake the order of magnitude of what we are dealing with. Our problems are primarily problems of macrophase biology, the integral functioning of the entire complex of biosystems of the planet.[2]

The complex biosystem that Berry speaks of is also known as the biosphere. It is our home that we are wrecking with our "plundering industrial life patterns," and the major engine of our civilization's short-sighted exploitation and destruction is the modern city with its flood of traffic, thirst for fuels and vast networks of concrete and asphalt. The car/sprawl/freeway/oil complex reproduces more of itself — a peculiar kind of economic "vitality" — while it paves agricultural and natural land, kills a half million people outright in accidents every year, injures more than 10 million, and is completely destroying a reserve of complex chemicals that took 150 million years to create — the so-called fossil fuels. It also consumes enormous quantities of steel and energy. In a 1999 television ad the Ford Motor Company asserted that it uses enough steel to build 700 Eiffel Towers every year. Seven hundred Eiffel Towers of steel racing about the countryside powered by flame, paving the earth, and transforming the atmosphere! And that's only one of a dozen major automobile manufacturers.

We have built 500 million cars worldwide and transform several million acres of land every year from agriculture, nature and more pedestrian-oriented traditional towns to sprawl. The car/sprawl/freeway/oil complex is destroying habitat, and directly and indirectly destroying animals and plants. Repetitive, small, car-dependent buildings scattered over vast areas, often made of wood from shrinking forests, not only require enormous quantities of gasoline to maintain, but share walls with no one and lose their energy of heating or cooling to the surrounding air after a single use. Thus scattered, small-building development wastes energy not only for transportation, but also for space heating and air conditioning. This four-headed monster of the twentieth-century Apocalypse — cars, sprawl, freeways and oil — is what we are building and what we are committing the next generation to live in. It is what largely defines our jobs and many other life activities. It commits us to one of the most expensive and dangerous common activities allowed, namely driving. The car/sprawl/freeway/oil infrastructure has enormous arms, in the form of shipping routes and pipelines, both subject to accidental disasters, and in the form of military forces that maintain constant pressure and, occasionally, go to war to keep petroleum flowing.

Because this monster is a whole-system structure, we can effectively attack it by taking on any one of its four main components. Working against cars, sprawl development, freeways and paving, or oil dependence will help bring down the whole destructive edifice. Even better, we know that if we provide positive alternatives to any of these components we will be starving the system and nurturing another whole-system creation, the pedestrian/three-dimensional system. We will be building a whole new infrastructure for a new civilization.

Paul and Anne Ehrlich[3] have suggested summarizing the situation in a simple formula: Humanity's impact (I) on the world's environment is roughly equal to population (P) multiplied by affluence (A) multiplied by technology (T). I = PAT. A large number of people with low consumption and benign technologies might have the same impact as a far smaller number of people with higher affluence and/or people with more damaging technologies. These three variables give us a way of thinking about the dynamics of damage to the Earth and its resources and life systems.

However something is missing from the formula — the anatomy of the built community. Land use and infrastructure are home to the population, the engine of most of the affluence, and shelter and organize the technologies so that they can function. Unless we take into account the city's physical structure and organization, we won't be able to solve the all-too-physical problems of a disintegrating biosphere and a rapidly degrading resource base for human sustenance. We can see cities, towns and villages as whole, functioning, potentially-healthy living systems, or we can get lost in the details as Thomas Berry warns us we may. The manner in which the city is laid out and organized is the foundation for virtually everything else. Without understanding urban anatomy we will fail to understand how population, affluence and technology relate to each other and to the environment. Impact (I) = population (P) times land use and infrastructure (L) times affluence (A) times technology (T). I = PLAT. One last refinement: "impact" is usually understood as negative. "Effect" (E) might be a better, more neutral word, but we could even imagine a benefit (B) arising from the healthy interrelation of P, L, A and T.

The urban planner Kenneth Schneider adds depth to this line of reasoning by saying, rather straightforwardly, that dealing with even the major issues rather than the system can preclude attaining the desired results.

> Despite the statements of many urbanists and environmentalists to the contrary, the central issues are not clean air and water, endangered species or environments, more money for housing and urban renewal, or even energy, certainly not in their separate capacities. These issues are relevant, perhaps necessary, but not basic. What is basic is the structure of the human environment, the city. Building a good city — a framework for all separate things to work harmoniously — is essential in order to alleviate each of the separate issues of development. Separate concerns considered separately merely trap us into building an even larger environmental destructiveness. [4]

It helps to see that the city is a particular creation, entity, organism, apparatus, meta-machine — by whatever name, a created artifact with certain characteristics and purposes. One of the clearest descriptions of the city's purpose comes from David Engwicht, Australian activist and planning consultant: "The city is an invention for maximizing exchange and minimizing travel." What is exchanged? Ideas, goods, food, money, friendship, hopes, fears, genes — virtually everything at the core of human culture and economy, genetics and evolution. The quality and the content of that exchange, and the influence of that exchange on the environment in which the city is placed, is very largely determined by the physical form and arrangement of parts. Seen in this way, the city is something like a ship for a journey into humanity's future. Better build it well.

A NEW SYNTHESIS ARCHITECTURE

At the European Eco-Logical Architecture Congress in Stockholm and Helsinki in August 1992, there was much discussion about a number of imaginatively designed "ecological buildings." These buildings featured renewable energy systems, built-in recycling, non-toxic building materials, interior greenhouse planting and rooftop gardens. Many had effective — even beautiful — natural lighting. One, the NMB Bank Building in Amsterdam, featured dynamically-sloped walls to bounce sound away from people and reduce wind effects, and small cataracts of fresh water running down grooves in the banister handrails. But with the exception of my own ecocity slide show, Paolo Soleri's proposed cities, and some traditional village architecture from desert regions around the Mediterranean described by the French architect, Jean Bouillot, each building stood like an independent entity, separate from the other functions of society and economy.

"Green buildings" have received increasing interest in the United States. In particular, those designed in the offices of Sim Van der Ryn, David Orr and William McDonough — respectively, the headquarters of Real Goods in Hopland, California, the Center for Environmental Studies at Oberlin College in Oberlin, Ohio, and the Gap Headquarters in San Bruno, California — are attractive and energy-efficient, since they are all largely passively heated and cooled by sun and shade and use a number of low-energy, non-toxic and recycled building materials and furnishings. The Real Goods Building in Hopland features straw bales worked into recycled wooden posts and beams in a particularly pleasant environment facing towards the sun on the south. It has a grape arbor that provides shade in the summer when the leaves intercept most of the sunshine, and, when the leaves fall off, lets light through in winter to warm the building. It has a pond and a constructed-marsh waste system full of plants and buzzing with dragonflies. But these American buildings called "green," "healthy" or "ecological" are only one story high (Real Goods) or two (Oberlin's Environmental Studies Center and the Gap headquarters).

Thus they address neither higher-density urban problems, nor transit and pedestrian solutions as do their taller European cousins among the Eco-Logical architects' buildings. A more fundamental problem with these American "green" buildings is that they do not physically knit together the life of the community. If ecology is not about the individual organism in its community of other living things, what is it about? If ecological buildings are not about their relationship to other structures, public open spaces, and the life of the whole community, what are they about? In the case of these buildings, the answer to the question, "Where's the community?" is, "The parking lot. That's where you go to connect with it."

In Stockholm and Helsinki it occurred to me that ancient cities such as Çatal Hüyük in Turkey, Jericho in Israel, the Minoan and Mycenean cities on the island of Crete, the pueblos of the American Southwest, the "lost city" of the Tairona in Columbia, and contemporary towns with ancient roots such as Shaban, Yemen, and others across the Casbah Belt from Morocco to Afghanistan, have reflected and served a synthesis of ecological and social needs. This Old Synthesis Architecture saw the building primarily as part of a whole community embedded in the natural environment. Enthusiastically praised by Bernard Rudofsky in *Architecture Without Architects,*[5] it was as much city planning as architecture. The architect Vakhtang Davitaia from Tiblisi, Georgia has described an art of building design centered on social gathering places, celebrating streets, squares, public monuments and schools, in which towns, as if growing out of the earth, assume the same form as the mountains of his home country. "Nothing could be farther from our philosophy than the English and American statement, 'A man's house is his castle.' We are a sociable people."[6]

Five hundred years ago, the European town was a cluster of buildings two to five stories high, many of them built up against or sharing walls with their next-door neighbors, with homes over stores and small handicraft shops, a walled section in the middle, a larger, fancier administrative building flanked by imposing residences, or perhaps a castle displaying fear of the outside and control within its bounds. Rising above it all was the church spire, spear-like and ready to fling the imagination completely clear of the Earth on its way to heaven. Close in on all sides were farm and forest, the former populated with domestic animals in pens and fenced fields, the latter partially logged and cleared but, connected by a few small roads to the town, an obvious source of sustenance and a pleasant green sparkle to the eye. This picture says something about the people and their relations to one another, to nature, and to the universe as they understood it.

In the Southwestern pueblo of the same era, the clustered pattern of mixed living-and-working habitat was even more compact, as if the whole town were one building of many separate rooms three, four or five stories high. Social order, perhaps cooperation, appears to have had very high value here. This community reveals an Earth-focused and season-conscious cosmology and daily life. Ceremonial kivas were dug into the sacred Earth. Openings in the architecture faced southeast to gather the sun's warmth in the morning and to cool in the afternoon. Gardens were small and variegated, indicating diverse production. The forest was partially cut, providing fuel for a few columns of smoke. Deer, antelope and rabbits lived in the valley and on the dry plateaus. Here, too, we can clearly discern a number of signs of the people's beliefs, values and life orientation.

In contrast, the present day city has almost no comprehensible form at all. Look out over today's typical city and the tangle of streets and freeways disappears into a gray jumble of low-lying buildings and the yellow-brown-gray haze of auto emissions. Over this miasma rise scattered tall buildings, most of them owned by banks, insurance companies and giant corporations. Looming above these symbols of money, security, consumerism and control, television transmission towers flash sci-fi red lights to ward off giant buzzing aluminum gnats full of jet-powered people. The towers are beaming images directly into houses sprinkled widely in random patches about the landscape. Therein people worship at the altar of diversion from nature and confrontation with themselves: television. The sprawl is tethered almost metaphysically to the towers by invisible electronic waves in the air bounced off satellites rolling around in freezing space that, after evening twilight or before morning twilight, trace spooky silent paths between the stars, high over the city. The whole scene is financed through the tall buildings inhabited for a third of the day by thousands of people who spend the rest of their time scattered over hundreds of square miles, or moving about that surface in metal boxes on thick rubber doughnuts.

Though modern cities and towns may have their origins in a kind of

Old Synthesis Architecture which brought together the pieces of the community into a whole, they have diverged and dis-integrated outward across the Earth's surface, scattered by ever increasing mobility. Cities provided the possibility of specialization and hierarchy on small acreage, but as transport became more dominant, buildings and clusters of buildings became increasingly detached from the whole and from the natural environment. Buildings began serving their own ends, for their own owners, in competition with, rather than in support of, the whole. This is not a completely bad idea. The districts of particular crafts, manufacture or service intensified the pursuit of particular activities, furthering lively exchange and creativity. At a certain scale, though, the spreading of the city meant that it took more and more time to get from one building or district to another. Ancient city builders were almost certainly aware of this and created compact development and narrow streets to deal with it. In a pedestrian world the notion of access by proximity was undoubtedly obvious and to build in a scattered mode would have seemed strange and impractical. With the use of animals and carts for transportation, and later, especially with cars, at some point a threshold of dysfunction was crossed. Problems mounted more quickly than solutions, while — and this is worth emphasizing — the increasing distances made it more difficult to see this. Contemporary accounts, from the cities of the 1700s, of the takeover of streets by horses expressed every bit as much outrage as today's road rage. Horse excrement, urine, flies and terrible smells played the same role as air and water pollution in today's commentary on car-dominated cities.

In recent times architects have designed for the egos of clients and themselves, usually in an attempt to make a unique aesthetic statement while creating solutions for their buildings' functional problems and clients needs. Not only does the design tend to disregard the whole, but often it intentionally contrasts with it. Frank Gehry's Guggenheim Museum in Bilbao, Spain, instantly and almost universally recognized as a masterpiece, is an example of contrast creating an enormously more interesting whole. When the part and whole don't function well together, however, this kind of design is dis-integrative, and this is the case with one-building-at-a-time architecture exacerbated by sprawl.

Looking at the buildings represented at the Eco-Logical Architecture Congress, I concluded that it was time to re-unify the dis-integrated city and bring the eco- and social- strains back together again in a New Synthesis Architecture. In this philosophy, the building is primarily conceived as a part of, not apart from, the rest of the larger built community, and positively related to the community of natural environments and life forms.

WILDERNESS AND THE WILDNESS OF CITIES

As much as I like European cities, after traveling to Australia and Brazil and reflecting on my childhood in the American West I began to realize that the ecocity should have an element of wilderness that is missing among Europe's manicured parks, its highly managed forests, and its working agricultural landscapes. People control nature in Europe, often with harmonious results, but results that nonetheless show the human hand and mind in every detail — every stone wall, every goat-nibbled meadow, every replanted forest. In contrast, people in western America are surrounded by a wilderness that, though by no means unadulterated, still has a pervasive presence. We need much more of it in and adjacent to our future cities, as well as in vast landscapes far from them. Somehow we have to give nature large zones of freedom right up to the urban edge as we design our built environments and give ourselves our own kinds of human freedom.

We need to establish the principle of restoration as the first step. Setting aside existing wilderness is a start, but we need to work toward preserving and recreating much larger, contiguous areas quite close to larger human populations. In and adjacent to cities, we should re-establish living ribbons of blues and greens, making a very serious commitment to restoring waterways, shorelines, ridge lines and wildlife corridors for continuous habitats of plants and animals.

Wilderness can expand as cities become restructured for pedestrians and shrink back to reasonable limits. Urban centers could coalesce around nuclei of activity in the suburbs, transforming bedroom communities into real towns with their own viable economies and cultural excitement. Establishing greenbelts is that pause in destructive growth, that moment of still reflection that hangs in time before the pattern is reversed and we begin withdrawing from car-dependent sprawl and restoring nature in a serious way. The first greenbelts were established toward the end of the 1800s. Depaving and withdrawal from car-dependent sprawl began toward the end of the 1900s. Now it's time to put both of these strategies on the fast track.

We will do well, first, to use nature as a model for designing our own communities, lifeways and technologies and, second, to give back to nature large areas for its own management. In this scenario, ecocities, ecotowns and ecovillages will flourish around the world in a wild profusion of forms — from Arctic fishing and hunting villages to sustainable logging and farming cities in the tropics, from oasis research outposts to great centers of manufacturing and commerce. But all of them will maintain enormous biodiversity in their surroundings, employ renewable energy almost exclusively, recycle assiduously, maintain regionally stable or slowly shrinking populations, and produce unique customs and artifacts. Continuous millions of acres of the metropolis will have been broken up into smaller, more compact settlements as asphalt and lawns are plowed under for crops or simply abandoned to the winds and rains and the seeds dropped by birds. Wildlife will move across the long-forgotten suburban wasteland between thriving villages and cities.

Four types of landscape might be recognized: one defined by the ecological city, town and village, another primarily for human support (mining, forest production, agriculture, fish farming), a third almost natural but inhabited by humans who know it intimately and are part of it, such as the Laplanders and the Inuit on the Arctic coast, and a fourth, nature's alone. Together these last two landscapes might cover more than three-quarters of the land surface of the Earth. Immense tracts of desert and agribusiness will return to grassland and forest. The productive landscape will make up most of the rest. The ecocity landscape will be small but packed with activity.

Nature will manage the two larger landscapes. Species will slowly and steadily increase in diversity, metamorphosing at the slow pace of evolution, with human intervention limited and always in defense of diversity. When whole species disappear it will be because they have been transformed through time into something else, or eliminated by some natural cataclysm.

People will manage the productive landscape. Soils will grow richer over time and the numbers of members of any species still surviving the ravages of the Age of Progress will increase, incidental to the variety of species nurturing and nurtured by people. Logging companies will manage lands with a wide diversity of economically-valuable trees, taking care to protect rare plants and animals and rotate harvest areas so that it is difficult to tell a natural forest from one used for production. Where an industry is actually extractive, such as mining, extraction sites will be repaired with aesthetic and species diversity as guidelines.

Finally, people will manage the ecocities, once again, using nature as a model. Land uses and the built infrastructure of buildings, streets, bridges, rails, wires, vehicles, and so on — the anatomy of the city — will determine the potential for life in it, rather as the genetic heritage of an individual provides for, but does not guarantee, full realization of that individual's potential. The city is a complex living creation, but if it is arranged and built for healthy metabolism of the society, economy and exchanges between nature and people, it should be comprehensible, not confusing. As any animal is a design of enormous complexity, it also makes sense in its basic structure. That sense is obvious in the structure of traditional villages and if the contemporary city is designed with that sort of integral logic, with its parts arranged to function harmoniously, largely on the organic model, because it is comprehensible it will be buildable.

Compactness — access by proximity — and diversity will be crucial. Today's car-dominated cities are flat, with holes (parks and parking lots) and tangled veins (arterials and freeways). They are analogous to a sheet of snail-eaten paper with a lumpy zone or two representing the taller buildings in the centers. An animal would be dysfunctional with such a shape, and so is a city. In contrast, the anatomy of an ecologically-healthy city will be characterized by walkable centers, transit villages, discontinuous boulevards (rising over wildlife corridors or tunneling beneath them), and agricultural areas close to the center. Compact and very diverse town and city cores and neighborhood centers will be universal. The metropolis will have become several pedestrian cities of walkable centers, linked by bicycle, with support for longer distances from public transit.

Major downtown and smaller neighborhood centers will be small enough to be easily traversed by most people on foot. Their size will be based on the size and speed of the human body, and thus we can be fairly confident that once we figure out the proper scale and form (which will be different for different populations and climates) we will have a human design truth that will last essentially forever. These centers will provide access to a wide variety of land uses and services in close proximity: housing, work space, food, hardware, clothes, education, places to socialize — the whole community in its basics. Many designers who think about pedestrian environments consider an area of about a quarter-mile radius the maximum for an active pedestrian center, and I think this is a good starting point. We can amend it in accordance with the stamina of the people, their willingness to use bicycles, the climate, and the overall functioning and total scale of the center.

For those few who must commute there will be transit, usually rail. Cars will be for specialized and emergency use or for rent. They will be rigorously restricted to limited areas on the city's fringe and travel a network of small country roads that cater mainly to farm and logging vehicles, some electric and some drawn by horse, mule or ox. Leisurely and time-consuming car trips will not be unheard of, but most long-distance trips in this scenario are by rail, airplane or bicycle. Country roads will be narrow and disappear among trees, or plunge into tunnels, sometimes for miles, weaving in and out of the surface like an embroidery thread through cloth. In cities, skywalks and bridges will connect public terraces and rooftops virtually everywhere. Public investment will be lavished on the pedestrian, who will be pampered with arcades, awnings, porches, verandahs and covered walkways. Mid-block pedestrian passageways at ground level, galleries and back alleys will become friendly commercial and garden-like lanes that create a fine-grained environment for people on foot.

Tall buildings around public spaces will be spectacular expressions of confidence in the future and a new faith in human creativity guided by responsibility. Large trees, visible for miles, seeming to float high over the city, will be enshrined in rooftop arboretums, supported by pillars built into apartment and office buildings. Movable greenhouse glass and windbreaks perched a dozen or two dozen stories above the streets will shelter and bring attention to plant, animal, songbird and human alike. Fruit trees, flowers and berry bushes will be everywhere in the streets, in window boxes, and on rooftops, attracting insects, birds, squirrels and lizards. New and old techniques will combine to store heat in adobe walls and hang solar greenhouse glass on the cascading terraces of the sun-facing sides of buildings. The gardens, cafes and sports centers high on the shoulders of buildings will be sheltered by glass walls that fold away

35

in pleasant weather or for whole seasons. People will gather there for the magnificent views and daringly move from building to building on bridges high above the streets.

Everywhere there will be water, with brooks, waterfalls and sculptural fish ladders, both natural and crafted, becoming focal points in the design of public spaces and the arrangement of buildings. Music from street performers will mix with the sounds of flowing waters and the murmuring voices of people sitting in spotlights of sun discussing and pontificating, whispering and laughing, where cafe tables and staircases pour out into the streets and plazas. The city will be so small on the land that all its limits will be visible from any central vantage point, and people will enjoy being close to nature.

A long-term balance with nature is anything but static or culturally predictable. "Sustainability" is a term strangely out of place in this world that loves real weather and the excitement of wilderness and the unknown, that enjoys surprise and the bracing stimulation of nature's power, calm and change. A dynamic and healthy balance with nature opens the door to infinite explorations of creativity in art, design and science, and to more authentic human relationships. The ancients of many traditions used the word "harmony" to describe the healthiest, most respectful relationship between humans and nature, and we may never come up with a better one.

The broad outlines of the task ahead of us should now be coming into focus, but one last point needs to be emphasized. Because the truths from which the ecocity idea emerges are based on the human body — its size, speed and requirements for nourishment, shelter, procreative and creative excitement and fulfillment — and on the relations of living organisms to each other and their environment, the principles of ecocity building are applicable forever and everywhere. They are not subject to any fundamental change due to changing tastes, styles, trends or fads. Once they are discovered, their possibilities are limited only by our own imaginations and abilities.

According to an ancient Chinese proverb, the beginning of wisdom is calling things by their right names. Noticing the absence of words to express ecocity ideas, some years ago I began making up my own words for them. I started with "ecocity," picked up words coined by others —

such as Bill Mollison's "permaculture" and Paolo Soleri's "arcology" — and reduced complex notions to formulas such as "access by proximity" and "shrink for prosperity." Part of the reason so many people miss the fundamental importance of their largest physical creation — the city — in the problems and solutions that dictate so much of our lives is the simple lack of a language with which to think effectively about city structure, about the functioning of the built community. Deeper than that, because the arrangement of parts of the city has not been well laid out in the dis-integrative phase of architecture and city design, there is little order in the ideas that describe it. Where is the science and art of investigating, describing, designing and building healthy cities? Not having found it, I have tried to spell out its beginnings here, and propose to call it "Ecocitology."

2

The City in Evolution

The city exists, like everything else, in an evolving universe. But it appears to have a special role in evolution that may have a great deal to do with how we build and use it. The theologian, Pierre Teilhard de Chardin, and the landscape architect, Ian McHarg, have written about this special role, but it's the architect, Paolo Soleri, who has been the most explicit about it. Perhaps the best way to begin, however, is with Thomas Berry:

> The changes presently taking place in human and earthly affairs are beyond any parallel with historical change or cultural modification as these have occurred in the past. This is not like the transition from the classical period to the medieval period or from the medieval to the modern period. This change reaches far beyond the civilizational process itself, beyond even the human process into the biosystems and even the geological structures of the Earth itself.
>
> There are only two other moments in the history of this planet that offer us some sense of what is happening. These two moments are the end of the Paleozoic era, 220 million years ago, when some 90 percent of all species living at the time were extinguished, and 65 million years ago at the terminal phase of the Mesozoic era, when there was also a very extensive extinction. [7]

Berry describes in rich detail the "lyric period" of life on Earth that followed, the Cenozoic era, in which flowering plants appeared in wild profusion, color and sweet fragrances over the land, and mammals expanded from a few obscure rodent-like varieties into the enormous diversity of warm-blooded, quick-witted species that came to fill the lands, waters and skies of planet Earth. Berry sees us as now entering an "Ecozoic era," in which life in all its ecological interconnections becomes an organism capable for the first time of attaining "reflexive awareness" or deep consciousness of itself. As we become aware, he says, through us the universe consciously awakens to its own existence.

This juncture between the Cenozoic and the Ecozoic is the point beyond which evolution consciously determines its own fate. By design or default human beings have become the agents of this transition, and in us the universe has acquired physical eyes and hands to see and shape the course of its own evolution. It has gathered and compacted into live physical beings a new creative force — Mind — at once a pilot and a builder of communities, technologies and transformed landscapes on the scale of planets.

Though most of the materials for this construction were produced by earth, water, air and other organisms long before humans appeared on the scene, we have arranged these materials in such a way as to constitute something new. Soleri calls it "neomatter," and it ranges from the relatively simple concrete invented by the Romans to the thousands of exotic chemicals introduced into the biosphere and their accidental combinations and by-products. Proposing what we should do with these new materials, powers and responsibilities, and in particular what to build, is the aim of this book.

It seems the universe began with a colossal explosion: the Big Bang. Brian Swimme, co-author with Thomas Berry of *The Universe Story*,[8] more poetically terms it "the Primordial Flaring Forth," and it sent rushing out into the void sub-atomic particles, quickly forming into vast, expanding clouds of lightweight gases, predominantly hydrogen. This happened around thirteen billion years ago in a process which Soleri identified as miniaturization/complexification/quickening. This process was immediately and everywhere established as one of the primary dynamics of evolution. Out of these vast clouds, atoms were pulled together through their own gravitational attraction to create masses of material that, when compacted enough to spark thermonuclear reactions, lit up as stars. Within these stars, a wide range of elements was cooked up over immense time and, in those of appropriate size, exploded again in mini-flaring forths called "supernovas," throwing a new soup of atomic particles and molecules into interstellar space. Relentlessly the process of complexification/miniaturization/quickening continued asserting itself as these particles, too, gathered together matter and energy in pinpoints in the vast dusty halls of the vacuum.

With these second-, third- and later-generation stars, much smaller and far more complex accumulations of elements and molecules emerged: the planets. On and in these planets, atomic decay and internal friction produced heat imbalances and convection currents that began mixing and sifting, sorting and distilling physical material in spatial volumes much smaller than the dust clouds from which the planets themselves had condensed. On the surfaces of these warmish newcomers, internal heating met the warming of suns and cooling of space, producing zones of the most complex mixing yet seen in the universe.

Here on the surface of our home planet, in environments of a complexity many orders of magnitude greater than that of interstellar space or the insides of stars or planets, solids, liquids and gases combined and were zapped by lightning and irradiated by sunshine, cosmic rays and nuclear decay. Here in this most complex and miniaturized of all realms of the universe heretofore, in a pattern seen since the beginning, a changing reality characterized in its broadest sense by a process of miniaturization/complexification/quickening was bringing something new into existence: Life.

Life gave rise to something so miniaturized and complex and rapidly changing as to be experienced much more in what it does through the living beings it animates than in itself: Consciousness. And I would say, at the same time, the other half of that same phenomenon: Conscience. In its wholeness, it's sometimes called the psyche, spirit or soul of the physical form whose reality it shares.

It is conceivable that much larger coherent systems, organisms by some reasonable definition, could exist with the same degree of complexity, covering much larger volumes of space, but such systems don't seem to be "buildable," either by nature or by humans. Proximity — closeness of parts, small scale — is necessary or the thing cannot hold itself together. Gravitational, chemical or atomic connections operate over certain distances beyond which they cease to bind. The evidence, in any case, does link the small-scale with the complex. There are, for example, no known beings of loosely assembled matter pacing between the planets with cells as large as thunderclouds or eyes the size of lunar orbits or solar systems. There seem to be no known forces that bind in a diffuse and yet complexly organized manner over great distances. We will be talking later about "access by proximity" as a principle of the ecocity, and it seems as good a description of chemical processes as it is a slogan for city building.

Paolo Soleri's *Arcology: The City in the Image of Man* has one of the most elegant statements on the subject I have discovered. "Any higher organism contains more performances than a chunk of the unlimited universe light years thick, and it ticks on a time clock immensely swifter. This miniaturization process may well be one of the fundamental rules of evolution."[9]

That last sentence may well be one of the great understatements, too, since there seems to be no evidence to the contrary anywhere, at any time. The miniaturization pattern in evolution is so fundamental, in fact, it seems to me we could think of it as the First Law of Evolutionary Dynamics. Scientists speak of the Second Law of Thermodynamics, the idea that all energy is in a winding-down pattern of entropy that will result in the heat death of the universe. At the same time there are forces of atomic, chemical and gravitational attraction conspiring to drag it all back together. Buckminster Fuller called this counter-entropic pattern "syntropy." Insofar as the stuff of the universe does get reassembled, it is toward more complexity all over again and in more compacted spaces — the Second Law of Thermodynamics encountering the First Law of Evolutionary Dynamics in a dynamic dance of entropy and syntropy that defines and organizes much (or all) of reality. I think of these two phenomenon, entropy and syntropy, as a set of dimensions, each of which, without the other, nothing. In the matter/energy universe, matter and energy just don't seem to exist separate from the other or separate from this dance of entropy and syntropy.

I would suggest condensing (miniaturizing) the term "miniaturization/complexification/quickening" down to a single word: "Miniplexion." The word "complex" comes from the Latin for weaving or braiding (*plectere*) together or with (*com*). Add "mini" for small. Complexifying, delicate, subtle weaving together, almost lyric, miniplexion. It's not just an important process of the universe, it permeates and characterizes all. Nothing exists separate from it.

In addition, in no way does unpredictability or catastrophe in any given biosphere demonstrate that miniplexion itself is stopped for even the shortest time. Because, after the impact of the asteroid, the retreat of the glacier, or the desiccation of the spreading desert, all systems that remain move toward further miniplexion. If local designs and innovations are lost in catastrophe, the biological and even chemical survivors remain as dedicated as ever to the process, being able, it seems, to do nothing else. In fact, the exotic comet smoke and debris from outer space, the finely-ground glacial dust, the radically-altered environment of the desert, can create new opportunities for evolutionary experimentation as microscopic amounts of rare elements contact living cells, large geographical expanses open up to reinhabitation on enriched soils, and desiccated landscapes provide environments for future species.

GAIA: THE SELF-REGULATING PLANET

In 1875 the Austrian geologist Eduard Suess proposed that all living creatures on the Earth constitute a sphere of life that he was the first to call the "biosphere." In the vastness of evolutionary time, the biosphere had emerged on the surface of the stony mineral continents and metallic hot core of the Earth's lithosphere, suspended in the watery oceans, rivers and lakes of the hydrosphere and bathed in the gasses and vapors of the atmosphere. By the 1920s the Russian geobiochemist Vladimir Vernadsky had realized that the Earth's biosphere had transformed the non-living material of the Earth into an environment co-evolving with, and managed by, the countless numbers of living organisms on the planet. Life and Earth, he pointed out, were together creating their future collective self.

Look at the chiseled walls of the Grand Canyon — thousands of feet of vertical geological text representing hundreds of millions of years of Earth's history colored by, largely made up of, once-living organisms. Look at the deep-rooted, high mountain ranges of limestone and marble once shellfish, the underground oceans of oil, and the vast regions of coal and tar sands once great marshy forests, even the immense deposits of iron and other metals long ago precipitated out of water by bacteria to become the ores used in building civilizations from the Bronze Age until today. Look at the blues and sunset colors, the crystal black night and feel the temperature of the sky — all as they are because of the activity of living organisms. This is the work of life on Earth already accomplished, turning human artifacts like the Great Wall of China and our giant cities into small, squiggly lines and smudges in life-built, geologic layers dozens of miles thick, encompassing a whole planet.

Vernadsky observed that the biosphere seemed to be self-regulating in a way that promoted relative stability on Earth. Oxygen in the atmosphere has been maintained by the biosphere at a level that permits its use by living organisms but not its abuse. Plants and animals seem to have struck a balance with the inanimate world in maintaining the proper concentration of carbon dioxide in the atmosphere to keep the planet at a temperature that is just right for a large variety of species.

Refining this idea further, in the 1970s the microbiologist Lynn Margolis and the atmospheric scientist James Lovelock described the processes by which living organisms transform Earth's atmosphere and geology and regulate the air's composition and chief properties so that life — the living organisms, the regulators themselves — can flourish. They dubbed the Earth/Life superorganism "Gaia" after the Greek titan of Earth.

Father Pierre Teilhard de Chardin proposed in 1925 that within the biosphere, through human communications and cultural artifacts such as books, music, art and radio, people had created an evolving "noosphere," or sphere of knowledge. He argued that cities brought together concentrations of people and their technologies as nodes of consciousness — nodes of intense complexity and enormous leverage for further evolution — in the evolving noosphere. From all these thoughts the notion emerges that the biosphere, or Gaia, is evolving a physical brain composed largely of our human-built infrastructure of cities and their support structures. We begin to see that humanity is part of a physical, living, thinking being composed of parts of the Earth itself and countless trillions of living creatures. Our specialty seems to be brain building for a collective version of Thomas Berry's "reflexive awareness."

Whether we accept this evolutionary panorama that Berry would call "The Story" and the place of the city within it, or adopt a more prosaic view of the city as functioning as a collection of buildings, landscapes, vehicles, people, animals and plants engaged in a mix of economic, cultural and natural activities under the partially conscious direction of people, the built human habitat sits squarely in the center of the human evolutionary drama. Whether the city is somehow thinking on its own in a way to which we contribute, or exists as a neglected, misunderstood tool for advancing evolution, there it is, functioning in the evolutionary context while changing that context in ways we can come to understand and participate in.

The Urban Comet

The city's role in an evolution that could bring on Thomas Berry's Ecozoic era is far from rosy. We are ripping vast patches out of the fabric of life on a planetary scale and rapidly degrading natural systems, up to and including the weather and climate upon which life depends. There is now, for example, more than a third again as much carbon dioxide in the atmosphere (370 parts per million by volume) as there was at the beginning of the Industrial Revolution (280 parts per million). Within fifty years, at current rates of increase, scientists are predicting a doubling for carbon dioxide from today's levels — which amounts to more than two and a half times the carbon dioxide of pre-industrial times. This is a major transformation of the atmosphere of the planet. Even with a just steady linear increase of carbon dioxide in the atmosphere, the great majority of experts believe that we can expect global heating, more extreme storms and generalized collapse of habitat around the world. In addition, cities are becoming "heat islands" typically seven or eight degrees hotter than the surrounding countryside. As their physical footprints expand and they come to constitute a significant fraction of the Earth's surface, they add to the heating of the Earth directly.

And it only gets worse. Research being conducted in Wisconsin, Michigan, Kansas, South Carolina, Florida, England and New Zealand is examining what the increasing levels of carbon dioxide hold in store for plants. In various chambers and semi-sheltered environments with carbon dioxide levels matching those expected in 2050, plants and animals from insects to sheep are being raised and studied. In a nutshell, most plants grow much faster but are rich in fiber and starch while very poor in nitrogen products and protein. Various caterpillars, for example, eat 20 percent to 40 percent more plant material but get much less nourishment, taking longer to grow and ending up on average — those that survive — about 10 percent smaller. An insect called a leaf miner is twice as likely to die in a double-today's carbon dioxide atmosphere. "Although they may eat more per individual, a lot of them die before they've eaten their fill," says Peter Stiling at the University of South Florida in Tampa. "The leaves are not rich enough to support them." As they struggle just to eat, these herbivorous insects and the plants they consume put out visual and chemical signals that make the insects more easily located by parasitic wasps and other predators. Add that to temperature change and major change in plant species distribution and the possibility of a world without many of today's species of butterflies and moths becomes a real possibility. Sheep eating the fiber- and starch-enhanced plants in the double carbon dioxide atmosphere of another experiment are having trouble digesting enough nitrogen compounds because the bacteria in their rumens have more work to do to produce the proper amount of protein. They need to pause in their eating to wait for the bacteria to catch up and complete digestion. Farmers might "solve" this problem by adding protein to their diet. Wild animals won't be so lucky.

The heat-island effect comes largely from city streets, parking lots and roofs absorbing solar energy — asphalt, concrete and roofing tar baking in the sun. The city built for cars is massively energy-consuming specifically for mobility. Most people are familiar with the direct results of automobile driving with regard to carbon dioxide production, and we hear over and over that driving less is one of the most important things we can do. Meanwhile scattered small houses consume far more energy per person served than buildings such as apartments and condominiums, since they share heating and cooling energy with no one before it is lost to the atmosphere. Beyond this, the manufacture of automobiles, gasoline, tires, highways, parking lots and structures, gas stations, and so on, the shipping of these items or their building materials, and the disposal or reuse of materials afterward is a very large share of the energy use of industry. Emissions, rubber dust from tires, asbestos dust from brake linings, and dust from aging roads falling on snow and helping to melt it earlier in the year all contribute to earlier seasonal warming. Sprawl that drives farming off rich soils close to city centers helps transform farming into an energy-intensive industry consuming on the order of ten times as many calories in fossil fuels as it produces as food. As the farmer/author Wendell Berry reminds us, the average distance that food travels from farm to American mouths is about twelve hundred miles. And we haven't even begun to look at the specific poisons associated with the city — the death of people, animals and plants in accidents, local air pollution, water runoff, ocean oil spills, and so on. The connection of the city and its particular structure to evolution by way of its immense impact on biology and climate should be obvious.

ISLANDS AND EXTINCTIONS

Our cities, farms, highways and dams are slicing natural habitat into ever smaller pieces. Island biogeography — a branch of biology that studies species living on islands — shows us some fascinating patterns. In *The Song of the Dodo*[10] David Quammen traces the history of the evolution sciences by taking the adventure to remote islands and following the scientific battles all the way to their conclusions in solid theory. Here are some of the patterns he has discussed:

Small islands have smaller numbers of species, and the number roughly doubles as the area of the island increases by ten times. Say if there are three species of beetles on a hundred-acre island, there will be about six on an island of 1,000 acres, twelve on an island of ten thousand acres, twenty-four on an island of 100,000 acres, and so on.

How frequently a new species arrives on an island from the vast biological supply house of the closest continent is proportional to distance and the vagaries of winds and ocean currents. Rafts of driftwood ripped by floods from the forests of the Andes, for example, brought reptilian settlers to the Galapagos Islands six hundred miles from Ecuador, but extremely rarely. For every animal that landed in 1,000,000 years, many hundreds drifted by, dying of thirst and hunger, some coming close enough to see the grass and shrubs or hear the clatter of roosting sea birds only to be blown by winds farther into the Pacific. A minuscule fraction coughed out to sea by storm-swollen mainland rivers made the journey and survived. The distance factor meant that no mammals could make the trip at all. With their rapid metabolism they simply couldn't last, or fast as long. The delicate skin of the salamanders and frogs could survive the salt spray and sun only very briefly. They are never found on islands that were not once connected by land bridges to continents.

Then, should other species have arrived earlier and settled snugly into all the niches on the island, the newcomer would have had to displace one or another of the old timers. In addition the new immigrant would have had the genetic disadvantage of inbreeding since only a small number, a pair, or even a single pregnant female would have made it to the beachhead to found a new species there. The resident species would have already learned genetically, and sometimes through parental teaching, how to mesh with the local ecology.

Old islands have relatively stable and large numbers of species; young ones have smaller but growing numbers of species. Old ones have a very slow turnover rate as species die out and new ones evolve from the locals or arrive from outside; young islands have a higher turnover rate as species jockey for position in the various niches and compete against the immigrants. Early arrivals on remote islands, once firmly established, undergo "adaptive radiation." A single species begins to establish itself in certain niches, and, if barriers are significant — as in Hawaii where the prevailing winds create deep forests on one side of the island and deserts on the other — tends to produce varieties, races and eventually completely different species adapted to different climates and different floral and faunal ecologies.

This process takes a while. When a species is driven to extinction, it will be a very long time before it is functionally replaced in its ecology, if ever. Removing a key species, introducing a foreign predator or disease, changing the climate, hunting a species to extinction, or driving it out with agriculture creates a cascade of extinctions, an unraveling of the fabric of life called "ecosystem decay." A hummingbird dies out, for example, because of a human-introduced mosquito, and the flowering plant that evolved with the hummingbird's pollinating beak and a battery of insect species dependent upon that plant for food and shelter follow.

As various forms of pollution increase and the sheer presence of people increases almost everywhere, cities, highways, farms, logging areas and lakes behind big dams are dividing the continents into ever smaller islands of life. It is therefore important for us to grasp the relationship between extinctions and evolution, to understand the role of cities and city-based civilization in evolution, and explore ways of reversing the process so that cities and their supply zones can allow natural areas to expand and reconnect. We can create islands of vibrant culture — ecocities in association with their working landscapes — instead of reducing nature to shrinking islands of isolation in a world of increasingly uniform culture of clutter. Says David Quammen, "Evolution is best understood in relation to extinction and vice versa. In particular, the evolution of strange species on islands is a process that, once illuminated, casts light onto its dark double: the extinction of species in a world that has been hacked into pieces."[11]

A fundamental pattern for understanding a city's impact is the relationship between its land area and the total amount of land required to provide it with its biological, material and energy resources — its "ecological footprint." Mathis Wackernagle and William Rees[12] estimate that the consumption level of a typical Canadian, for example, requires approximately twelve acres of land per year. If a Canadian city has 100,000 citizens, then it will require 1.2 million acres of trees for wood and paper, mines for ore, farms for food and fiber, plants to absorb carbon dioxide generated in energy use, and so on. This island called a city is more ambitious in its exploitation than a colony of birds on an oceanic island. The city's ecological footprint is proportionally much larger than that of the birds' rookery.

The higher the density and diversity of a city, the less dependent it is on motorized transport, and the less resources it requires, the less is the impact it has on nature. As the city is designed to conserve energy and materials while turning wastes into resources, building soils like a compost box, the ecological footprint implodes as the physical footprint shrinks toward an optimal size for its population. When the city is actually building more soils than it is consuming and helping species to survive — actually giving back acreage to nature and creating new resources for its healthy evolution — the negative ecological footprint is turned on its head and the conversation changes character fundamentally.

The car city not only takes up more land area per person, but makes even greater demands on the Earth's resources. The transit-driven city rises higher from a smaller physical footprint and has a more than proportionally smaller ecological footprint. The bicycle city continues the pattern with its yet smaller physical footprint and far smaller ecological footprint, and the very high-density pedestrian city, probably the truly ecological city, will not only take up much less space on the surface of the planet but require far fewer material resources. It might even return a net evolutionary benefit to nature.

The Australians Jeff Kenworthy and Peter Newman, examining cities around the world, have developed extensive data on this subject.[13] In their writings we see the almost mathematical relationships of density and diversity of cities in relation to pedestrian areas, bicycling, transit, cars and the health of local and global ecologies. Their work amounts to an urban corollary to the kind of relationships developed in island biogeography.

Perhaps the largest pattern created by human beings on the geographic tapestry is the drowning out of natural life in vast swatches. Though islands exhibit a wide range of variation in plants and animals, it is among a modest number of species. The real reservoirs of biodiversity are the continents. However, human settlement is swamping the coastal areas and the valleys, leaving ever smaller natural environments. As people occupy ever more land it is as if the oceans were rising. Mountain ranges become isolated, then ridges and, finally, higher peaks turn into separate shrinking islands. At the same time global warming is reinforcing this pattern by driving cooler climate species up and out of existence off the tops of mountains. Civilization would be far wiser to emulate the extraordinary diversity of the islands of the world by becoming islands in a sea of biodiversity. If we value the variety of life on Earth, cities should similarly be semi-isolated and highly tuned to their immediate hinterlands and local ecological conditions.

The density, diversity, form and function of cities, and the awareness of their citizens in this regard, are now key factors in evolution. On the positive side, the very form of the city, by providing access to culture, resources and nature, has the potential to raise consciousness of evolution to new heights. Though the effects on biology and evolution of today's enormous sprawled cities are grim, learning about such cities and about the alternatives to them gives us the tools to solve many urban and evolution-sized problems.

THE CITY AS ORGANISM

Just as exploring the patterns of evolution helps us to understand cities, so does the analogy of a living organism. Viewed as a whole system that is part of the larger whole system of the biosphere, the city seems to have a number of parts:

* A skeletal system, for support (architecture, bridges, telephone poles).
* A muscular system, for locomotion and internal movement (vehicle engines, fluid pumps).
* A digestive system, for transforming stored energy (food or fuel) into more usable forms (food-processing plants, gasoline refining facilities).
* An internal communications system of wires and fiber optics, with communications receivers (radio and television receivers, computers, post offices) and communications broadcasters (radio and television transmission towers, computers).
* Circulatory systems for internal transfer of materials (streets, gas and water lines, storm and sewage lines).
* Edge membrane to separate the organism from the outside environment (city walls or "limits," sometimes a natural feature like a river or a constructed one like a boardwalk).
* Portals to allow selective entry and exit from the whole system (city gates, or lacking these, the first gas stations at the freeway ramps).
* Systems of filtering and recycling (compost boxes, chemical or biological wastewater treatment ponds, recycling systems).
* Storage and retrieval systems (warehousing, water reservoirs and cisterns).
* Information storage systems (books, libraries, CDs, tapes, records, hard drives).
* Excretion systems (sewage outfall, waste incinerator, crematorium, freeway to the landfill)
* And reproductive systems (colleges and construction companies preparing to build more of the same — or perhaps ecocities).

According to James Miller[14] every living system has nineteen irreducible subsystems. Miller includes among his living systems, in both physical form and corollary functions, the cell, the organ, the organism, the group, the organization, the society, and the suprasocial system. He could easily have used complex buildings, cities and bioregions as examples. All have analogous subsystems and functions and are related in analogous ways to their environments. In addition, the interrelations of the subsystems and their processes within the whole living system follow closely analogous patterns from one living system to another.

The city, then, is a system somewhere between the human animal and the bioregion and biosphere in size, a living system in which we reside. The organism mutates and physically evolves over thousands or millions of years and countless generations directed by ever-so-slowly changing DNA. The traditional village also mutates into something different very slowly, its subsystems having functioned dependably for thousands of years directed by traditions relatively stable in human affairs. But the city has mutated rapidly, directed by commerce, creativity, greed and colliding concepts of the good and beneficial — and the bad and detrimental. All are living systems with the subsystems and functions Miller identifies. Understanding this hints strongly that the city needs to work at the extraordinary efficiencies that only the miniaturized, three-dimensional pedestrian city can deliver.

PRACTICE

In the late 1950s Paolo Soleri, living in the desert outside of Phoenix, Arizona in a place called Paradise Valley, was drawing, building models and writing about better ways of building cities in that climate and topography. The city he proposed, called Mesa City, covered a great expanse, but he imagined that there would be considerable concentrations of people in much of it. He recalled the kind of vitality he had experienced growing up in European cities, and he knew that a certain density of population and intensity of activity were required for a vital economy, a healthy ecology and an involved community. Thus the wide-open spaces of Arizona played off against the compact hill towns of northern Italy. Expansive land uses and compact vital centers stretched out and pulled together in his imagination. Following the planning *modus operandi* of the time, Soleri labeled various parts of Mesa City "housing," "industry," "civic center," and "education," like organs of a living system, in generous landscapes of specialization.

Then, rather suddenly, his thinking shifted, as if his stretched-out city had gathered together into a single springy, three-dimensional form with all its various parts lying adjacent to, over and under, rather than simply beside one another. Now the drawings included "sections" (vertical slices viewed from the side) through the town with "housing" above or around "education," and "industry" below that, and so on. Soleri realized immediately that such a three-dimensional city, though large for a single structure, could be very small for a city. Such a city would bring enormous complexity into very close proximity. It could cover one-tenth the land, and consume one-twentieth the energy, making renewable energy systems immediately practical and making massive, polluting energy systems anachronistic. It could recycle at extraordinary efficiencies and produce virtually no pollution. It could completely liberate its citizens from automobile dependence and its costs and hazards and do all this while creating a far superior container for a creative culture.

Interviewing Soleri in 1970, I asked him when he first made the urban/evolution connection. He told me that shortly after the dawning of his three-dimensional consciousness he read Teilhard de Chardin's writings on evolution, which had been suppressed by the Catholic Church but had become available shortly after his death in 1955. Lying near a swimming pool while taking his afternoon siesta, in the play of imagination about evolution and the city, he suddenly realized that the three-dimensional city was an instance of evolutionary miniaturization/complexification/quickening, and that if built it could be the instrument of the next quantum step in evolution. The three-dimensional city was the new physical form, the mutation, to take evolution to its next plateau. The formula for gravity came to Newton, the story goes, while he was sitting under an apple tree contemplating falling apples. Charles' law relating gas volume, temperature and pressure came to him in a dream that he recalled and wrote down with a pencil and paper next to his bed. Similarly, after rigorous preparation, seeing the pattern came almost effortlessly for Soleri. I said, "That must have made you rather happy." He answered, "Happy? I was ecstatic." De Chardin had seen the broad outline of the city's role in evolution but not the physical form it would have to take. Soleri identified that form and recognized that such a city would have to emerge from creative intent.

The new outpouring of city drawings, models and writings emerging from his workshop was radically altered in form, very three-dimensional. Soleri called his concept "arcology" for the fusion of architecture and ecology — architecture that becomes a new ecological reality and architecture that is part of, and participant in, evolving ecosystems. He adopted terminology from de Chardin and made up some of his own, arguing that humanity was developing a "technosphere" producing "neomatter" that must now come into balance with the biosphere through conscious direction of the evolving "noosphere."

Each Soleri town was designed as a single structure — a single complex building or a condensed and consolidated whole community. A village might rise to five stories, a small town might be twelve stories, a large city 150 stories high. Not everyone was enchanted by his schemes. Critics called them file boxes — never mind that his drawings and models showed generous semi-interior spaces, panoramic vistas opening up to nature, and expansive cathedral-like pedestrian environments. Rather than claustrophobia, to many, including myself, they conveyed new freedom in their vistas and in the possibility of simply walking out of the compact city and into nature.

Most detractors made assumptions that did not cover the range of possibilities, stating their own assumptions about his work as if they were Soleri's proposals. It was Buckminster Fuller, not Soleri, who suggested putting a giant climate controlling dome over Manhattan. Soleri built one small residence set into the cool earth of the hot desert and drew only two or three cities set partially into the landscape in a similar way, yet half the people I talked to about his work over the next twenty years said, "Oh, you mean the guy that wants to build underground cities." On his identification of the role of cities in evolution his critics were almost completely silent.

Where are the environmentalists who care so much about the fate of the Earth now that the idea of building for a radically-reduced impact on nature is circulating widely? Soleri's experimental town in Arizona — Arcosanti— could be built for a fraction of the cost of an aircraft carrier or major freeway expansion and what we would learn from it would be extremely important. Soleri learned early that support for the ecologically-healthy city is very limited relative to the needs of our times. "There's an enormous gap between interest and commitment," he has said. Build a better gewgaw, doodad or thingamajig and the world will beat a path to your door; design a better future and it will suspect and marginalize you.

Soleri has received virtually no work contracts or assistance from government, business or foundations. The sale of wind bells made at Arcosanti, his books and talks, and the steady flow of students earning college work/study credit for helping to build Arcosanti have provided almost all the funds and labor for his work. But the lessons that might be learned from his relatively purist approach can be applied to changing existing cities in many different ways. The support is so low and the importance so high it's a national disgrace.

LESSONS

Evolution biologists tell us that in all the history of life on Earth there has never been a species in the general size range of the human being with a population even close to ours. In fact, says Edward O. Wilson, human numbers are now more than one hundred times greater than the runner up. With our food animals, tree and agricultural crops, and human body biomass, humans appropriate as much as 40 percent of all solar energy accumulated by life on the land surface of the Earth, and 25 percent of that accumulated by all life on the planet, including life in the waters.

The lesson from the immensity of evolution, ironically, is to think small. The concept of the small, tall city will come back over and over to help us think through the means to a better future. Complexity in those smaller, taller spaces will translate gracefully into "diversity" — diversity of human uses, economic activity, cultural systems, ecological building features and species. Whether it's small and tall in Soleri's single-structure city or in the vital neighborhood center going from one- and two-story buildings to three- to five-story buildings, this city will be a model for reshaping civilization.

Earlier I mentioned the forces that hold things together in the evolving universe and the distances at which they operate. Similarly, people are united by certain forces of attraction for personal and mutual benefit, whether it is for economic transactions and education, or for delight and reproduction of the species. Physical nourishment, shelter, security, curiosity, affection, sex, personal and social fulfillment — all these forces have distances in space and time beyond which they fail to function. The community simply can't be scattered too thinly. Gasoline is the most typical substitute for the social forces that bind community when the distances get too large, and it doesn't work very well. In fact, it's a disaster measurable in social segregation by distance, human alienation, atmospheric pollution, death on the highways, habitat destruction, species extinction and change of climate — that same old list of victims of myopic collective design and planning. From the evolutionary perspective, sprawling suburbs have to go. The relentless spread of humanity, in sheer numbers and in two-dimensional spread across the landscape, has to be reversed, and the restoration of nature has to proceed on a grand scale. We need to roll back sprawl and rebuild civilization.

The lesson of the end of the Mesozoic Era and beginning of the Cenozoic 65 million years ago, when the dinosaurs disappeared, is the same one with its own twist: the large and violent are not necessarily well treated by evolution. Now we humans, roughly in proportion to how well we understand our place in the noosphere and biosphere and are able to transform the instrumentality of our changing evolution, have a once-in-the-lifetime-of-the-planet opportunity to transform a grand mistake of consciousness into one of its finest achievements.

3

The City in Nature

Although the form of most cities today is destructive of nature, it has not always been and need not continue to be so. Parts of many cities today function far better than other parts. If we were to consider the whole and put the best parts together in a city it would be vibrantly healthy. A compost box, a simple device built and managed by people, is a modification of the forest floor where organic matter is transformed from waste to a great new resource. Similarly, a city could build soil and support biodiversity if it were designed, built and maintained for the task.

Many city dwellers show a deep appreciation for nature. This appreciation may come from a nostalgia for nature lost, but it may also be caused largely by the city itself — by its sociability and its gathering together of knowledge. Possibly the urbanite's appreciation of nature is taught by the physical form of the city — the fact that it functions something like a living, natural organism, even if this lesson is largely subliminal.

Appreciation for nature takes many forms among city folk. The average city is a complex botanical garden of trees, bushes and flowers from all over the world — on streets, in parks and yards, in containers on porches, in lobbies and living rooms, hanging from macramé, attached to chunks of dried peat moss; from tiny lobelia and Johnny jump ups to giant sunflowers and towering redwoods, from showy palm trees to bushy ferns loved passionately by their owners. Aquariums, terrariums and bird cages are perennially popular. Biodiversity in cities, despite the acreage given over to buildings, barren rooftops and asphalt streets and parking lots, is very high, surpassing that of many environments where few or no people live. Dogs, cats, guinea pigs, hamsters, snakes, geckos, chameleons, tarantulas, ants and worms are all living in our homes and schools.

Cities are perhaps most exciting when storms hit, windows shiver, thunder and lightning crack the night, lights go out, snow silences the streets, stars come out sparkling — and birthrates are statistically higher nine months after a power failure or blackout. Even moderate earthquakes and volcanoes at a just slightly dangerous distance, like Mount St. Helens erupting within sight of Portland, are exciting, breathtaking experiences that create respect for nature in most of us. As Ian McHarg says, "We need nature as much in the city as in the countryside."[15] Most urbanites, and in fact suburbanites, too, spend a good deal of time and energy dreaming, planning and doing something about getting out of town in quest of more nature. Suburban life in itself is an expression of the desire to have both an urban and a rural life at the same time.

THE NATURE OF THE CITY

In understanding the nature of the city, distance is a key factor. The principle of access by proximity applies to living organisms and cities alike. Gathering people together reduces distances, which in turn reduces the need for travel and expenditure of transport energy, the level of pollution produced and the quantity of land paved. If cities are fulfilling an evolutionary and environmental purpose of some sort, it is better that they be trim and energy-efficient in their activities, as natural ecological systems invariably are.

Country people who actually live off the land and do no harm in the process, who don't commute, travel only rarely, compost, recycle and use renewable energy technologies have little impact on nature. But the typical energy requirements and pollution production per person in the country can be very high. The rural lifestyle in which a house stands alone, sharing no walls, common spaces or tools with others, and in which long-distance travel is required for sustenance and socializing, appears to be settled gently into nature but in fact is a major cause of environmental degradation.

In building a city, as compared with a rural or suburban infrastructure, the investment per person is far smaller — another efficiency in the nature of the city that benefits nature. The building materials, streets, rails, transportation vehicles, pipes and power lines required are far less per person than in sprawled suburbs and rural areas. Services are more compacted spatially, too, allowing speedier delivery and less expenditure of money and energy. The postal delivery person serves many more people in a day's work in the city than in the country, delivering mail to dozens of people at an apartment building or two when those dozens might take five, ten or twenty times as long to serve in the suburbs or country — requiring the post office to buy more trucks and gasoline and hire more delivery people for any given number of deliveries. Fire trucks and ambulances arrive more quickly, and far more people with serious injuries in the country die than in the city because of the time it takes to get to medical assistance.

Cities are blamed for the sheer quantity of population, pollution and demand for energy and other resources they generate, but if the same number of people with the same level of consumption were more dispersed their impacts would be far greater. When people blame the city for environmental damage they fail to distinguish the all-important element of density of population, lumping dense, diverse communities with sprawling suburbs. Compact cities can actually constitute a long step toward reducing a population's assault on nature. Reducing overall population, reordering the built community, cutting demand, changing the technology, or any combination of the above will help solve the problem. When city building becomes ecocity building, all approaches will be taken at once. (Impact = Population times Land use/infrastructure times Affluence times Technology.) When all these parts are brought together in the logic of a well-tuned organism, then we will have a synergistic combination with far greater benefit than otherwise conceivable.

The well-formed city is a kind of economic/social machine of very high efficiency. People live in cities partly because the very structure of the city means that they can get more done there with less energy, effort, time and financial cost. The city is a natural pattern of organization for cultural living, as much as anything else about us might be natural. When built and functioning well, the city can be an excellent tool for bringing culture into harmony with nature. It's just that nobody has bothered to pursue its design and construction as such.

ELEPHANTS IN BERKELEY?

Berkeley's natural historian and expert on Native American history, Malcolm Margolin, has described the rich tapestry of living creatures, landscapes and local microclimates that characterized the Berkeley-Oakland area before the Europeans arrived, at a time when the local Native Americans managed the landscape with fire. Grassy hills on the east rose over a gently sloping savanna dotted with occasional oaks. These sloping flatlands terminated in the west at the marshes and sandy beaches of San Francisco Bay. The canyons in the hills were covered with gigantic redwoods and fragrant bay laurels. Many creeks, emerging from the hills, took roughly parallel courses across the flatlands to the bay, connecting the ridge line to the shoreline with green strips of mixed bushes and willows and occasional larger trees. These colonnades of trees seemed to pour out of the canyons through the year-round grasses, past the scattering of seasonal ponds and freshwater marshes, toward the salty realm of crabs, shrimp, salmon, sturgeon, seals, otters and whales.

This was the most popular avian resort on the migratory flyway of the west coast of North America. Seabirds and inland birds by the millions blotted out the light in dark, swirling clouds, raising the sound of thunder with their countless wings. Hawks cut their way through the confusion to rodents and rabbits while enormous California condors hovered and wheeled overhead. Elk, antelope and bear moved across the landscape with other large mammals, not the least of which were people.

The Oakland-Berkeley Hills firestorm of October 20, 1991 swept away whole neighborhoods — 3,375 homes — with such intensity that concrete foundations crumbled into softly rounded stones. Despite my having known the landscape so well, so complete was its transformation that I found it hard to remember what had been there before. When, a few days later, I asked Margolin, "What was the landscape like here before the Indians arrived and began managing it with fire?" he paused for a long moment before answering.

"I don't know. I don't know if I've ever thought about it."

In the next few days I kept asking the question of friends until one of them, a remarkable naturalist named Sterling Bunnell, said, "Well, it probably looked a lot like East Africa does now, because it was managed by elephants."

Elephants in Berkeley? That was a mind-expanding idea. Probably, Sterling suggested, the landscape here before the Indians, before about 15,000 to 10,000 years ago, was very complex and richer in biodiversity than the same land the Indians inhabited later. There were two species of elephant, a giant camel, a giant ground sloth, a giant bear, a very large dire wolf, the American lion (slightly larger than the African lion today) and horses. The Indians, he said, seem to have eaten them all (maybe not the wolf and lion) and were probably the main cause of their extinction. In addition there would have been the animals the Indians lived among when the Europeans arrived, such as elk, deer, antelope and grizzly and black bear.

The elephants' role? They rummaged about tearing up trees, creating large areas of open space and trampling paths in wild but logical patterns across the landscape, clearing portions of forests in some areas, slicing through brush lands, leaving trails that many other animals could use. Elephants have a knack for knowing where water is located just under the surface. They rip into the soil with their tusks, throwing the earth to the side, and dig down to the shallow water table. Thus they create ponds that they and many other species enjoy for drinking and bathing. In other words, they manage the land like a special kind of gardener who somehow, without a stated plan, ends up creating tremendous biodiversity. Furthermore, in Africa they are known to deforest very large areas of land, giving rise to a whole new sequence of ecological zones, with the forests growing back over many decades. They act something like great fires rotating around immense landscapes creating variety over long periods of time as well as large geographic areas. It seems they are bent upon creating diversity in almost every way they can.

What the elephants do on their canvas of millions of acres over hundreds of years, said Sterling, is essentially to create convoluted edges between various habitats and time periods. Edges are far richer in life than large habitats of a single type or ones existing in the same condition without change over time. He added that the appreciation people have for landscapes with edges (a forest edge on a meadow, a moist oasis up against cactus desert) which are called "ecotones," is probably the source of some of our aesthetic sensitivity and comes from the fact that they are full of possibilities for things to eat, building materials for nests and places to escape from predators. I asked Sterling, "If elephants are gardeners of this sort, creating such rich environments, could people do the same?"

"Undoubtedly," he answered.

Margolin[16] has described how people can insert themselves into a natural environment and create subtle changes in that environment that make it richer in wildlife. In *Earth Manual: Working Wild Land Without Taming It* he writes of collecting seeds from native plants, carefully labeling them, then planting them strategically at proper times of the year. In the same breath, however, he may propose chopping down a tree or even cutting half way through the trunk and toppling it over so that, in the late winter and early spring when food can be desperately scarce for deer and rabbits, animals can browse in its twigs, buds and bark. This tree cutting is based on the assumption that there is no scarcity of trees in the area, but it is still startling — except for the fact that we can see in it the elephant gardener at work. Similarly, he suggests gathering broken limbs and arranging logs and rocks to create cover for small animals so that they can more easily avoid predators. He also advocates damming watercourses far more enthusiastically than I had anticipated, saying that it is hard to go wrong creating more bodies of water and land/water edges provided that proper fish ladders and special diversity-maintaining strategies are employed. Cataracts should be saved. Flooding scarce habitats and beautiful features should be avoided. As Sterling Bunnell points out, an aesthetic sense helps us identify the areas of most diversity — again, the elephant at work, or maybe in this case the beaver.

Permaculturists, with their subtle design approach to a "permanent agriculture," agro-foresters and organic farmers all use design principles to produce rich harvests, although the biodiversity here is likely to be mostly among non-indigenous food plants and animals. Crop rotations, companion planting, the use of manure and composting have the potential, taken together, to get enormous production out of the soil while leaving it as rich as, or richer in nutrients than before.

NATIVE AMERICANS AND INVADERS

Sterling Bunnell theorizes that Native Americans remember with regret, in their ancient oral traditions, the earlier days when their ancestors hunted and exterminated the great Pleistocene mammals of North America. He thinks it likely that the traditions that focus such reverence on nature come from such an understanding, and that a determination to avoid any such future catastrophe is partially responsible for their eco-logically-informed philosophy and lifeways. By this theory, the Bay Area Native Americans managed their landscape with fire specifically for maximum species diversity, that is, for the preservation of all species. Other students of the subject say that the warming and drying of the continent in the waning centuries of the last Ice Age, which coincided with the appearance of humans with relatively advanced hunting weapons, was the more important cause of extinction and that, in any case, there is no way an oral tradition could preserve memory over such an enormous time span. In either case, some people knew a lot more than the European immigrants and their descendants about their environments and used that knowledge in arranging their lives and communities. We can learn from them.

Kirkpatrick Sale and David E. Stannard both speak of the relationship between the white conquerors of the Americas and those they conquered, and contrast their perspectives on nature.[17] For those who think that recent industrial society is the first to abuse nature and that the science of Newton and the philosophy of Descartes represent the biblical fall from grace, these scholars' work opens up new territory. The poison has long been alive and well in a form as damaging as today's and goes back far beyond Newton and Descartes. In fact, it is biblical and even earlier. In many ways the pre-industrial conquest of peoples and nature was more intentional than today's environmental destruction, which is often a by-product of preoccupations so far removed from the site of exploitation that the beneficiaries of the exploitation scarcely know it is happening, and, furthermore, don't want to know. The older style of exploitation was far more personal and intentional. People just went out and killed, stole and extracted with a righteous rationale, clad in armor, by the strength of the flailing arm, with blood and wood chips flying everywhere.

"When Colon [Columbus] set foot on his landfall island he brought this ecological heritage with him," says Sale.[18]

> We must begin, alas, with Europe's fear of most of the elements of
> the natural world — a fear based, as it always is, on simple
> ignorance. ... The church offered no encouragement for any

investigation. ... Common lore ... was not much better, filled with either mundane and stereotypical views (lambs are meek, lions brave, wolves crafty) or fanciful and erroneous ones (toads suck cow's milk at night, woodpeckers are dangerous predators, beech trees deflect lightning ...) ... All this platitude and misinformation about the real world was glued together with nonsense about the monstrous and fantastic world, and held to with the same level of credulity by even the most inquiring minds of the day: Laurence Andrew's very popular bestiary *The Nobel Life & Natures of Man, of Beasts, Serpents, Fowls & Fishes That Be Most Known*, for example, the first printed work on animals in the English language, lists with equal credulence 144 known animals, 8 entirely unknown and 21 strictly mythological."

The Alps that we tend to think of as so beautiful today, draped in snow, looking up at us from coffee-table books and down from wall calendars, were "distorted," "chaotic" and "hideous" to commentators at the time of the early European colonial conquests. The forests were full of monsters, criminals and diabolic forces. The sooner they were cut down and put to use the better.

And that they were. Sale estimates that Europeans were consuming a ton of wood per person per year by 1500.[19] John Perlin documents forest after forest falling faster than they could grow back in Europe from Roman times on. This followed a legacy two or three thousand years older in the Middle East, where deforestation upstream from the Mesopotamian Valley helped drive one civilization after another over the edge and into oblivion. By Columbus' day many European countries were searching outside their borders for the natural resources that had become scarce or unavailable because of over-utilization. Just in time, a whole new rich and relatively defenseless world was discovered.

As the state and church controlled life and afterlife in the Europe of the time, so when the Europeans confronted the wild areas of the world they saw them and their people as dangerously out of control and needing to be disciplined, civilized. The word "wild," Sale points out, comes from "willed," that is, "self-willed, self-determining." People and living things that functioned on their own without adherence to higher authority were somehow out of line in a proper cosmology, and therefore their exploitation and destruction was of no particular concern.

> This separation from the natural world, this estrangement from the realm of the wild, I think, exists in no other complex culture on earth. In its attitude to the wilderness, a heightening of its deep-seated antipathy to nature in general, European culture created a frightening distance between the human and the natural. ... To have regarded the world as sacred, as do many other cultures around the world, would have been almost inconceivable in medieval Europe — and, if conceived ... punishable by the Inquisition.

In addition to ships, guns and a willingness to kill, steal and rationalize, says Stannard, "It has been estimated that, because of its animals of transport and burden, fifteenth-century Europe had a source of power five times as great as that of China. If one considers the almost total absence of large domesticated animals in the New World, it might be said to have had as much as twenty times that of the Americas."[20] Noting that no wheels were used in the New World except, oddly, on toy animals for children, we can see another advantage to the Europeans in conflict with Native Americans.

But the conquest and subsequent colonization of most of the world by Europeans was perhaps based even more on cities. First, the city itself was an invention that made possible extremely rapid exchange of ideas, resources and tools, and provided immediately available work forces. We seldom hear that the city itself conquered nature and the more nature-based cultures of the world, but the suggestion was not lost on the conquerors themselves. Their entire enterprise was named for the city and very consciously called "civilization." It was held in such high moral, mythological, even cosmological esteem that it became the ultimate rationale for exterminating or expropriating all cultures, species, properties, habitats and people in its path. The objective was to bring civilization to all people and to tame the wild for industrial and agricultural production with the city at its center. Heaven itself was the City of God, and it was its streets, not the rural paths in the woods, that were paved with gold.

In contrast, indigenous peoples lived more harmoniously with nature. For over 1,000 years the Kogis of Colombia have lived high on the forested mountain slopes twenty-five miles from Santa Marta on the Caribbean coast. Since they melted into the forest to escape the Spanish in the 1500s they have been practically unknown to the outside world. A 19,000-foot mountain massif eighty miles on a side called Pico Cristobal Colon, or the Sierra Nevada de Santa Marta, is the glacier-draped center of their world and, they say, ours as well.

In the 1970s, with their glaciers receding, waterfalls drying up and species disappearing, the Kogi elders (the Mamas) trained one of their own to become their spokesperson to plead with the outside world to restore balance to human/natural affairs. Coincidentally, at about the same time, a grave robber digging for the gold of the Tairona, the Kogis' ancestors, wandered into a particularly forbidding and wet section of the lower mountains, and there, just fifteen miles outside Santa Marta, stumbled upon a stunning "lost city." The anthropologist who directed the early excavations of the city, Alvaro Soto, said, "What Indian mind wanted to show was that it is possible to have a good density of population in a very beautiful environment without destroying it. They adapted the city to fit this environment perfectly."

Despite over four hundred years of potential erosion by water and disruption by plant roots in this dense, wet jungle, the stone work is only slightly damaged. The Colombian Director of Indian Affairs, Martin von Hildebrand, said of the city, "It was a whole, integrated organism. It is the interrelation of these sites that keeps the world in harmony, and it is the duty of the Mamas to see that the world remains in harmony. If you excavate … you take out part of the system. Each part is integrated into the whole. They consider that fundamental."

Said the Mamas, "People were made to care for the plants and the animals. If we act well, the world can go on." Their directions for restoring the well-being of the world included the request that anthropologists, gold seekers and others leave their lost city so that they could return to it and restore it to well-being and, in so doing, increase the well-being of the world. Their request was honored, and they have begun to reestablish themselves there.

Close-ups in a film about the Kogi provide some notion of how building in that location could be substantial and long lasting. Rocks in walls and walkways on the steep slopes and ridges lap in such a way that dripping water from the frequent rains falls free of the walls rather than running down cracks where stones meet. The gardens of the Tairona and the

Kogi appear to be a cross between complex companion planting and a kind of forest management. They plant in the forest while caring for the self-propagating plants that they value for their many different uses. What they are doing amounts to: cutting trees selectively, choosing carefully to maintain species diversity and enhance their usefulness to people; introducing special food plants and carefully managing the ones already present; protecting favored animals from predators; feeding individual animals and plants in need; clearing small areas to get extra sun to flowers considered especially beautiful, and planting to give more shade to another; adjusting rocks to direct rivulets in times of rain to dry plants; and moving large rocks from dry stream beds to create ponds. All this and more than we can imagine is the reality there in this landscape that ranges from rain forest to desert, fog forest to icy tundra, palm-fringed beach and tidal pool to blue glacier and frosted waterfall — all separated by less than twenty-five miles.

The lost city of the Tairona, the center of this culture, was, of course, strictly pedestrian and so were the other ancient New World cities and towns. Their citizens probably didn't think much in terms of "compact development" because, given a foot-transportation reality, they simply built so that people could get to one another and out into the countryside. It must have seemed natural — as natural as clusters of cliff-swallow nests, beaver dams, honeycombs and caterpillar tents.

Not only the environments and cultures in the Americas, but also the types of community were extraordinarily diverse. Many of the works of Native Americans were formidable by any standard. The Adena culture, beginning 1,000 years before Greece, came to cover an area from Vermont to Indiana and from New York to Virginia. Its people built "towns with houses that were circular in design and that ranged from single-family dwellings as small as twenty feet in diameter to multi-family units up to eighty feet across ... in close proximity to large public enclosures of 300 feet and more in diameter" called sacred circles by archeologists "because of their presumed use for religious ceremonial purposes."[21]

The Hopewell culture that followed it covered a territory from New York to Kansas and from the Northern Great Lakes to the Gulf of Mexico. Like the Adena, it had intensive horticulture and large monuments to the dead. Says Stannard,

Literally tens of thousands of these towering earthen mounds once covered the American landscape from the Great Plains to the eastern woodlands, many of them precise, geometrically-shaped, massive structures of 1,000 feet in diameter and several stories high. Others — such as the famous quarter-mile-long coiled snake at Serpent Mound, Ohio — were imaginatively designed symbolic temples.[22]

The fantastic carvings and paintings of the Northwest Coast Indians, adorning totem poles, large communal buildings and seafaring canoes, are relatively well-known. But even in the supposedly barren lands of the Inuit the seas, shoreline and skies often seethed with life, and the people built not only the well-known igloo but also, Stannard points out, "the huge, semi-subterranean barabara structures of the Aleutian Islands, each of them up to 200 feet long and fifty feet wide, and housing more than 100 people."[23]

The classic urban people of North America were the Anasazi of Arizona, New Mexico, Colorado and Utah. In Chaco Canyon, New Mexico,[24]

more than 1,000 years ago, there existed the metropolitan hub of hundreds of villages and at least nine large towns constructed around enormous multi-storied building complexes. Pueblo Bonito is an example of one of these: a single, four-story building with large, high-ceilinged rooms and balconies, it contained 800 rooms, including private residence for more than 1200 people and dozens of circular common rooms up to sixty feet in diameter. No single structure in what later became the United States housed this many people until the largest apartment buildings of New York City were constructed in the nineteenth century.

Today's Hopi people, who claim the Anasazi as their ancestors, live in much the same manner. Vernon Masayesva, Chairman of the Hopi Tribe, describes their cities:[25]

Some of our pueblos date back to 900 A.D. and some of our oldest villages pre-date that period. Oraibi is the oldest continually inhabited community on the North American continent. The only message I can give you is what Hopis have accepted as their responsibility for the privilege of living on this Earth. We are concerned for all living things; our architecture reflects this same spirit of reverence for what we call Mother Earth. Hopi villages have pueblo-style housing. We were the first known apartment builders constructing houses about four stories high.

The Hopi village always has a plaza, which is the heart. A village to Hopis is a living entity, and so the center, the plaza, is the heart where all sorts of public ceremonies are performed, where children are entertained. Many religious ceremonies were reserved for special places called kivas, built in outlying areas around a village for special ceremonial purposes. The old villages, old houses, were not necessarily built by men; many were built by women, because it was like giving birth to a house. The Hopi architecture was built by the people, for the people. This is an important point to make because I've been through several cities, and the new architecture seems to me to be all science. It's all brains and no heart. They aren't cities where we can grow and be sensitive to our environment, where we nurture our values, where we can teach our kids the important values we never want to forget.

When the Americans came they wanted to make us in their image and they brought with them schools and their style of architecture which was pitched roof, tin-covered, square box houses. And they built these houses primarily to entice the Hopi leadership to move down off the mesas and into the houses, the new houses, the white man houses. It was a way to break up the community in the villages. The buildings that they built had no relation to what the Hopi values were. ... So eventually we forgot that communities can be built in such a way that they're environmentally sensitive. If the Hopi has any message for future cities, it is to keep these things in mind. Building should respond to the needs of mankind, and the need of mankind today is to be stewards. So the ecocity is not just the city of the future, but is also the city of the past. Because they all have to now be tied together.

How can the Kogi and the Hopi, with such modest technologies, consider themselves the keepers of the Earth when they lack the powers of industrial society to mine, techno-farm, alter enormous landscapes and build gigantic edifices? In the same way that the bacteria in the oceans 3 billion years ago managed to change the atmosphere of the entire planet and transform its stony shell to the depths of many miles — by small acts of commitment sustained over a long time all going in the right direction. Small things can replicate. Small steps toward ecocities can add up to a healthy planet.

The Kogi and the Hopi actively seek the ear of the outside world because they identify with the patience of nature, knowing it well, and understand the power of the deceptively small thing, the idea, the thinking itself. Oddly, we in the technological world around them, steeped in massive flows of information, give very little credit to thinking itself. What really counts in this high-consumption world is the bottom line, how much wealth, power and supposed resulting pleasure we have accumulated. Those who know the power of a true idea are different, and they have included many Native Americans. They have what I call "conceptual integrity," which believes as it does not because it has high ratings, big sales, voter support, multiple endorsements and popularity, but because it seems to be true in its own right. A few good words at the right time are like a minute cosmic ray on its trajectory toward a strand of DNA about to bring on a positive mutation, create a new species and thus a new world, not out of arrogance, but simply by being there heading in the right direction, at home in the universe, doing the right thing. That which the Native Americans understand and we don't, quite yet, is the big secret for a healthy future.

BIOREGIONS, HINTERLANDS AND CITIES

A natural system that expresses a kind of unity is known as a bioregion — a landscape within natural bounds, often a watershed, made up of a distinctive set of species in interrelationships specific to that region. The demarcations can be very subtle, as a rich grassland fades into a desert, or abrupt, as a mountain ridge cuts a sharp line between dense upwind forest and downwind desert. Within a bioregion there may be extremely complex and highly differentiated smaller environments, such as a river with all that it supports in its waters, a marsh system, or a grassland valley, each with fish, birds, insects and large mammals, some of which overlap into the adjacent environments.

Peter Berg of San Francisco's Planet Drum Foundation has added the human dimension to earlier notions of the bioregion, and he acknowledges that cities can fit comfortably into a bioregion. Just how has not yet

Where city centers meet the bioregion, small plazas can be created and paths into the hinterlands.

been thoroughly worked out, partly because detail is of the essence and it takes a long time for the complex detail of a bioregion to be organized into clear, large patterns of order in the mind of any person living there. But the fine threads are weaving together (miniplexing) right now. We are learning bioregions by long, sensitive study, observation and careful participation in trial, error and course correction. Traditional indigenous cultures have had a strong tendency to respect their elders, in part, because it is in the nature of much of the knowledge that counts that it is complex, detailed and takes time and patience to learn.

Jane Jacobs, bringing her keen observations of urban life to bear on the bioregional perspective, links cities intimately with what she calls "the hinterlands" — the basis in nature providing resources for the city while the city provides the vital economy for both itself and the hinterlands. Summarizing economic theories of recent history, she points out how difficult it has been to apply these theories to reality. It seems that all of them have failed to function as predicted. In fact, economic surges and disasters have come and gone in a pattern so much their own, so independent of control or clear understanding, that theory is little improvement over muddling through by habit or tossing dice. "In the face of so many nasty surprises," says Jacobs,[26]

> ... we must be suspicious that some basic assumption or other is in error, most likely an assumption so much taken for granted that it escapes identification and skepticism. Macro-economic theory does contain such an assumption. It is the idea that national economies are useful and salient entities for understanding how economic life works and what its structure may be; that national economies and not some other entity provide the fundamental data for macro-economic analysis.

What she offers instead is the concept that cities, generally the relatively large and economically diverse ones, are the key organizers of economies, the basic units of economic prosperity. It is in the nature of vital cities to produce a great variety and number of products for their own people and trade actively with suppliers in the hinterlands and with other cities. Cities can do this because they have assembled many productive, creative people and their tools, facilities and resources close enough together to allow frequent exchange with each other, sharing ideas, and providing raw materials and parts and services for one another. Without all the parts, including the people, linked and actively participating together in a vital city, the economic processes cannot thrive. Some people — the Shah of Iran and Peter the Great of Russia, for example — have tried to buy "development" without assembling the parts of a city, including the traditions of innovation, but it has never worked. Lewis Mumford, advancing the same thesis twenty-three years earlier, argued that "the industrialization and commercialization we now associate with urban growth was for centuries a subordinate phenomenon, probably even emerging later in time."[27]

Jacobs also points out that the city depends on the hinterlands from which food and resources come. The people in the hinterlands in turn receive from the city tools, cultural items and access to markets. If the city and its hinterlands can thus be mutually supportive, ecological diversity in the country can be encouraged via increased variety of markets, which encourages diversification of products paralleling biodiversity from the hinterlands. In one case she mentions, in Japan, rare mushrooms attracted the attention of farmers and began to be harvested for sale in a nearby city. After that, the mushrooms and their associated environment thrived under the stewardship of people selling to the markets in the city. With the mushrooms as a new source of prosperity, the people reduced forest cutting and invested some of their new income and liberated time in imaginatively expanding their range of products even more, while obtaining new tools and information from the city. They discovered a vested interest in natural biodiversity and launched initiatives to preserve it. In this way complex cities can assist in restoring and maintaining complex ecologies.

At the core of the dynamic of cities are the various business and production activities Jacobs calls "import replacement": producing the variety of items that makes the community thrive, instead of buying them from others. She considers import replacement very basic, going so far as to say that, to exist at all, a vital city needs a preexisting vital city producing what it needs but is not yet able to produce. She traces cities slowly emerging out of the early unknown in ancient times and overlapping one another temporally, more recent ones firing up on the basis of responses to their earlier trading partners. She speaks of lonely Venice, established in the seventh century off the Adriatic coast of what is now northern Italy. Retaining knowledge of boat building and other fading memories of Rome and Greece, its citizens found refuge from the barbarians on the European shore who had failed to learn from the empire they had helped destroy, had no ships, and simply couldn't get at them. But there was a city that Venice, struggling up from the mud and sandbars of the Great Lagoon could trade with: Constantinople, 1400 nautical miles away, maintaining the functions of a vital city. Venetians, says Jacobs, were clever enough to begin replacing their Constantinople imports by making many of them for themselves. Virtually all they had to trade was salt evaporated from the shallow waters around Venice, but the people in Constantinople wanted it. As they got good at replacing their imports by making the products themselves, the Venetians began trading their new products with later European cities in the same parenting role that Constantinople had played for Venice.

Later European cities, launched largely by Venice centuries earlier, played the same parenting role for American cities. The Native American cities parenting one another in this manner couldn't influence the new wave of cities after Columbus because, simply put, they were summarily and totally annihilated.

Says Jacobs,

> City import-replacing is not all that economically glamorous. The replacements are usually small initially, frequently involve items that in themselves are frivolous, and in many cases are absolutely imitative — but nevertheless, in the aggregate, they add up to momentous economic forces. ... Indeed, as far as I can see, city import-replacing is in this way at the root of all economic expansion.[28]

This may provide something of an explanation for the nature of cities as they go about exploiting nature and other cities for their own self-development. But another question immediately comes to mind: Where do the imports that get replaced come from originally? Some cities may be replacing imported computer keyboards in the 1990s and supplying themselves and their region with them, for example, but cities weren't doing this in 1940 because these items didn't exist yet. Who came up with the original? On this even more basic level of creativity it seems that the city is at least as important as it is in the import-replacing business, serving to gather resources not just for imitation, but for the genius of creation itself.

At yet one level deeper we can ask how was the city itself created? Thomas Berry, the theologian of the Ecozoic, says that the most creative period of history was the Neolithic village-making phase. Perhaps the basic building blocks of today's economics, the germ of the first city, began then with the simple gathering of homes together into the first village that added a few community buildings with special designs for special functions. The Agricultural Revolution, with its domestication of animals and plants and slow buildup of items — stone tools to copper to bronze to iron, baskets to clay pots to metal pans, sun-dried brick to fired brick, dry-stacked stone to stone and mortar, and so on — initiated much of the basic village creativity, which was elaborated and refined later in cities. The logic of the whole community-building venture, including the social and economic dynamics of it, was probably as unconscious then as it is now for almost everybody. The creativity of the myth building and spiritual awakening that concern Berry predates cities and grew up as language — another immense cultural creative product — complexified. All this was sheltered and facilitated in the early organizing unit that was the village in its natural hinterlands.

All these elements and the village itself grew, and grew very slowly together. Mumford believes that, "The city of the dead antedates the city of the living."[29] Nomadic people, he argues, came back to burial grounds to remember their loved ones and their past, set up temporary camps nearby, probably noticed discarded seeds from earlier visits sprouting into berry plants and fruit trees, set up permanent camps after that, and, voila! There is evidence, too, that the complexifying village was a creation of hunting and gathering societies predating agriculture. In this view, the magic of "access by proximity," and perhaps an organized sort of leisure facilitated by the village, led not only to the culture of complex cities, but to agriculture, too.

BUFFALO COMMONS

Today many towns and rural areas do not flourish without massive subsidy from outside, usually provided by a national economic policy establishing an extractive economy. In a sense they are "unnatural" and are forced into a non-reciprocal relationship with the land, climate and biota. Usually they are in economically-dependent mining, logging or cattle-raising regions that Jane Jacobs calls "supply regions," often far from the cities to which they deliver resources or products. Without a national policy to support it, habitation of such supply regions would barely exist, since nature can't support it and distances from a vital city economy are too great to be conveniently bridged. But nation-states are another thing. They look for defense resources, cultivate national pride, want to extend the common language and customs, are fixated on grand economic strategy, believe in the conquest of nature and savages by civilization, want more wealth for their rich people, power for their politicians, dreams for their poor, and so on.

The Great Plains of the United States give us an example of what a nation-state, as contrasted with a city/hinterlands system, want to extract from the country — in this case wheat and Indians. Grain agriculture was the economic idea initially, and an Indianless frontier the racist cultural one. Whatever it was didn't last very long.

In 1937 the painter Thomas Hart Benton wrote, "Cozy-minded people hate the brute magnitude of the plains country. For me the great plains have a releasing effect. I like the way they make human beings appear as the little bugs they really are. Human effort is seen there in all its painful futility. The universe is stripped to dirt and air, to wind, dust, clouds and the white sun."[30]

Frank and Deborah Popper of Rutgers University's Urban Studies Department think it's time to face up to the reality that that portion of the United States called the Great Desert on early nineteenth-century maps is simply not economically substantial enough — and far too far from places that are — to be anybody's hinterlands but their[31] own. They write,

> At the center of the United States, between the Rockies and the tallgrass prairies of the Midwest and South, lies the shortgrass expanse of the Great Plains. The region extends over large parts of ten states and produces cattle, corn, wheat, sheep, cotton, coal, oil, natural gas and metals. The Plains are endlessly windswept and nearly treeless; the climate is semiarid, with typically less than twenty inches of rain a year.
>
> A dusty town with a single gas station, store and house is sometimes fifty unpaved miles from its nearest neighbor, another three-building settlement amid the sagebrush. ... Although the Plains occupy one-fifth of the Nation's land area, the region's overall population, approximately 5.5 million, is less than that of Georgia or Indiana.
>
> The Great Plains are America's steppes. They have the nation's coldest winters, greatest temperature swings, worst hail and locusts and range fires, fiercest droughts and blizzards, and therefore its shortest growing season.[32]

This starkly beautiful, big-sky country, with its ferociously unforgiving weather, has absorbed and flung back wave after wave of government-subsidized settlement. First the 1862 Homestead Act sent a flood of farmers and ranchers into the Plains with large subsidies, not the least of which was the clearance of the Plains Indians by massacre and starvation via destruction of their food supply, the buffalo. Exterminating the buffalo helped the future homesteaders also because, as a friend of mine once said of the vast stampeding herds, "Those guys don't stop for fences, you know." The intense blizzards of the 1880s and the drought and financial panic of the 1890s drove out most of the first wave of homesteaders.

During World War I, with competition reduced and demand increased because of Europe's collapsed agricultural production, there was another subsidized boom. But even before the depression of the 1930s, the economy of the Plains was collapsing again. Then came the Dust Bowl.

From the 1950s through the 1970s dams were built with federal funds, lands purchased or reclaimed from the second wave of departing homesteaders, and rented below market to new farmers and ranchers: the third wave of subsidy. In the 1970s oil and natural gas were extracted, coinciding with a quadrupling of the value of these fuels due to OPEC's increased oil prices, creating two hundred energy boomtowns. Today we are in another bust cycle and the Poppers are asking why throw good money after bad? Water supplies are diminishing in the area. The enormous Oglalla Aquifer, a veritable underground sea supplying 11 million acres of farmland in Colorado, Kansas, Nebraska, New Mexico and Texas, is being depleted far more rapidly than it can be replaced by rain soaking into the terrain. Many counties in this region are in poverty conditions, with virtually all their young people departed. Median age is more than fifty. Meanwhile buffalo ranching is becoming firmly established. When cattle freeze and stiffly topple over dead in the harsh Alaskan winds, the buffalo just hunker down in little clusters of deeply-matted, furry insulation many inches thick while land values fall, schools, banks and whole towns close down.

Restoration of some of the wild lands has worked already. "Beginning in 1937," say the Poppers, "the federal government bought up 7.3 million acres of largely abandoned farm holdings of the Plains (an area bigger than Maryland), replanted them, and designated them national grasslands. Today the national grasslands are used primarily for low-intensity grazing and recreation. Often thick with shortgrasses, they rank among the most successful types of federal land holdings."

Why not support what works? say the Poppers. Why not take nature's hint and reintroduce what they call the Buffalo Commons — a gigantic swath of the United States from Texas to Canada where wire fences snap, curl and rust into the ground; where wooden posts dry, crack, fall and disappear beneath wildflowers from horizon to distant horizon; where the plodding of cattle hooves recedes into oblivion as the thunder of bison returns? In this wild landscape, a few oasis-like small towns could be cultural watering holes for hearty Indians, buffalo-boys and occasional eco-tourists from distant cities. The Poppers predict that we will in fact learn from those past mistakes:"[33]

> During the twenty-first century, the American frontier will expand and become more visible. Large chunks of the rural West will be privately preserved — for instance, by ranchers who discover they can do far better by renting their land to hunters for part of the year than by laboriously running cattle on it year-round. The Nature Conservancy and similar preservation organizations will make extensive land purchases. The ecological restoration of land damaged by previous extractive use will be big business; so will ecological tourism. ... The combined rise of preservation and decline of extraction will present a remarkable chance to undo the nation's past mistakes. .... We are no longer a frontier nation, but we are still a nation with a frontier. And it will be a frontier that will expand far into the next century."

So said the Poppers in 1991. Ten years later, they are seeing their Buffalo Commons metaphor moving toward reality. It makes sense in this place. In a new flurry of scholarly papers they are now touting the use of regional metaphor to create themes that will shape sensible relations between people and their natural and cultural foundations. A metaphor like the Buffalo Commons, they say, is "soft planning." Its objective is not to write laws and ordinances, General Plans and zoning codes, but to create the almost poetic images and understandings that lead such political agreements into a world where our imaginations do right by the place where we live.

LEARNING FROM NATURE, LEARNING FROM CITIES

The cultures that lived close to nature rather than behind the walls of cities, suburbs and layer upon layer of technology, of course, learned something from nature. They had to to survive. But with our whole-systems sciences, like ecology and evolution biology — and let's not forget "ecocitology" — we can break through the barriers, the concrete and asphalt and automobile habits and learn even more.

Perhaps the nature of cities was more accessible to those living in the first of them, the logic of access by proximity arising "naturally" before humans had the technologies of transportation that made ignoring spatial relationships possible. In the earlier indigenous ways of learning the logic of nature and nature of cities, important relationships with wild animals and native plants were obvious, respect for such large-scale concepts as conservation and recycling was basic. As cities increased in size, however, their citizens forgot many of those lessons, exploiting to the extent of expunging the basic ethic of conservation and recycling, sweeping it away with the exhaustion of numerous resources, thoughtlessly dumping waste and even laying waste entire rival cities. Now we can see a whole second-generation list of lessons from nature, from the subtlety of ecological interconnections reinvigorating the old lessons of conservation and recycling, to the recognition of the place of our civilization in evolution.

Hints are available from the deeper layers of biology, too. Nature shows us a sequence of events in healthy biological relationships that we ignore only at great risk. Here the idea of the "builder's sequence," which I will discuss in more detail later on, can be useful. Just as in building a house we have to start from the foundation, so we have to start healthy cities from a foundation in good land uses and build up from there to specifics. This model applies not only to the sequence of evolution, from which we can learn much, but to the fact that, "Ontogeny recapitulates phylogeny" — that the whole evolutionary life of a species (phylogeny) is played back all over again in a kind of shorthand as an individual living creature develops (ontogeny). We don't just appear as full-blown, tiny human beings immediately after conception, getting larger for nine months in the womb. Instead we look rather like a jellyfish at first, then later develop shark-like gills, then amphibian flipper lobes, then a reptil-

78

Learning from nature. One pattern in many forests is the sequence of unique environments laid out vertically, one above the other. This can be a model for city structure.

ian tail, and so on, step-by-step turning into humans, building physically upon a pyramid of life going back more than 3 billion years. Skipping any of our earlier evolutionary stages in the recapitulation means extreme deformity or death.

Building upon a 3.5-billion-year biological foundation, as well as 15 billion years of cosmic evolution, we are all made of twenty-nine basic molecular building blocks: various amino acids, sugars, nitrogenous molecules and fats.[34] Later evolution does not create new building blocks of exotic materials from somewhere off the band of organic chemistry or even a different set of organic chemicals. It uses the same old ones that are in all of us, from paramecium to redwood tree, from deep-sea squid to Albert Einstein. Unless those building blocks get stacked up in a particular sequence and order the organism doesn't even get started, much less attain any kind of health and success among the living. All or almost all of James Miller's nineteen subsystems of "living systems" have to be present, too.

And so, within the realm of our freedoms and rights, the lessons of nature suggest that we need profound grounding in very specific sequences of development and have a duty to honor that biological history. If we neglect it we will very likely forfeit our freedoms and rights while inflicting immense damage upon the rest of our biosphere. Regarding cities, this will mean respecting the builder's sequence and carefully watching its playing out.

A final lesson from nature is that all organisms — from the bacteria that laid down the bands of iron ore on the ocean bottoms to human beings building civilizations — intervene in the rest of nature no matter what we do. Julian Huxley once said that we've got the job of managing evolution now, whether by design or default, so we might as well get good at it. We might learn from nature in the form of fires, floods and the disruptions of elephants as they go about creating high biodiversity that at first glance looks like destruction. The lesson here is that deeper knowledge gained from observation is very important to long-term health. We may thus learn that we need not be especially timid in altering certain particular environments, but must understand life systems with some real sensitivity before taking action. With our growing planetary, even evolutionary, consciousness guided by the timeless conscience of contemporary ancients, and aided by modern scientific inquiry, can we build cities in balance with nature? If we learn from nature, assuredly we can.

4

The City in History

The quest for the city in balance with nature has almost certainly been part of a dream of human fulfillment since cities first emerged. But cities worked so well, so efficiently, that production became overproduction, and then surfeit and treasure enough to distort the saintly. Once established among its more nature-loving kin, the villages, the city swept its citizens away in confused passions, love of arts, materialist greed, creative brilliance, power hunger, service to humanity, war. Perhaps in looking at that history, we will discover that now is the time to pull those two historic lines of development — city and village — together again.

VILLAGE FOUNDATIONS

Brian Swimme and Thomas Berry[35] say that the Neolithic village of some 11,000 years ago represented humanity's greatest flowering of creativity. As the village was invented, so, too, were the first basic small containers — baskets, pots, granaries and cisterns. Weaving and the beginnings of metal tools and weapons originated about then, probably in early villages. The use of animals for transportation and work and animal husbandry and horticulture also began in this period. Says Lewis Mumford, "Historic man has not added a plant or animal of major importance to those domesticated or cultivated by Neolithic communities."[36]

Ilara, Turkey. Traditional town structure with all basic functions of life within a short walk. Çatal Hüyük, occupied 7-8,000 years ago, was near this site.

This period appears to coincide with the first flowering of complex and subtle language — an awakening from unexpressed memories and dreams and a launching into the manipulative arts that co-evolved with language. The universe, through humans, suddenly awoke and began talking about what it saw, weaving myths and tales, trying to figure everything out for the first time. The first simple stutterings toward solving the great mystery of life and the universe, which took place in the hunter/gatherer Paleolithic, were a crack in the door that in the Neolithic village was flung open to the light of discovery and invention. And the invention of the village had the potential to allow people to establish materially productive and satisfying human communities in a relatively healthy relationship with nature. With the considerate use of agriculture, human needs could be met with reduced pressure on natural flora and fauna. The early village was potentially very close to a real ecovillage.

More complex towns and cities appeared among the villages 8,500 years ago. Çatal Hüyük in present-day Turkey appears to be the oldest. (Jericho, in present-day Israel, a substantial village of around 2,000 people, preceded Çatal Hüyük by about 500 years but was far simpler.) Thirty-two-acre Çatal Hüyük, which sheltered an estimated 5-10,000 people, was more than a large village since it featured many specialized structures and revealed far more complex material culture. Here we find the earliest known fired pottery, woven cloth, earthen building blocks and some of the oldest copper, lead and gold implements. The first mirror, made of polished obsidian, was there along with murals of people, animals and birds. Sculptures of bull's heads built around actual skulls with horns intact protruded from walls into what appear to have been ceremonial rooms.

In many ways Çatal Hüyük was the first expression of the urban age, but that age didn't really erupt upon the scene until almost 2,000 years after it was abandoned. Then, around 5,500 years ago, the cities of the Mesopotamian Valley appeared, with populations of several tens of thousands each, with kings, slaves, high arts, wars, written language, epic forest cutting, abstract science, exhaustion of soils by the hundreds of thousands of acres and fantastic architecture.

Though the Neolithic village represented an unprecedented flowering of creativity, the inhabitants of such a village would have seen few novelties in a lifetime. If the ancient villages were similar to the ones anthropologists studied in the late 1800s when such villages were far less tainted by the outside world than our remaining "primitive" villages today, and when anthropology was in its early thriving, then not much that was novel was readily accepted. Having lived in a remote mountain village in New Mexico, I know from experience as well as legend that it takes three or four generations to become accepted, and you are not really one of the locals until your family history is lost in antiquity, more or less equally with all the others. It helps speed things up for your children's children if you marry into old-time families. The village perspective can be as narrow spatially as it is enduring temporally. Says Lao-Tse of villagers, "To delight in their food, to be proud of their clothes, to be content with their home, to rejoice in their customs. ... They might be within sight of a neighboring village, within hearing of the cocks and dogs, yet grow old and die before they visited one another."[37]

Village culture has always cherished continuity and resisted change, and in this it has been extraordinarily successful. As Mumford puts it,[38]

> The village multiplied and spread over the entire earth more rapidly
> and more effectively than the city; and though it is now on the verge
> of being overwhelmed by urbanization, it maintained the ancient

folkways for thousands of years and survived the continued rise and destruction of its bigger, richer and more alluring rivals. There was sound historic justification, Patrick Geodes pointed out, for the boast of the village of Musselburgh: "Musselburgh was a burgh when Edinburgh was nane, and Musselburgh will be a burgh when Edinburgh is gane."

A major reason for this is evident: Villages didn't have much that cities craved. Other than humble food and shelter and a small undependable tax base, villages provided little to make of them worth conquering. When damaged, they also had much less to re-create in their recovery. Happily for many, that kind of history passed them by.

The creativity of the village was collective not only in that many people acting together were doing something new, but in that the process involved more people than were even alive at any one time. In urban society today we are used to amassing considerable resources to launch any venture. Prototypes are expensive. In the village a very different dynamic prevailed. Creative innovation in a short period of time would have been difficult partially because amassing almost anything was contrary to village values. Says Jules Henry in *Culture Against Man*,[39]

> In primitive culture as a rule, one does not produce what is not needed. ... This helps to give primitive culture remarkable stability. The primitive workman produces for a known market, and he does not try to expand it or to create new wants by advertising. ... Related to our contemporary dynamics is the lack of a property ceiling. Most, though by no means all, primitive societies are provided with intuitive limits on how much property may be accumulated by one person, and the variety of ways in which primitive society compels people to rid themselves of accumulated property is almost beyond belief. Distributing it to relatives, burning it at funerals, using it to finance ceremonies, making it impossible to collect debts in any systematic way — these and many other devices have been used by primitive cultures, in a veritable terror of property accumulation, to get rid of it. ... The fact that our society places no ceiling on wealth while making it accessible to all helps account for the feverish quality Toqueville sensed in American civilization.

EMERGING CITIES

Though things moved slowly in the village, what it created it created very well. Perhaps that collective, careful and slow-moving village creativity in itself, a dimension of evolving consciousness, was exactly what made the next kind of creativity possible. With the cities emerged that other kind of creativity, one so flamboyant that it has blinded us to the earlier kind. This original Renaissance, village begetting city, probably saw its first glimmerings in Çatal Hüyük. By the time of the Mesopotamian cities it was driven by the creativity of individuals thoroughly aware of their own powers — the creativity of personality identifying with the powers of the universe, the gods of the city itself, or, in later days, a single, individualistic, creative God. This was a creativity discovering and expressing itself through art, science, manufacture, political and institutionalized religious power, grand waterworks for agriculture and, of course, city building.

Villages satisfied the needs of the body and celebrated the mysteries of the universe. But the cities — they ran away with the imagination and sought to solve the mysteries while creating new miracles. They were genius and madness, creativity and destruction, generosity and greed, love and cruelty wildly intensified. From their beginnings they symbolized — they were — the physical manifestation of human passions, fruits of the Faustian bargain. Sibyl Moholy-Nagy writes,

> Man has built and loved cities because in the urban form he constructs the superimage of his ideal self. The common denominator of cities, from Nineveh to New York, is a collective idol worship, praying for power over nature, destiny, knowledge and wealth. The gods of cities are supermen, of whom Don Marquis wrote, "And he clothes them with thunder and beauty. He clothes them with music and fire, seeing not as he bows by their altars, that he worships his own desire."[40]

As the cities made possible the highly productive economy of which Jane Jacobs speaks, they generated a new, very dangerous and often exquisitely beautiful kind of creativity: specialized, narrow, blind to its long-range effects, and powerful in its new integration of ideas, tools and products. It quickly produced magnificent architecture and sculpture, writing, math and astronomy, dangerous concentrations of power, the sweet smells and moist airs of gardens, shady luxury with occasional fine things to eat and drink, pungent marketplaces, and hot dusty streets filled with strangers and acquaintances in a pact to accept one another. The city was like no other environment on Earth: Imagine walking into one when there was only one or a few and the whole rest of the world was the hot valley bottoms and rolling mountains of Asia Minor. City creativity was part and parcel of specialized groups playing different roles in a hierarchical economic order, the emergence of systems of privilege, centralization and bureaucratization of power, the development of military weapons, social and economic classes, slavery, greed and rampant egotism to the point that high leaders regularly proclaimed themselves gods.

It's doubtful this kind of creativity could have crept upon the scene. Instead, it strode into the room and kicked over the table. In all likelihood it was incarnated as men with weapons who wanted to take over, allied with creative individuals tired of being told they couldn't create. Patron and innovator, civic despot and artist, proto-industrialist and intellectual, power-wielding priest and earliest astronomer — together they established a new order to lay claim to the powers and secrets of the universe. They were not necessarily very nice, but they did inspire a good deal of imagination and admiration, and not just in themselves, but in the individual everywhere — who could avoid severe subjugation.

Bridging History, Nature and Evolution

At some point as the city began to emerge from the village, large enough numbers of people would have been gathered together with appropriate tools to cause the pace of change to quicken. Close proximity (access by proximity) and cross-fertilization of ideas, tools and products would have stimulated creativity to an unprecedented degree, bringing the novelty of conspicuous change into the short span of a single lifetime, and giving people the experience of witnessing personal creativity right before their eyes. This was a form of creativity rejected as dangerous in the village but recognized, utilized and honored in the city. It represented consciousness evolving with little conscience — a kind of creativity more than willing to exploit, in some cases even destroy, the village and much of nature in its service. In the village the idea of cutting down a tree might have caused the elders to point out the value of the tree to useful and beautiful birds, to children who liked to climb in its branches, to villagers who benefited from its shade in the summer. But the city's style of creativity would have seen the potential for wood to produce more housing, tools and furniture, and as fuel for firing pottery and melting gold and bronze.

With this new kind of creativity came a new kind of time. The cyclical sense of time endlessly returning was transformed into a vector later thought of as Progress. In the brief cycle of one life the personality could now see itself as participating in the process of change in society and nature, experiencing a tiny shred of earthly immortality and god-like creativity, causing something to actually happen and be part of a permanent change. It must have been fun, the dawning of the idea of personal creativity. Its products, which might have been regarded as deviant and dangerous in village cultures, would have become adopted in the early city, even celebrated. Feelings of personal mastery and joy in creation and the discovery of math, writing, astronomy and engineering must have been a heady brew. It is understandable that early urbanites tended to ignore the restraints of village culture, of those who waved a finger at novelty, calling it dangerous to nature and the society of people. "I don't know about this newfangled idea," in the village gave way in the city to, "Why not just try it out?" — a rhetorical question meant not to be considered too thoroughly.

What happened as the city emerged can be viewed in evolutionary terms as the emergence of conscious personal creativity out of the conscience that preceded it. Conscience is intuitive, synthesizing, integrative, emotional, limitless, complex, concerned with endless chains of subtle causes and effects in a very personal way that feels care, guilt, love and affection, and so poignantly that consciousness is a bit embarrassed. It is poetic, willing to entertain far-flung, personally enriching inference and analogy. It is often aware of how everyone is feeling and sees itself as essentially part of a community of other beings. It has little need for material props, and cooperates well. It is not just self-conscious, but often painfully, responsibly and sensitively so. Consciousness is more logical, unemotional, limited, purist, scientific, concerned with particular affect, applications, testable results, expediency. Aware that it is aware it has a strong ego and competes well.

These two patterns of thinking, as I am contrasting them here, are obviously not mutually exclusive. Many people of conscience, such as the Gandhis of the world, are highly conscious, and many of the most conscious, such as the Einsteins and the evolution biologists, are among the most powerfully motivated by conscience. But some intriguing distinctions can be drawn that parallel the distinctions between thinking in villages rooted in nature and the thinking going on in nature-exploiting cities. Conscience gave us the Neolithic village with its reluctance to rock the holy boat of nature and the sacred home of community. Consciousness, the second to evolve, constructed marvelous cultural structures rationalized for the sake of enjoying its new glories and avoiding criticism that might slow Progress. Conscience feels, then consciousness builds and rationalizes. Consciousness invented paradigms to make its work more manageable, constructing not only coherent frames of reference for knowledge and experience, but firm preconceptions and conclusions to screen out and limit disturbing information. Consciousness was highly educated, but in some areas, intentionally ignorant. Conscience and consciousness should have evolved together as the unity of both, the emergence of a kind of "conscienceness" in the universe, in cities and villages, in a rich exchange with each other and in balance with the Earth. Perhaps in at least one case they did.

Minoan Crete seems to have evolved from village to city and thoroughly integrated both conscience and consciousness. The ancient culture on the island of Crete lasted about 1,400 years, contemporaneous with the ancient cultures of Mesopotamia and Egypt and ending about 700 years before the Greek "Golden Age." Riane Eisler calls the Minoan culture a "partnership" culture, as contrasted with the "dominator" model followed by the other ancient city cultures in the region surrounding the eastern Mediterranean Sea.[41] The cities of Crete had no defensive walls, its art had no depictions of war and weapons but many of exuberant sensuality and sport, including acrobatic gymnastics with dangerous bulls being pursued by young men and women alike. Writes Nicolas Platon, who began modern excavations in Crete in the late 1920s, "All the urban centers had perfect drainage systems, sanitary installations and domestic conveniences. There is evidence of large-scale irrigation works with canals to carry and distribute the water ... viaducts, paved roads, lookout posts, roadside shelters, water pipes, fountains, reservoirs, etc."[42]

"Cretan palace architecture is also unique in civilization," says Riane Eisler.

> These palaces are a superb blend of life-enhancing and eye-pleasing features, rather than the monuments to authority and power characteristic of Sumer, Egypt, Rome and other ancient war-like and male-dominated societies. There were vast courtyards, majestic facades and hundreds of rooms laid out in the organized "labyrinths" that became a catchword for Crete in later Greek legend, ... laid out over several stories, at different heights, arranged asymmetrically around a central courtyard.

The irregular form of this architecture contrasted sharply with the rigid order of the walled fortresses on the mainland.

The Creator was seen as female, says Eisler, rather than male, and depictions of ceremonies and celebrations on walls and ceramic ware indicated that women held high, often the highest positions of status and decision-making. Despite female leadership, there appear to be no signs of oppression of the male in Minoan Crete — hence Eisler's classification of the society as a "partnership" society. Meanwhile, in the "dominator" societies surrounding Crete geographically and following it temporally, depictions of exploitation and oppressions of the female, along with numerous images of war, are in evidence everywhere in the archeological record.

On Crete, says Nicolas Platon, "the fear of death was almost obliterated by the ubiquitous joy of living." In any case, much about peace and vivacious ways can be surmised from their artistic history.

Ultimately Minoan civilization was destroyed, apparently by a mix of colossal geologic convulsions — volcanic explosions and earthquakes — and invasion by warlike neighbors with iron weapons and little regard for a "partnership" culture.

Looking back at these two divergent streams, village and city, and an inspiring exception that seems to have held the best of the two streams together for several hundred years, might it not now be possible to forge a partnership between conscience and consciousness, village tradition and city tradition, people and nature, civilization and the Earth?

MODERN TIMES

With the emergence of the city, the functioning structure of the village expanded into large buildings or whole quarters of the city dedicated primarily to a single craft or profession — weaving, brickmaking, leatherworking, woodworking, food handling and storage, trade and marketing, social and political events, defense and administrative control, and education of the elite. Residences ranged from palaces with gardens for the rich, to hovels for the poor and the slaves.

War was a major shaper of cities in the Middle East and later in Europe, dictating walls, which defined and compacted cities, until firepower could breach the thickest defensive shell. When nation-states emerged out of city-states, they pushed the walls of defense out dozens or hundreds of miles to national borders. The Great Wall of China was the ultimate expression of this. When city walls dissolved in the 1600s and 1700s in Europe, the city frayed out a bit at the edges, encroaching in a minor way into natural and agricultural lands.

In the United States, colonial city-builders had so much more firepower than the Native Americans that walls were barely featured at all. By 1750 cities contained a mere 3 percent of the population despite their disproportionate economic and political power. By the early 1800s a small number of urban people who could afford horses and carriages chose to live farther from the madding crowd, thus becoming early commuting suburbanites. In the mid 1800s, starting in England, trains made the suburbs accessible to more middle-income people, and small towns were linked with larger towns and cities. Significant commuting had begun. In such villages and small towns close to cities most people lived a short distance from the train station.

In Scotland, coordinated with the early rise of industrialism, the Enclosure Acts starting in the 1700s tested the rights of the poor to raise animals on the commons against the rural landlords and found, as the law often does, that public rights were less important than private. The wealthy were then legally empowered to enclose much of the commons as private holdings and evict the poor. This idea spread to England, and thousands of people were excluded from self-sufficient agricultural life, rendered poverty stricken and desperate just at the time that expanding industry sought larger numbers of workers at the lowest possible wages throughout Britain. Former agricultural workers had to move to the city or starve on country roads. This "coincidence" of rural land use policy and urban history is repeated in variations on the theme to this day as people in the Low Consumption World (my term for the "Third World") are being forced off their land by governments representing the wealthy. Thus population growth has often been forced upon cities by policy decision. As industrialism gained momentum and Progress became the secular religion, slums appeared near the factories, and industrial pollution began spreading over thousands of urban acres.

In many cities, daily escape to the suburbs began to look like a very good idea for those who could afford it, and the single-family house with its own vestigial, foodless farm or slice of nature called the "yard" became Home. In that mythical, ever-so-private shrine lived the middle-class family, at first "extended" and later "nuclear," which proved fissionable into yet smaller units: single-parent families and individuals at home alone.

By the late nineteenth century, improved construction methods and the logic of efficiencies of proximity began expressing themselves in taller and taller buildings, creating economies of scale otherwise inconceivable. In America, home of pioneering big buildings, immigration was encouraged by policy. Over 5 million immigrants arrived in the decade after 1880. New York became the first city in modern history to pass 1,000,000 in population, and possibly the second in all of history, the first having been Rome 1,400 years earlier.

Technological development shaped cities profoundly. Elevators pulled cities into the vertical dimension while trains and streetcars spread them out horizontally. Hoisting devices had been in existence since the pyramid builders in Egypt, but in 1854 Elisha Otis invented the safety elevator. With his new device, if a cable were to break the elevator would immediately lock itself against a pair of ratchet tracks along the walls of the elevator shaft. This invention made passenger travel possible beyond the four stories considered the tolerable maximum for stairs at that time. Three years later Otis got his first order for two passenger elevators for a five-story china-and-glass company in New York City, and shortly thereafter buildings up to ten stories were being constructed in New York, Boston and Chicago. By 1883 there were over 2,000 elevators in the apartments and offices of Boston. Thus, many years ahead of other countries, the United States took the lead in vertical growth of cities just as, about fifty years later, it would lead the way to sprawl. The cable car system introduced in San Francisco in 1873 was a brilliant mechanical device that used the weight of cars going downhill to help pull the other cars on the same single cable going up hill many blocks away, thus requiring an absolute minimum of energy. Cable cars spread around the country, but soon they were outpaced by electric trolleys on rubber wheels and street-cars on steel wheels and tracks.

Thomas Edison invented the electric light bulb in 1879, and two years later his power station in New York City, the first in the world, came on line for the public. The electric light bulb soon brought inexpensive and relatively safe light to the deep insides of buildings far from windows, replacing the sooty gas lights of the Victorian era and increasing the potential depth of buildings just as elevators had increased their height. After the 1880s and 1890s the whole city, with trains and streetcars, elevators and electric lights, had the means to expand many times over, to a scale never dreamed of just a generation earlier.

The apartment building, common in Paris since the mid-1700s, was frowned upon by American society at the time and for the next 100 years. "You know that no American who is at all comfortable in life will share his dwelling with another," said a typical 1880s developer.[43] But wooden tenements, built from 1840 through World War I, shoehorned dozens of families into three- and four-story buildings. By 1879 some developers were ready to shift their experimentation to the wealthier classes, who also wanted to be near the businesses and cultural life concentrated in cities. In New York, one of the earliest of these was the eight-story Dakota Apartment House of that year. (John Lennon was living there at the time he was shot to death at its front door, just one block from the site of the first fatal automobile accident in American history on September 13, 1899.) This spacious, stately building, with its large rooms and high ceilings, was anything but cramped. Almost upon introduction, these more expensive apartment houses became extremely popular, and in New York City hundreds were built in the 1880s.

New, mass-produced, high-compression brick took office buildings up to considerable heights, but the thickness of the wall at the base dictated a structural limit. One of the last of the tall, brick office buildings constructed in Chicago, in 1891, supported sixteen stories on walls five feet thick at the base. As brick and stone were reaching their zenith, along came iron and steel, introduced in tall buildings in Chicago in 1884. Five years later New York built its first steel building, and the race between the two cities was on. In a novel set in 1890 called *The Cliff Dwellers,* these early large buildings were described as cities unto themselves. "A tenant could eat, drink, have a haircut, obtain legal advice or consult a real estate broker without leaving the building."[44]

The tallest early buildings were the houses of commerce, especially insurance buildings, rising to heights that cast church spires into deep shadow, rendering insurance in the hereafter inferior to insurance for the here-and-now. By the 1930s New York had gone from the cloud-scrapers of the turn of the century to skyscrapers like the Chrysler building and the 107-story Empire State Building. Forces of economic efficiency and cultural access, aided by vertical and horizontal transportation and light-ing technologies, reached a pinnacle in New York in the 1930s. The mili-tary pressure for urban consolidation was long gone, but the city had become compacted anyway, without walls.

Many forces pushed or pulled in the other direction at the same time. One was a simple reaction to the pollution of the industrial city and the intense competition and expense of cosmopolitan living near the cen-ters. Escape was an outward push, whether the reasons were ecological or sociological. Tuberculosis was rampant in sooty cities in the late 1800s and early 1900s. An architectural element that attempted to address the problem, the sleeping porch, became common; the idea was to breathe the fresh night air. It didn't work very well since daily contamination didn't settle out that fast, thus this was also the time of rural sanitariums for rest and recovery. The first American national park, Yellowstone, established in 1872, was largely justified as a sanitarium of fresh air, an escape from the urban world for reasons of regaining health. The outward pull had elements of nostalgia for country farm living, which in the early 1900s was still only a generation or two back and a few miles out from down-town in any direction. Frequent and profound contact with nature, too, was the dream of thousands of Americans, dreaming of the frontier, read-ing Walt Whitman and Henry David Thoreau.

Probably at the deepest level there was also a certain unconscious urge for none other than the ecocity. This, after all, is nothing but a re-fined urge to live both city and country life simultaneously, which I call the "ecocity impulse." Perhaps this urge is also a profound nostalgia for community in harmony with nature, remembered almost mythologically, even genetically, from the early village. For Americans, especially urban-ites greedy for life and with new technologies ushering in a world of all possibilities, why not have both lives simultaneously? There must be a way. For this unstated dream the car would be the instrument of deliver-ance. But rails first.

If the train-created suburbs were functionally disconnected from the Earth, they at least created residential areas on a close to walkable scale, with diversity serving domestic purposes. Rarely did their econom-ics remain grounded in the countryside itself. Some towns with strong ties to the land, when linked to cities by efficient, frequent trains, were to varying degrees transformed into dependent bedroom communities.

Smaller than trains, streetcars make more stops and have a shorter practical range than trains. Rather than seeding new towns in the coun-try or connecting earlier ones at a distance, they tended to expand the fringe of existing, modestly-large towns. "Streetcar suburbs" were a short ride out from the center and were generally compact, often with taste-fully designed, small apartments and two- and three-story homes cater-ing to the entrepreneurial, professional and upper clerical classes. But these first inklings of sprawl were nothing compared to what loomed in the future. The automobile, allied with its usually unacknowledged co-con-spirator, the bus, became the definitive shaper of urban form.

The automobile was invented and taken out for its first test drive by Karl Friedrich Benz in Mannheim, Germany in 1885, and by 1909 Henry Ford had set up the first automobile assembly line. The vehicle went from a luxury plaything for the rich to common usage in the United States in less than a decade. By democratizing the car Ford become the chief de-signer of the urban, suburban, even rural American landscape, and in-ternationally his influence continues to spread as cars induce sprawl ev-erywhere.

Ford declared that the most beautiful things in nature were the highly efficient creatures from which all excess weight had been stripped. On this natural model he conceived the assembly line, which was a marvel of efficiency but produced a product that ended up being the most ineffi-cient transportation invention in history. In retrospect we can see the positive lesson of the assembly line as well as the negative lesson of the automobile: minimizing motion maximizes efficiency. The idea of efficiency as a problem of modern life is largely a misconception. Much of what we think of as efficient is just getting things done quickly. Sometimes they prove to be pointless or dangerous and therefore shouldn't be done at all. The lesson as far as city structure goes is that if we end up covering long distances, moving about constantly, we will be leading wasteful lives, wasting resources and time and laying waste to land, air and water. But all this was not yet evident when the Model Ts and As were pouring forth from the factories, a car for every garage and a chicken for every pot. Prosperity was for all, and nature was so endless in America that it could soak up any punishment people could dole out.

The changes wrought by the automobile in a single generation were epochal. In all but the strategically, commercially indispensable centers like Manhattan and downtown San Francisco, town centers withered. Very quickly the "doughnut" phenomenon and the bedroom community became realities. Doughnut: At night and on weekends everybody took their dough home to the encircling suburbs and left a hole in the middle. Civic irresponsibility thrived. Bedroom community: a place where people slept and occasionally entertained and, from the early 1950s on, watched lots of television, but seldom lived in a cultural, urban or village sense. Downtown: a place which, if not derelict and boarded up, was, with rare exceptions, a money machine by day and ghost town by night. As the dominance of the automobile became established, the hole in the doughnut became ever more literal as parking lots, new and used car lots and gas stations pushed out most other land uses other than daytime business. Maps of cities came to look like Swiss cheese, but with square and rectangular instead of circular holes, and this pattern was crisscrossed by broad and unforgiving bands called arterials and freeways.

"But," say the defenders of the American Way, "people love their cars." Well, they loved their streetcars, trains and ferries, too. I have to point out that auto love was not enough to satisfy the auto industry, and neither was intensive advertising or glorification in the movies or national economic policy and patriotism. ("What's good for General Motors is good for America.") What would it take to get enough? Conspiracy. During the period from 1927 through 1955, General Motors, Mack Manufacturing, Standard Oil of California (now Exxon), Phillips Petroleum, Firestone Tire and Rubber and Greyhound Lines shared information, investment money and management activities — in violation of anti-trust law — for the purpose of maximizing profits and eliminating ground transportation competition in the United States. The net effect was to destroy urban rail transportation in over 100 cities. To do this, the conspirators set up several front companies in which they invested their money. These companies bought up and then tore up the streetcar lines of a gigantic nation, leaving citizens stuck with no transportation alternatives of note other than cars and busses.

Those who were shocked to see their favorite streetcar lines suddenly replaced by diesel-fuming busses were told by the conspirator-owned bus companies about the virtues of busses over trains and streetcars. They were modernizing, they said. Busses worked better, more "flexibly," than streetcars because they could follow the car out over the flatlands.

Shocking though it may sound to fans of public transit in general, the reality is that busses were losers from the start, requiring major subsidies from government for the simple reason that it is impossible to cover large, thinly-populated areas with frequent, convenient service. This is a problem of geometry and human numbers on the surface of the Earth. Efficient, economical public transportation can't work in sprawl. Ever since those first days of conversion from rail lines to busses, the subsidies to the car have been astutely hidden, while ever-cleaner smog devices have been celebrated with fanfare. In the meantime subsidies to the busses and disparaging comments on their incorrigibly bad breath have been trotted out so that people can throw pies in public transit's face.

But if National City Lines, Pacific City Lines and American City Lines (the three major front companies) and their investors couldn't make big money on busses, why did they tear up and scrap rail lines that they had paid good money for? Because that money was a pittance compared with how much they began making on cars, trucks, tires, gasoline, asphalt and highway building. And, of course, they also made the busses and the bus tires and the diesel fuel for the busses that they sold to themselves (their bus companies). Later, claiming intolerable losses, they sold the bus companies themselves to municipalities trying to help their lower income people get around. An internal memo at Mack Truck that surfaced at the conspiracy trial explained it tersely: The "probable loss" for the investors in the bus companies would be "more than justified by the business and gross profit flowing out of this move in years to come."[45]

Finally, in 1955, after this conspiracy had been going on for almost three decades, federal prosecutors figured out there were less than honorable motives behind this strange disappearance of almost an entire country's urban rail system, identified the conspirators and took them to court. The companies and their representatives were charged with violation of the Sherman Anti-Trust Act and found guilty in Judge William J. Campbell's U.S. District Circuit Court in Chicago. Each company was fined $5,000 plus the court costs of $4,220.78, and each individual was ordered to pay $1.00 for his role in the conspiracy. Thus did big-time urban planning proceed to a successful if guilty conclusion. Thus was America's car dependency intentionally designed into our lifestyles to maximize profits for the car/sprawl/freeway/oil system. Thus was the flat urban form called sprawl not just the drift of public desire — far from it — but planned.

THE AESTHETIC TRADITION

Ecocity aesthetics go back to the Hanging Gardens of Babylon and beyond, to the wall paintings of Çatal Hüyük depicting soaring birds and rampaging wild bulls. They go back all the way to villages where folk crafts took up natural themes in decorating dwellings, granaries, ceremonial lodges, shrines and monuments purposefully, reverently orienting toward the warmth of the sun or signs in the stars. In Europe, on the eve of the colonization of most of the rest of the world, however, any aesthetic akin to that of ecocities was nearly nonexistent. Kirkpatrick Sale describes the European attitude of the times, quoting passages that illustrate the prevailing lack of aesthetic sensitivity to nature:[46]

> It is there in such celebrations of urban form as Piero de la Francesca's Ideal Town, an entirely lifeless human construct without a single blade of grass or shadow of tree, dominated by that most controlling of all inventions of Renaissance art, perspective. ... But of all the images of control, the most pervasive and most revealing is that of the formal Renaissance garden, whose style was perfected and popularized ...with such careful artworks as the gardens of Compton Wynyates in England (1520) and Tivoli in Italy (1549). Here it is the hand of man and not the grace of nature that is ever-

present: bushes and small trees trimmed in rigid geometric shapes
to look like wedding cakes or perfume bottles, closely clipped
hedges along geometric walks, blocks of flower beds in uniform
colors, carefully edged lawns and artfully distributed statues,
benches, fountains, pools and bridges.

Here there was no possibility of the "unweeded garden that grows to seed," that Hamlet described with typical disgust, where "things rank and gross in nature posses it merely."

The purveyors of Western civilization learned a little from those they conquered. The British picked up the shady wraparound porches that kept buildings cool in hot climates, the "verandahs" of India, and took them to other hotter parts of their empire. The Spanish adopted the mud brick or adobe building from North Africa, where the material moderated temperature admirably, and brought the idea with them to the New World, where some of the natives who had previously built in stone adopted it from them. But generally very little having to do with living and building sensitively with nature was learned from the natives. Instead, whether they fit well or not, European building styles were imported. In North America north of Mexico formal gardens, hedgerows and fences were built, demarking northern European ideas of land ownership and aesthetics simultaneously. Lawns were introduced to make an Old World of the New.

In America the industrious habits of the Colonists and relative defenselessness of native flora, fauna and people translated into a rapid industrialization that placed buildings in any arrangement that seemed expedient. Some architects, craftspeople and artists adopted some elements of native culture or exhibited appreciation of the land they had acquired, but not many. The land was tamed into usefulness, not lived with and understood. To the high-powered juggernaut of Manifest Destiny, as the forests were cut down and soil of farm after farm was used up on the march westward, as the raw energy of industrial exploitation, steel tracks and iron horses pressed on, aesthetic refinements garnered from the original inhabitants or nature herself would have seemed close to ridiculous. Inside towns there was the inward pull of the mechanisms of exchange — access by proximity — in economics and culture. The opposite and outward pull of transportation put space between people almost reflexively, as did the psychological desire of a people longing to breathe free, free from other people of the sort they were leaving behind as they escaped persecution and hard times in Europe. These factors, more than art, and much more than any attributes of nature other than its beckoning vast openness, were the shapers of the village, town and city.

The gridiron layout of streets, usually north-south, east-west, made it possible to build with minimal time-consuming thought. As Kenneth Schneider says, "The gridiron assured easy access to every property and set forth the image of democratic equality. No plan could have met the unknown requirements of industrialization and rapid urbanization as flexibly. The straight streets forming square or rectangular blocks could be set out and surveyed without agonizing decisions."[47]

There was, however, a minority tendency in the other direction. Thomas Jefferson and others tried to adapt an architecture to America's needs, borrowing from the democratic Greeks and the imperial Romans. The architecture itself and the arrangements of order and landscaping it fit into had less to do with nature than with the golden mean and other geometric abstractions and classical traditions. At the same time some buildings were placed carefully in settings that were close to natural. In the Jeffersonian distrust of cities and idealization of rural agricultural America there was more than a glimmer of nature-appreciating aesthetics. The campus of the University of Virginia, designed by Jefferson himself, was centered on a quadrangle of lawn surrounded by a library at one end, classrooms and housing along the sides, and an opening to nature on the fourth side opposite the library. It is hard to be more architecturally explicit about celebrating both culture and nature than by placing a library and a natural view opposite one another on a central green.

Working with nature was expressed in the small, locally-viable towns, in the farmhouses attached to barns in New England, and in the two-story saltbox houses with a wind-breaking roof sloping down from the second floor on the windward side. Evident in these cases are the clustering of functions for practical reasons and the orientation of the buildings for climate moderation. Often the design of these towns and modestly complex buildings attained a level of real aesthetic sensitivity to the natural environment.

The City Beautiful movement, launched by the World's Fair in Chicago in 1893, took the words of the Fair's chief planner-architect, Daniel

Burnham, to heart: "Make no small plans. They have no power to stir men's souls." After that the monumental arrangement of streets, large public squares, imposing buildings, colossal sculptures, triumphal arches and grand reflecting pools became the desire of cities the world over. The movement codified and refined the themes of the great city going all the way back to Mesopotamia and Egypt. Its palette included broad avenues for impressive displays of autocratic and military power, tempered by the Renaissance garden, filled out with buildings in the American Roman or Imperial Federal style, focusing on splendid open spaces demarked by dramatic colonnades. Typically these buildings and spaces were festooned with Isadora Duncan-like statues and enormous vases overflowing with cast concrete or (in the case of temporary expositions and fair grounds) papier-mâché flowers. The columns, arches, sculptures and reflecting pools were aesthetic products of a domineering culture, but the mirror pools caught the clouds and blue sky, framed views and trees and accentuated something of nature in that almost excruciatingly sensuous way of a Maxfield Parish painting — but too large. In its exercise of contrasts, the City Beautiful style was an odd, rather oblique celebration of nature.

That these grand designs were not more universally adopted by larger cities was a result of construction costs and their disregard for the dynamics of gathering people and functions together in small areas. The patches of open space and broad bands of avenues and boulevards were just not cut to the smaller size of the human body. Great for military displays designed to discourage revolution and stir pride in national grand designs, they were neither inviting nor very functional for economy and culture. The contemporary technologies of tall buildings — strong structure, elevators and electric lights — which attracted the action toward smaller areas of land and into the sky distracted from the panorama of spacious boulevards and large, building-defined spaces. In the United States tall buildings literally rose up and over the aesthetic and psychological effect of the City Beautiful. One kind of grandeur contradicted the other as two kinds of skylines vied for the same aesthetic space. Ironically, at the same time that Burnham was saying, "Make no small plans," the tall-building planners were making yet bigger ones that cast shadows over his creations and influence.

The Garden City idea, originating at about the same time, was an attempt to create what might have been called an ecocity if the word "ecology" had been in general usage then. With its requisite greenbelt, the Garden City was developed from the turn of the century until shortly after World War II, and is still studied in architecture schools and influential in new town and large development planning today. The idea in Ebenezer Howard's 1902 book *Garden Cities of To-Morrow*[48] was "to wed city and country." Garden City advocates rejected the suburban idea of bringing city and country together by placing private houses in "yards." They were thoroughly concerned with creating lively community, economy and culture, not escaping from them. Howard and his many associates and followers hoped to have a natural and agricultural zone — the greenbelt — around the town, and planned for densities about twice the average of today's American suburban communities. Housing was planned to be a short distance from a city center in which commercial jobs were located and not too far from civic amenities and internal parks. Industries were to be located on the fringes, adjacent to the greenbelt. The general average size was proposed to be 1,000 acres of development in a natural and agricultural reserve of 5,000 acres owned by the city and supporting 30,000 inhabitants.

Several such cities, among them Letchworth and Welwyn, in England, were built. Although reasonably lively, they have lacked the vitality of larger or older cities. Both of these cities are somewhat smaller than planned, and they seem to do well according to many criteria, including financial. While housing in England is chronically in need of government subsidy, Letchworth and Welwyn have never needed assistance. The concern of the founders for equity resulted in a community ownership plan in which the residents buy shares proportional to their living space limited to 5 percent dividends per year, with any excess going to community uses.

Lewis Mumford points out that there has been stiff criticism of the built Garden Cities and many claims that they have failed. "This is surely a singular kind of 'failure.' What other new conception of city improvement has resulted in the layout and building of fifteen New Towns, in Britain alone, to say nothing of similar foundations, either achieved or in process, in Sweden, in the Netherlands, in Italy and in Soviet Russia, ... from Scotland to India?"[49]

In my opinion, the Garden Cities mark a moment when the idea of the ecocity appeared and was consciously, if partially, expressed and actualized. These towns sparkled with promise and cried out for further development and experimentation, but they were neglected in favor of stronger movements in economics and aesthetics, and passed by.

At about the time the Garden City movement was gathering momentum, interest in nature and good solid craftsmanship was evident in the one-building-at-a-time approach. The Arts and Crafts Movement was characterized by strong, honest lines and an appreciation of natural materials and motifs. The ideas of the Arts and Crafts Movement found expression in architecture and in interior and exterior decoration, furniture and textiles — even in tile, pottery and kitchen-utensil design. Trees, flowers, leaves, birds, animals and sometimes people were abstracted into essential lines and motifs. Parts of buildings and furniture and other handiwork were strengthened with design lines or actually built stronger, with thicker material near joints and at bases where, in nature, wood or muscle might need more bulk to support a branch, hold a tree firmly to the ground, or support an animal where limb meets torso. A certain simplicity and functionality was celebrated, and a sense of calm and peace was a goal, often attained. Individual houses, from bungalows to mansions, nestled into the landscape with sensitivity, or appeared along tree-lined neighborhood streets, unpretentious but beautifully crafted. Public schools, churches, exhibition halls and other buildings were built in the style. Around the world, a similar deep respect for natural materials and craft traditions has produced beautifully conceived and built adobe houses, buildings of stone and row houses of brick, and clusters of wooden or wood-and-thatch buildings in villages, all in their own way establishing the foundation of an ecocity aesthetic.

The modern architects Walter Gropius, LeCorbusier and Frank Lloyd Wright appropriated the technology of the times and aspired to create marvelous new realities. Drawing from Cubist painters like Braques and Picasso, from industry, from the expedients of engineering's straight lines and urban gridiron layout, from their fascination with new construction materials like glass and steel at a scale and strength never seen before, and from their own imaginations, they created a world of crisp right angles and generous fields of simple, uncluttered, efficient, honest form and surface.

Gropius, a leading spirit of the Bauhaus school in Germany, wanted to harness industrial productivity to house workers honorably and inexpensively, liberating their time for leisure and creative achievement and reducing social inequities. In many ways, though often dreary and repetitious, the resulting buildings under his influence did serve millions of people, placing them near inexpensive transit, and giving them access to jobs, parks and whatever cultural and economic benefits were provided by their particular cities. This international style of architecture became the most pervasive reality of new, higher-density urban development after World War II. Its monotonous ubiquity was condemned by people of higher income and more refined, parochial, traditional and pastoral tastes. The undifferentiated scale of its larger buildings seemed dehumanizing, and partly because of this many people have rejected medium- to high-density development ever since. In redevelopment areas, such buildings were repetitious and monotonous in design, cheap in construction and stuffed with more than their fair share of desperate unemployed people, frustrated youth and occasional outright criminals. The buildings were blamed for the social problems that such low-cost and volatile concentrations of poverty and pain produced.

Even some that were not so poorly conceived were built, for example, without eaves, covered porches or awnings to shelter pedestrians from the weather. The modern style was supposed to look "clean" (without pointless decoration and superfluous detail), and functional (in terms of simplicity and economy of materials). Those clean lines were good for cleaning the sides of buildings with rain and the clothes of people in the streets while they were still wearing them. "Functional" often worked better in theory than in practice. Yet the intention was socially responsible, and remains the reason why millions of people still live in such "apartment block" housing. Some economies of scale are genuine. It provides shelter and access to transit, jobs and social life. True, it often lacks the fine-grained detail of rich ecological and social relationships, but it might regain these with some serious redesign and a little more judicious investment.

LeCorbusier, with his plans for enormous slab-and-block buildings fifteen and fifty stories high, rising from the African savannas where humanity descended from the trees and learned to walk upright and free, imagined a superworld for the superman of the future. He drew stocky, slim-waisted, square-shouldered figures to decorate his walls, shapes of the New Man and New Woman who could crack granite with judo chops.

His women, like Michaelangelo's, were actually men with breasts appended, as if with Velcro. His buildings were likened to male erections rising through sensuous though barren female lakes and glens. He imposed a vision of buildings on nature that made the monumental plazas of the City Beautiful shrivel and blanch into parochial inconsequentiality. The linear city he designed for Rio de Janeiro was a single, long, winding building dozens of stories high with a freeway on the roof. It would snake through the primordial upwellings of stone that rise through the jungle and curving beaches. Fortunately it wasn't built. There is a place to be big and splendid in constructed edifice, I am sure, but this is a place to be careful and in awe. No apartments looming up to compete with Half Dome in Yosemite Valley or sports arenas on the side of Mt. Fujiama, please.

LeCorbusier's schemes were not, however, simplistic. His Marseilles Block, a sixteen-story apartment building with a shopping "street" halfway up and rooftop sculpture gardens and children's playground, and many of his other buildings, consciously brought together many aspects of full community life. If the same elements were assembled in his buildings with more consideration of nature's workings in that particular place, they would have constituted a significant step toward the ecocity.

Frank Lloyd Wright used the horizontal expanses of the American Midwest and Plains to organize the lines of some of his buildings. He also borrowed Aztec themes, abstract geometries, Art Nouveau shapes, patterns from nature and building materials produced in economical industrial repetitions for creations that sometimes worked in poetic counterbalance with nature. In his Broadacre City plans, in which everyone could afford to have a house on an acre of land and get there by car or helicopter, were the seeds of an intellectual and aesthetic justification for sprawl. He meant helicopter, too, and we'd be narrow to deride the notion knowing what we know of jammed freeways, nervous breakdowns of air controllers, and the Peter principle which says that if something can go wrong it will. In those days the idea was bold, brilliant and cheery. Now it's time to learn from it that some things worked ecologically and some did not.

If we draw out the lessons of the efficiencies of the assembly line, the striving for industry in service to all the people, the building of whole communities cognizant of access by proximity; if we select the best of village social creativity and urban personal creativity, thus reuniting conscience and consciousness in the enterprise of building cities, we can develop a whole new aesthetic and begin weaving together the essentials of the ecocity.

5

The City Today

Individualistic civilization in the United States was launched upon perhaps its last great binge at the end of World War II, when people felt they had a right to a separate house — usually rather nondescript, even humble, with a moat of grass and picket-fence battlements — and a car to get where everything else in life happened. True, this doesn't have the grand sweep of history's wars, depressions and struggles for empire, but the damage to nature through cars, sprawl, freeways and supportive systems may be even more immense than through any conventional war. With about 20 million people killed in car crashes in the twentieth century, and a similar number by car pollution, the casualty list of the car war ranks it roughly equivalent to the other two big ones. Its effect on nature in terms of species loss and climate change ranks it as apocalyptic. The period from World War II to the present has brought us to the point of finally having to begin a conscious, worldwide effort to rebuild our civilization. The first step in this effort is the rebuilding of our physical, constructed environment on the basis of ecological principles.

We may well be standing now at a point in time in some ways analogous to that of the Neolithic village about to be transformed into the city. I doubt that anyone at that time had any clear idea what the city would become. They were almost certainly unconscious of the larger pattern that would develop into the future. Today, with stores of important tools and information in random disorder, we are fumbling our way toward the next reorganization, which, in this case, may yield the ecocity civilization. Just as the Neolithic villagers were unaware of the process of city building they were about to spawn, we seem to be unaware of the ecocity we might well create in the next few generations. This time around, however, if we aren't very conscious of what we are doing the consequences will be dire. Perhaps even more important, if we don't explicitly recognize the role of conscience as well as consciousness in this process, we won't be able to harness the process for anything close to what we generally think of as good. For our next step in the pattern of healthy evolution, the two modes of thinking — consciousness and conscience — need to be seen as a whole.

REBUILDING AND THINKING — IN THAT ORDER

The war was over, all its horrors retreating into the past. Americans suddenly realized that they had about 6 percent of the world's people, 50 percent of its wealth, and 50 percent of its cars. What was to be done with by far the largest unscathed industrial machine on the planet, and with America's 11 million men in arms about to be liberated? They set out to build the ecological city. Theirs was the ecocity impulse to have both society and nature, both of them healthy and prosperous, simultaneously. But because this impulse was uninformed by urban ecological principles, it produced sprawl on a stunning scale. Within eighteen months of the end of the war, the American military had shrunk from 11 million to 500,000 and perhaps the biggest war-to-peacetime economic conversion program ever had begun. It was the construction of suburbia, facilitated by the National Defense Highway System, the limited-access "freeways" pioneered by Adolf Hitler's autobahns, and the mass manufacture of the automobile.

Where did all the soldiers go? Largely they went to build cars and suburban houses and roads, and to college on federal money to learn how to do more of the same. They were consciously building a new and modern country and world and unconsciously attempting the ecocity. Very few of them knew about the Garden City movement, but in their own way they were striving for a similar ideal. Everyone was to be humanized by grass, trees, roses, robins, butterflies, clean skies and quiet starry nights. The vast majority thought it was a good idea. Linking semi-rural suburbs to the city with roads, cars and television seemed harmless enough. The air was still crystal blue from sea to shining sea, with a few industrial exceptions and an occasional unfortunate incident in the Los Angeles air basin. If everybody could have a car and a house at a reasonable price they would just solve the next problem as it appeared.

That Americans had not yet processed their own destruction of Native Americans, who were far better connected with nature, had not yet thought about the dynamics of the city and lessons of ecology, and had not heard of other relevant strands from recent history, prevented the ecocity venture from moving from impulse to insight to something healthier than suburbia. In addition, most people were personally compromised, bought off. By the mid-1950s tens of millions worked for the auto/sprawl/freeway/oil industrial complex, or were in debt to it or hooked on its products. This made them blind to the pitfalls and contradictions of the development patterns enveloping them. No one seemed capable of comprehending the implications of the rapidly multiplying number of cars and acres of sprawl. Few people even today comprehend that.

The Marshall Plan was busy rebuilding European cities while America was building suburbs on its land on the urban fringe. The first attack of Auto Sprawl Syndrome, that circular disease of cars creating sprawling suburbs, and suburbs demanding more cars, began to produce serious degenerative symptoms. Slums spread and city centers began slowing down economically. Defining that first episode of Auto Sprawl Syndrome in the 1960s was the pattern of commuting from suburb to city center. Defining the second episode, coming in the 1980s, was the pattern of commuting from suburban home to suburban work place, both randomly scattered about a vast landscape.

Ecological consciousness rose as problems became too large to ignore. Rachel Carson's *Silent Spring*, published in 1962, launched an activist reaction to industrial and technological assaults on the environment. DDT was killing birds, beneficial insects and other organisms from pole to pole. With a politically difficult but relatively easy technological shift in production, DDT was outlawed. Industry cranked out new substitutes amid much noisy complaint. No lifestyle change or consideration of the structure of communities was required for this early environmental success.

While *Silent Spring* was making history, awakening ecological conscience and saving a considerable number of species, back in the city the simple, big-box megabuilding emerged as the villain of enormous, slum-clearing urban renewal projects. The expensive, tall apartment buildings of New York, San Francisco and Chicago had their happy residents, but their more homely cousins were widely maligned. In a few cases, as with the enormous Pruitt Igoe urban renewal project in St. Louis, buildings were eventually dynamited at the request of their own residents. This was not an auspicious time for Paolo Soleri to be introducing the concept of the large building as city. The fact that his proposed structures contrasted radically with megabuildings in terms of diversity and relationship to nature and community was lost on a society thinking in terms of 200-horsepower cars and enormous areas of uniform zoning. Kenneth Schneider offers some insight into the nature of the times:[47]

> Both the faith and the sense of historic suddenness were vaguely
> with me in 1952 when I chose to join the relatively new profession,
> city planning, which I felt could be a renaissance profession
> destined to shape urban history and help maintain the faith. A few
> years taught me that the profession was far from performing acts of
> renaissance. Alas, it became clear to me, city planning was destined
> to push paper for the established way of exploitation. ... Planners
> operate without a conception of an ideal city. ... We look vainly for a
> social ideal. Despite a fifty-year debate about the neighborhood
> unit, the concept remains incomplete and exists only partially in a
> few locations. ... Urbanity, the quality of environments that
> stimulate a rich cosmopolitan life, is almost absent in the literature,
> except as a reflection of particular architectural settings. ... While
> medicine operates with a vision of health and law with a distant
> image of justice, city planning exists without such a goal.

Schneider adds that the process engaged in by the city planner helps hardly at all. "Any process which does not serve a deep cultural ideal in-evitably serves the raw power of those who wield it. Most planners try to make planning serve a public purpose by focusing upon the process of planning" and inviting public participation. In practice this gives repre-sentation of a sort to interests in addition to the financial, but this repre-sentation is almost inevitably lacking in knowledge of city functioning, environmental implications, and an overall vision, that is, a whole systems perspective or ecology of the city. The planning process broadens the range of input somewhat — usually by adding more self-serving influences. The democratic "methodologies," says Schneider, "allow urban ideals, but do not envisage or promote them. Urban processes, no matter how democratically based, are dangerous until a commonly accepted ideal of the city gives them specific content and direction."

Although Soleri's ideas were based on an ideal — the city built to play its proper role in evolution — and although his theory of miniaturization/complexification/quickening laid powerful theoretical foundations, his single-structure cities were unfortunately timed. His models and drawings of arcologies looked foreign to almost everyone. Environmental issues at that time were chemical and conservationist rather than issues of urban land use and abuse. Also the main thrust of his writings represented the new-town approach — building a whole city at once. He had little interest in transforming existing cities where they stood. Very few embraced Soleri's work when it was new, and, lacking an understanding of its foundation concepts and evolutionary context, critics have expressed amazement that, thirty years later, he still advances his arguments when "other megastructure architects" have long since given up. But there is an enormous qualitative difference between the megastructure building and Soleri's whole-city arcology, and people have been slow to understand that his exploration of a basic life principle is beyond fad and fashion.

Misunderstanding on the architecture and city planning front notwithstanding, by the 1960s and early 1970s good things were happening. Largely as a reaction to the Vietnam War, grinding poverty, racial injustice and political assassinations, the peace, civil rights and women's rights movements all made rapid progress. Environmental consciousness was rising, and Gandhian principles of nonviolence and civil disobedience were being methodically applied in the peace and civil rights movements. Millions found cooperation with the establishment so "odious," in Mario Savio's words, that if they didn't "place their bodies against the gears and levers," they at least "tuned in, turned on and dropped out."

With Earth Day 1970 and subsequent environmentalist actions and legislation, ecologically-informed policies, programs and personal actions were gathering momentum. Within twenty-four months of Earth Day, the Clean Air Act, the Clean Water Act, the Environmental Education Act, and the Occupational Safety and Health Act were passed. DDT was banned, and the supersonic transport was stopped. The youth culture, with its wanderings into metaphysical realms influenced by Eastern mysticism and psychedelic drugs, health food and yoga, and with its wanderings back to the land in hippie communes or organic farms and out to the world in Peace Corps programs, created a condition of readiness to confront major lifestyle changes. Some came to Soleri's experimental city, Arcosanti, to live, work and contemplate building a better world. These people were prepared to experience change. Later expressions of this experience took the form of "simple living" lifestyles, urban homesteading and a more honest assessment of the impacts of our lives on society and nature. The words of the cartoon character, Pogo, immortalized in 1970 Earth Day events, were taken to heart and acted upon with good humor. "We have met the enemy and he is us." To this the young people who were willing to experiment with their own lives could add, "We have met the ally too, and he is also us."

It was perfect timing, then, one might think, that almost precisely as the OPEC oil embargo slammed into American experience like the front-page fist fights that erupted in the gas station lines of 1973, a powerful document from on high hit the press. A study called *The Cost of Sprawl*[50] was undertaken by three U.S. agencies — the Council on Environmental Quality, Housing and Urban Development, and the Environmental Protection Agency — and released in the spring of 1974.

Gathering data from all over the United States, the study compared low-, medium- and higher-density communities, and measured their impact on schools, fire and police services, government facilities, roads and utilities. It demonstrated that higher-density communities required 50 percent less land and 45 percent less investment cost in infrastructure (buildings, roads, landscaping and utilities), caused 45 percent less air pollution and a similarly reduced amount of water pollution runoff, and used 14 to 44 percent less energy and 35 percent less water. Costs of fire, police and other government services were similarly reduced in the higher-density community.

The high-density model, as the report defined it, was a mix far from the extremes of Manhattan, Hong Kong or Paris. In fact it included two- to six-story buildings and nothing taller. It left out the cost of the automobile entirely and it did not mention the savings from using transit in higher-density areas. It also omitted any architectural and technological features — from ones as simple as enhanced insulation to ones as flamboyant as solar greenhouses — that might make real contributions to cost and energy savings. If these features had been considered, the costs of cars factored in, and the extrapolation to yet higher densities calculated — if, in other words, the next logical step had been taken — it would have been apparent that the agencies were really on to something. Namely, the whole-cloth ecocity concept.

The Cost of Sprawl had profound things to say. If not the last word on the subject, it was one of the earliest and best reports. However close it came to a breakthrough, it nonetheless slid quickly into oblivion. The report on urban density and form, the opening into ecocity thinking, gathered dust in the Jimmy Carter years while attention and support went to initiatives for developing specific technologies that would have been far more useful had they been attached to ecocity thinking and development. Then, under Ronald Reagan, most of that modest effort was scrapped. The crack in the door to ecocities was shut at a potentially historic juncture. Thus, in the late 1970s and the 1980s, the big message about the city and the environment was ignored, and urban form and whole-community awareness drifted deeper into the back of the mind. Simpler changes came online: car mileage went up, as did energy efficiency in buildings and appliances. And now, decades later, the shape of cities in America and most of the rest of the world is worse than ever.

APPROPRIATE TECHNOLOGY

A new willingness to experiment in technology, agriculture and architecture emerged during the period from the time of the oil embargo through the early 1980s. This willingness found particularly strong expression at the federal government level when President Jimmy Carter put solar collectors on the roof of the White House and established the Solar Energy Research Institute. In California, Governor Jerry Brown set up an Office of Appropriate Technology and abandoned the Governor's mansion and the attendant commute for a modest apartment within walking distance of Sacramento's downtown offices. He appointed Huey Johnson, founder of the Trust for Public Land, to head the State Department of Resources and the innovative architect, Sim van der Ryn, to head the Office of the State Architect. These moves helped create a powerful

Architect Bill Mastin's "Integral Neighborhood" drawing, showing a highly mixed-use ecological neighborhood using appropriate technology and associated lifeways.

wave of experimentation, putting alternatives like solar and wind energy on the map.

The British economist E. F. Schumacher, who had been studying small-scale industries and Buddhist economics for years, published his book *Small is Beautiful* [51] in 1972, and his timing was as good for his message as Soleri's was bad for his. The establishment of the first Ecology Center in the United States in Berkeley in 1969, Earth Day in 1970, the United Nations Conference on the Environment in Stockholm in 1972, and the oil embargo of 1973 all prepared the soil for Schumacher's message of small-scale, decentralized, self-reliant and relatively simple technologies, businesses and lifestyles. He did not live long enough to exercise his rising influence and feisty leadership, but his ideas affected policies and practices in the United States, Europe and other parts of the world.

"Appropriate technology" was, in Schumacher's words, technology with "a human face." It came to include solar, wind, geothermal and biological fuels; energy conservation measures such as extensive weather stripping and insulation; recycling of all sorts; soil building through composting; agricultural practices such as integrated pest management and companion planting; and more efficient transportation systems such as bicycles, public transit vehicles, transcontinental railways and electric cars. If the technology seemed appropriate to a healthier world, it qualified. Could there be an appropriate technology embracing all or most of the others, giving them shelter, access, order and healthy relationships? It's the ecocity, of course.

In bridging from appropriate technology to ecocities we had an example that clarifies the continuity: the Montgomery Ward Building, built in stages from 1923 through 1927 in Oakland, California. Although it was exemplary for working well with public transportation and for energy and land conservation it was demolished due to the shoddiest of local politics. It could have been an ecological landmark building illustrating how working intelligently in the third dimension solves numerous problems in one compact and elegant design.

At eight stories, the Montgomery Ward Building covered most of a two-block area and was the largest and tallest industrial building in Oakland until January 2001. Oakland resident and Berkeley city staff planner Sandy Grube, in leading an effort to save the building, won listing on the National Register of Historic Places. The designation was largely on the basis of the building's Art Deco styling and Arts and Crafts detailing, but its story is much larger than that.

Goods arrived on the first floor by way of a short spur off the regional rail line that came right into the building and were transferred to the upper floors by freight elevator. Customers arrived at the second floor showroom, looked over the displays and placed their orders at the sales counter. Then their orders were written down, rolled up and slipped into a canister that was placed in a pneumatic tube and sucked up to one of the six stories of warehousing above. Next, a clerk picked up the order and, on roller skates, zipped off to the correct shelves to locate the item and bring it back to a spiral delivery chute, which in turn delivered the package to the show room by gravity, generally in less than two minutes. The customer paid for the item and carried it out the door a few feet and, usually, to transit home. If the package was large, it could be delivered by a truck making the rounds.

Today, instead of goods being warehoused on a relatively small, local piece of land over both display room and arrival docks, they are stored in giant one-story sheds covering hundreds of acres of land ten, twenty or even forty miles from Oakland over two ranges of hills and in the California Central Valley. They are serviced by a fleet of trucks clogging the freeways and burning millions of gallons of fuel each year. The customer arrives by car and parks in a gigantic land-gobbling lot and walks to the big box facility, also one-story. There he or she haplessly wanders the storage shelves alone, trying to catch the attention of clerks, pushing a cart, spends considerable time locating the item, then carries it back to the checkout line. Finally it's back out to the car and the long drive home.

Permit me to say it is an insane waste of fossil fuels, asphalt and concrete, accompanied by massive quantities of air pollution and the consumption of millions of hours of people's time and millions of dollars of people's money to move products in today's manner as compared to taking transit to the old Montgomery Ward Building and having goods delivered to your hands by roller skates and gravity. Compounding the insanity, as Grube pointed out in defending the building, was the destruction of thousands of tons of building materials and all the energy that went into creating the building. The structure could have been remodeled successfully, as in fact old Montgomery Ward buildings have been recently in Portland, Chicago and Baltimore. It could have remained one of the best examples of urban ecological design and efficiency, of appropriate technologies united by appropriate architecture and urban layout.

PARADIGMS AND PERMACULTURE PRINCIPLES

While appropriate technology was dawning, systems theory was coming on strong, with Thomas Kuhn's *The Structure of Scientific Revolutions*[52] in 1962 and Fritjof Capra's *The Tao of Physics*[53] in 1975. Their "New Paradigm" involved experiencing and understanding life as the interrelation of whole systems — organisms, businesses, conceptual frameworks — as part of larger whole systems: societies, ways of life, economies, bioregions and, ultimately, the whole Earth and universe. A paradigm is a set of perceptions, concepts, convictions, habits and lifeways functioning in the environment in its largest sense. Largely, what a paradigm sees is what it allows itself to see. A paradigm is not just the way we think and experience, but also a screen erected by the mind using previously ordered experience that, like the receptionist outside the doctor's or lawyer's office, admits or rejects newly arriving experience or information.

The New Paradigm, as some of its promoters capitalize it, amounts to lifeways and patterns of perception and thinking that recognize and relate to whole systems, not just isolated items and events, over very long time periods, not just for the duration of something's "usefulness" for immediate purposes. As human consciousness is aware that it is conscious, so New Paradigm thinking is aware that paradigms exist and create a dynamic that can be understood and worked with. We can see, for example, that as new information builds up suggesting that an older system of thinking or "Old Paradigm" is no longer answering questions, a breakthrough to a new understanding, a new set of theories, may be imminent. For example, Newtonian physics seemed incapable of explaining ever more phenomena as technology and experience advanced in the sciences. Then, at a certain point, Einsteinian relativity matured and coalesced into a consistent body of information, perceptions and systems of order that created a whole new paradigm.

In this book I am suggesting that this is exactly what we see happening in the realm of design of human habitat. The old ways, ideas, perceptions and information screens are failing us and we need to go beyond trying to repair the car and its infrastructure and instead build the ecocity. It's noteworthy that, just before the dawning of a new paradigm, resistance typically reaches its peak and pitched battles are fought to keep people from even considering new information. But then the weight of evidence becomes overwhelming and rather suddenly, everything makes sense in a new way and the new paradigm not only blossoms forth in its own right, but acceptance becomes almost universal. As they say of a new idea, even more a new paradigm: It is initially derided as ridiculous, then opposed violently as dangerous, and finally embraced as self-evident.

A whole-systems approach to agriculture that leads into aspects of ecocity design and goes a long way toward fleshing out a new paradigm is called permaculture. The term was coined by the inventor of the concept and founder of the movement, Bill Mollison. His definition goes like this:

Permaculture (permanent agriculture) is the conscious design and maintenance of agriculturally productive ecosystems which have the diversity, stability and resilience of natural ecosystems. It is the harmonious integration of landscape and people providing their food, energy, shelter and other material and non-material needs in a sustainable way. Without permanent agriculture there is no possibility of a stable social order.

Permaculture design is a system of assembling conceptual, material and strategic components in a pattern which functions to benefit life in all its forms. The philosophy behind permaculture is one of working with, rather than against, nature; of protracted and thoughtful observation rather than protracted and thoughtless action; of looking at systems in all their functions, rather than asking only one yield of them; and allowing systems to demonstrate their own evolutions.[54]

Although Mollison started by sculpting landscapes to create ponds, planting trees, bushes and vines, and building rural homes, some of his associates have been impatient to expand the concept to embrace more aspects of human environmental design. According to the architect Declan Kennedy,[55] "The term, permaculture, originally described a permanent agriculture. Nowadays, the concept encompasses much more: a planning and design method with the aim of creating stable self-supporting systems, a sustainable culture based on ecological principles, which not only supply wholesome food for people, but energy, warmth, beauty and meaningful pursuits."

Permaculture emphasizes fruit and nut trees, and berry and vegetable plants that bear year after year or reseed themselves, rather than annual crops that are sown and harvested every season. Arrangement and proximity are essential: Trees are planted to shelter buildings and gardens from wind or to avoid shading areas that should get warmth and light. Plants that are most frequently used, such as salad greens and herbs, are located closest to the kitchen, with occasionally-used main course vegetables farther away, seldom-harvested grains, berries and fruits farther yet, and the distant woodlot, harvested only annually, farthest of all. Beyond the semi-natural woodlot, nature is mainly in charge: a healthy reservoir of life that in the form of bees, butterflies, hummingbirds and many other animals and plants delivers the service of pollination, occasionally provides game for the farmer's dinner, and supplies completely untended wild fruits, nuts and berries for the picking. Beyond that there is natural wilderness where people are non-interfering observers. Right on the windowsill, for color, fragrance and inspiration, is the window box with flowers. We see here again the principle of access by proximity. Dogs and cats are not particularly useful in the eyes of permaculturists. At the permaculture village of Crystal Waters in Queensland, Australia, they are banned and as a result the village is alive with hundreds of natural birds and frequently visited by native bats, reptiles and marsupials.

The permaculture homestead follows the same principles in architecture, with the home sited for shelter from the winds provided by trees, hills or berms, and oriented to collect or avoid direct sun, depending on the climate. To the already complex house with attached solar greenhouse, the permaculture designer might also attach a chicken house and composting bin that share heat with each other and the main house. Worms may be busily composting kitchen waste in the basement side by side with a dry toilet that is preparing an annual dose of fertilizer for appropriate parts of the garden. When it rains, the roof collects water with its gutters and downspouts and cisterns store the water beside the house, ready for use inside or for watering the garden. A pond may be carved out of the yard on the sunny side of the house to reflect added light and warmth into the greenhouse and provide for ducks, which delight in eating the snails that are doing their best to eat the crops before the people do. The permaculturist can provide hives for bees, for honey as well as pollination services. All this, again, represents access to diversity at close proximity.

A key principle, according to Mollison, is, "Trust the chickens." It's impossible to predict how all the elements of your house and garden design are going to interrelate, he says, but you can try it out and carefully watch how it works. The chickens will deliver eggs and meat. They will rid your garden of certain grubs and other pests, but they will also pick at some of the plants you like, and they may need to be fed something in addition to kitchen scraps, local bugs, occasional weeds, and so on. If a clear pattern of benefit emerges with any element of the whole — chickens, worms, greenhouse, wood stove — many other benefits are likely to emerge unexpectedly. In building my own solar greenhouse in Berkeley, I was expecting food production and heat for the house, but to my surprise I also got peace and quiet. The greenhouse glass virtually eliminated the considerable street noise that had formerly plagued our place. We are familiar with the vicious circle, in which one bad thing begets another. This, in contrast, is the virtuous circle, in which good things beget other good ones. Putting beneficial things into mutually-supportive relationships often has this delightful effect. Trust the chickens.

Permaculture amounts to the mixing of appropriate technologies and agriculture according to design principles that accomplish high orders of integrity in complex whole systems. Urban permaculture amounts to the application of these same design principles to urban habitats, to produce a yet higher order of integrity.

One of my favorite examples of urban permaculture was designed by Margrit Kennedy, Declan's wife, as part of the International Building Exhibition in Berlin in the mid-1980s. In the very dense Kreutzberg neighborhood — typically 900 to 1,200 people per urban block, in buildings averaging six stories in height — there was a large city parking structure used by people with work or appointments in the neighborhood. These motorists were few relative to those living in the neighborhood and, living elsewhere, were not local voters. With cars threatening the lives of the residents' children every day, there came a time when the locals decided to close down the parking structure and do something more socially useful with the building. The International Building Exhibition, held within a few blocks of the Bauhaus Museum, was at the time identifying sites around Berlin that would showcase new and socially-conscious architectural ideas and styles, serve citizens, attract positive civic attention and participate in architectural history. Margrit Kennedy, who was asked to submit ideas to the International Building Exhibition for projects that might be built, identified the parking garage conversion as a promising site for an urban permaculture project. She was selected by the exhibition organizers and sponsored by the city and federal government to work on the project. Three years later the house for cars became a nursery school for children.

First the neighborhood organized support and took the proposal to Berlin City Hall, which decided to proceed using some of the capital earmarked for the International Building Exhibition. In good recycling tradition, the basic structure was preserved. The sloping ramps were left intact, with an awkward staircase built into the shallow slope —two steps forward, one step up. A masonry saw was taken to the three levels and a central atrium created by simply slicing out and removing the center of three floors of concrete slab. Classrooms were built by inserting divider walls perpendicular to the central opening, and the atrium itself was glassed over with a skylight and filled with dozens of plants. On the roof of the building a playground and garden were built behind a secure fence, and a small pond was added to support aquatic plants, insects, fish and frogs. Around the outside of the building a trellis was constructed, and when I visited in 1989 vines had just started to wind their way downward from the roof and upward from street-level, past the roof and up the fence that surrounded the rooftop playground. What kind of food production came from this building/garden/trellis system I have not heard, but even if token in this particular case, the educational value and the soft tempering of sun and shadow would constitute powerful instruction for children growing up there.

Permaculture is a system with a number of principles guiding its practice. Among the most important is the notion that one component of a design serves best when it serves several purposes at once, such as a solar greenhouse that warms a house, provides a nursery for starting plants early in the season, creates a quiet environment and helps keep chickens and compost at proper and stable temperatures. To provide these services, the greenhouse has to be oriented properly toward or away from the sun, depending on climate and local sun aspect, and must be attached to the house, chicken coop and compost box in a reciprocally beneficial manner. Another important principle is that edges between zones are especially rich in potential productivity and services to people, agriculture and natural species. They can be created by design, and even more, if convoluted, like the edge of a scallop shell, can become yet richer and even more productive.

Mixing architecture and town planning three-dimensionally with complex agriculture shaped by the bioregional realities of climate, weather and sun angles becomes a context for real thriving of appropriate technology and the human community. All of this has been technologically and conceptually available since the early 1980s, but until today only the smallest steps have been taken in this direction.

"Improved" Suburbs, Revitalized Downtowns

One of the things that does get built these days is the "improved" suburb, and among their builders are the "New Urbanists." Andres Duany and Elizabeth Plater-Zyberk designed the 80-acre Seaside in Florida and the 352-acre Kentlands project in Gaithersburg, Maryland. Peter Calthorpe designed the 1,100-acre Laguna West project south of Sacramento, California. Other New Urbanist projects are built or under construction, and building codes for the entire U.S. are being adjusted somewhat to allow the sort of features they promote, such as older-style, more narrow streets with smaller intersections. Says one of their prime movers, architect Peter Calthorpe:[56]

> Urban Development is ideologically a strong and compelling alternative to the suburban world, but it doesn't seem to fit the character or aspirations of major parts of our population, and many businesses. Mixed-use new towns are no alternative, as the political consensus needed to back massive infrastructure investment is lacking. Growth therefore is directed mainly by the location of new freeways systems, the economic strength of the regions, and standard, single-use zoning practices. Environmental and local opposition to growth only seems to spread the problem, either transferring the congestion to the next county, or creating lower and more auto-dependent densities.

In response to this problem Calthorpe has proposed the "transit village" or "pedestrian pocket." He describes this as

> ... a balanced, mixed-use area within a ¼-mile walking radius of a light rail station. The uses within this zone of approximately fifty to 120 acres would include housing, offices, retail, daycare, recreation and open space. Up to 2,000 units and 1,000,000 square feet of office can be located within three blocks of the light rail station using typical condominium densities and four-story office configurations. These pockets could be implanted into existing suburban fabric by the creation of a new light rail line and a corresponding up-zoning at each of its stations. ... The goal would be to create an environment in which the convenience of the car and the opportunity to walk would be blended. The Pedestrian

Pocket would accommodate both the car and the economic engine of new growth, the back office [an office in the suburb remote from the city center]. Parking would be provided for all the housing and commercial space.

In the early 1980s New Urbanist thinking began with recognition of the healthy aspects of the "traditional" small town with modest density, which we tend to remember as more typical around the 1940s, a time not yet swamped with cars. Such towns had total densities two or three times as high as suburban developments. They had residential areas of modest houses with porches, private back yards, public front yards, ample side yards, often an alley in back with a garbage can behind the house. In the center was a town square or plaza surrounded by buildings one- to four-stories tall, sidewalks everywhere, and cars parked at the curb to protect pedestrians on sidewalks from moving cars and thus make them feel comfortable. Calthorpe and his allied architects refined and updated the genre, proposing to make it somewhat more dense, putting a residential unit over the garage in recognition of the fact that more people these days live alone, or as part of a couple without child, or as a single parent with a child or shared child. Rail access was proposed for the centers when possible, or they were sited near existing commuter rail lines. Called "neo-traditional" development early on, this approach became known as the "New Urbanism" as it evolved, although originally it was neither new nor really urban. An association called the Congress for the New Urbanism was founded to refine and promote such work.

But how well can slightly more dense suburban centers work if the assumption is that cars will be needed in addition to whatever transit is encouraged? Calthorpe has called New Urbanist strategy a bridge strategy. De-emphasizing the car to some degree may be the beginning of a bridge to a better urban structure, but that's not much and it will be helpful only if it is understood in that way — which hardly seems to be the case. A few generations of people could easily live and die in such developments swearing it's where they had arrived, not a step to somewhere else, all the while consuming 80 percent or 90 percent as much gasoline as the people in the conventional development next door. In the New Urbanists' own manifesto,[57] which they call the "Charter of the New Urbanism" the point is made quite clear, in fact, that they don't want to cross over that bridge. "In the contemporary metropolis," it says, "development must accommodate automobiles. It should do so in ways that respect the pedestrian and the form of public space." Elsewhere in the Charter they say, "Communities should be designed for the pedestrian and transit as well as the car," as if the process of design starts with the car but we should remind ourselves not to forget people.

Calthorpe was on a better line of reasoning in the early 1970s when he wrote an article called "The Solar Shadow" for *Progressive Architecture* magazine. In it he noted that with compact urban development in which living units share walls ("party walls" among architects) more energy could be saved than with solar passive design — solar orientation and greenhouses. Furthermore, he noted the enormous differences between the energy consumed by VMT — average Vehicle Miles Traveled — in suburbia and in the city. Independent thinker Michael Phillips at that time put the pieces together and compared the energy consumed by the average suburbanite to that consumed by the city dweller that didn't own a car at all, and showed a much greater level of energy conservation and time and money saved. He figured in the manufacture of cars and highways and calculated that the suburbanite consumed about ten times the energy of the car-free city person. The bottom line: appropriate technology produces only an illusion of efficiency. Something more fundamental is needed; the built environment has to be reshaped.

The New Urbanists did go on to do that, but with so much acquiescence to the automobile that one wonders if the purpose was mainly to convince people they had done enough when, in fact, they had done very little.

If the New Urbanists want to build an improved suburb, there are others who want to improve downtown. Roberta Brandes Gratz and Norman Mintz epitomize the approach.[58] Their prescription is not to pursue big development projects, but to work with what is there in the past and present to produce a transition to a lively future by reviving the downtown's sense of community. This is a matter of detail — one improvement in one business at a time. The overall strategy is to promote and allow a return of diversity. Eschew "convention centers, stadiums, aquariums and other headline-grabbing, budget-straining projects," they say. Quoting H. L. Mencken: "For every complex, difficult problem, there is a simple, easy solution ... and it is wrong."[59] They champion small-scale innovation and say that reinventing the wheel is fun and provides creative practice to the community. They advocate being careful about tenants, avoiding big parking lots that obliterate the continuity of shop fronts, and providing new street light fixtures to make people feel safe. They advise creating districts — and in this they are consistent with models at least 5,000 years old — of clusters of shops and businesses that complement one another even while, often, competing with one another. Not the leather working or pottery districts of past eras but, for example, offices, copy shops, stationery stores and lunch delis — several of each. Other examples: restaurant areas and arts districts. Cultivate the "third place," they say, the informal public gathering place. (The first place is home and the second place the work place.) It "must be within walking distance from home, [a place] where one feels valued as more than a faceless consumer; where socializing, loitering and lingering are recognized social assets, not commercial liabilities; where conversation and camaraderie prevail; and where the hot political issues and the latest football scores gain equal attention." Gratz and Mintz say that these places are returning, and in many cities so are sections of, or whole downtowns.

Improving suburbs and downtowns, creating pockets of charm, may be a step in the right direction, but what about improving the whole thing? Approaches to the whole city, as a rule, must take into consideration the whole city's land use patterns, the architecture built upon those patterns, and the way in which these are connected with the transportation system. Part of the land use "element" will be the restoration and preservation of agriculture and nature. And in some places this genuine, whole-systems approach is actually being put into practice. In fact, in essence, this is exactly what the planning departments of cities are attempting, and most of their tools, such as General Plans, zoning ordinances and building codes, have significant potential for ecological benefit if written for that purpose. Many city-employed planners wish they could do more in this direction but are hampered by a lack of ecological insight in the community. In a few cities, however, many healthy ideas are deeply imbedded in the community and supported by skilled leadership, and, therefore, their plans are beginning to solve larger ecological and urban problems.

COMMUNITIES ON THE CUTTING EDGE

Whole cities, among them Curitiba, Brazil and Waitakere, New Zealand, are taking on a wide range of ecological issues, and being self-consciously called "ecological cities" by their own leaders. Many are establishing greenbelts, constructing new urban rail lines, restoring natural areas and building "greenways" or nature trails. Portland, Oregon, has removed a major motorway along the Willamette River to create a public promenade and park. Many are promoting bicycles and are doing ever better at recycling. Waitakere has a program for planting several trees for each new baby — a "baby forest" that the parents plant themselves. On a smaller scale, many intentional communities that call themselves "ecovillages" are being established, and many of them are united in a loose-knit organization called the Global Ecovillage Network, which vigorously promotes their values and strategies.

One of the most inspiring experiments in urban design anywhere has been taking place over the past thirty years in Curitiba, Brazil, the country's eighth largest city at 1.6 million in the municipality, 2.5 million in the total metropolitan area. Under the leadership of Jaime Lerner and other recent mayors, this city has become a model for solutions to intractable urban problems afflicting cities on every continent. Lerner was an architect and city planner. When he was appointed mayor in 1970, he brought along a number of innovative colleagues — and a team of inspired professionals launched into action.

Curitiba's success had a good deal to do with the considerable imagination and contagious enthusiasm of the mayor and his remarkably creative crew at the newly opened school of architecture. He launched a new institution, IPPUC, the Institute for Urban Planning and Research of Curitiba, which has endured through several other mayor's terms as well as Lerner's, lending stability and maintaining pioneering ecological innovation to the city for thirty years. Happily, many of IPPUC's founders had visited Europe and recognized that pedestrian areas and public transportation can work beautifully. Unhappily, they saw their closest urban neighbor, Sao Paolo, clogged in cars and fumigated in smog. They were ready to try almost anything to avoid such a plight, even sensible ideas like creating pedestrian streets. With an influx of agricultural workers who had been replaced by farm machines, they expected the city to grow rapidly from its population of 600,000. The stakes were high to get it right.

Their rare insight at the time was to make the land use/transportation connection work from the very beginning. They planned for future expansion of the city along five high-density corridors stretching out like arms of a giant starfish and served by frequent and inexpensive busses traveling quickly down streets dedicated to them alone. Other cities in Brazil were using federal money and their own to build subway systems. Curitiba decided the benefits of a subway just were not worth the extreme expense — 300 times more costly, said the planners, than simply paving five dedicated streets. Private companies would get to build tall buildings along the corridors using their own capital and make good profits while the bus companies would have the riders living and working within a short walk of the main "speedy" lines. Full and frequent busses meant profits for the bus companies too, without subsidy from government. Bus riders got access to jobs, housing and open space all in the same package. The low cost of building the bus system also meant that a great deal of money was saved to be invested in other things: purchase of land to restore rivers and expand parks, launching of social programs of a wide variety, and building of neighborhood libraries called "lighthouses of learning," which have four- or five-story towers that look like lighthouses and inspire the affection of citizens.

The imagination and enthusiastic civic spirit of Curitiba's ecological and social policies have been its hallmark. It's not just that the city has achieved 70 percent recycling, the record in South America, but that old and broken down busses have been towed out to the slums of new immigrants to become schools for entry-level skills useful in the city — recycling busses as well as trash. Recycling hit a high point with the filling of several old quarries with water, creating beautiful lakes, and the building of major public institutions there, including the Free University for the Environment and the Wire Opera House (called that because the graceful metal-tubing and glass structure almost looks like an open wire structure).

By whatever means — sometimes taking it to the television audience in personal appeals, sometimes drafting school children to lecture their parents on environmental issues — Lerner's administrations have unclogged traffic, greatly reduced residents' travel time, established a 300-mile-long bus system and a 125-mile bicycle and foot path system. Curitiba's fuel consumption has been reduced by 20 percent compared to other similar-sized Brazilian cities. It has the country's lowest traffic-accident death rate per capita, and air pollution is remarkably low. According to Lerner, "There is little in the architecture of a city that is more beautifully designed than a tree," and with that philosophy his administration initiated a program that had planted more than 4 million trees by the time I visited in April, 2000. Street children are finding jobs through city programs; garbage collection and recycling are being accomplished in shantytowns; food shortages are being alleviated through city programs to trade agricultural gleanings for recyclables; and a twenty-four hour health clinic for the poor has been opened.

Early in his first term as Mayor, Lerner built Brazil's first pedestrian street despite protesting business owners — who later flourished financially as the project spread and turned into a twenty-seven-block system of pedestrian streets. That famous first Monday after Lerner's Department of Public Works put up the barriers at the ends of a downtown block, protesting car drivers arrived on the street intending to remove the barriers and keep the street for cars. But city employees were ready with long rolls of drawing paper and hundreds of school children laid out the paper on the street and began drawing. The drivers backed off, the shop owners decided to wait a few days, and sure enough, it worked out just fine. For the young and restless, one of Lerner's administrations built the country's first "twenty-four-hour street": a glass covered pedestrian street sheltered by one of Curitiba's characteristic metal tubing and glass structures of big semi-circular arches (similar to the Wire Opera House), which provides space for round-the-clock snacking, socializing and courting. In the shantytowns, where narrow footpaths wind between ramshackle hovels improvised from recycled materials, garbage collection and municipal recycling were beyond the reach of trucks. Lerner proposed a "Green Exchange": The people themselves separate recyclable materials and garbage and take them to pickup points where they can be exchanged for food provided by the city. The city then takes the garbage to the dump and markets the recyclables to help pay for the system. To get the populace into the swing of things, Lerner promoted the slogan, "Trash That Is Not Trash," and went on television[60]

> ... to convince residents to separate rubbish into organic and inorganic waste. With a mix of public relations savvy and

leprechaun spirit, he had garbage trucks painted green. And he kicked off the campaign by donning overalls and doing a day of collecting recyclable trash. "Shantytown kids ran after the garbage truck, tauntingly calling me 'trash collector'," says Mr. Lerner. "But that was my idea. If it's not beneath the mayor to collect trash, it shouldn't be beneath them to separate it."

Next, the city recruited four actors, dressed them up in foliage, called them the "Leaf Family," put them on TV, and then sent them out on a tour of the city's schools to teach ecology and trade pictures of famous comic book heroes for non-degradable trash such as batteries and toothpaste tubes. The kids were excited to see them and listened attentively — largely because they'd already seen the Leaf Family on television. That TV personalities would actually visit their school to talk about ecology — that was exciting.

Confronted with a car population growing faster than the human one, Lerner increased bus routes, frequency and convenience. In a truly remarkable stroke of genius, he designed the spiffy "tube stations" that are now internationally famous, solving technical problems while inspiring the public with a stylish kind of urban feature somewhere between architecture and furniture. These glorified stations are in the shape of giant glass bottles on their sides with both ends cut off. Bus riders can walk up a few steps, enter a turnstile, pay an attendant the equivalent of 45 cents, and go anywhere in the city. No longer does the driver have to fumble with change or worry about who puts how much into the money box. The tube station celebrates the bus riders, its design announcing that the city cares about them. When the bus arrives, wide doors open and a wide plank drops from the side of the bus to the platform, allowing people to exit and enter the bus quickly, four abreast. Inside the tube stations, people don't get rained on. Upon installation of the tube stations, time for travel on the bus went down 24 percent and ridership went up 20 percent, virtually overnight. Says Lerner, "If city dwellers used their cars less and separated their trash, half the city's problems would be solved."

How was Mayor Jaime Lerner able to accomplish all this, and in a country of modest means? With enormous imagination, flexibility and determination. And most important, as just suggested, he got the city reshaping project off to an excellent start. The compact development provided for efficient, inexpensive transportation and left room for recreational open space, natural restoration and money for services to the people.

Not everyone is happy in Curitiba. Poverty is a problem that is being solved only slowly despite innovative approaches. Cars are now beginning to glut city streets as ever more people become prosperous — largely because they have been able to save money due to the excellent bus service. But as Marc Margolis has put it, whereas "in Brazil most mayors start out their terms as fabulously popular celebrities and finish them barricaded behind palace doors, dispatching press releases and disclaimers and ducking the press, Lerner can walk the streets with impunity."[61]

Said one of Lerner's critics, "The only thing lacking is for people to say that the sunsets here are nicer since Jaime Lerner took over." But as the smog clears and the distant pink clouds show through, this may well be true. Vote for better sunsets. Vote Lerner.

Vancouver, British Columbia is well on its way to becoming an ecocity. It has 2 million people, of mostly British ancestry and tradition but rapidly shifting toward Asian. The third-fastest growing city in North America, it has an intense, very three-dimensional but very friendly downtown with 60,000 residents. Says Larry Beasley, co-Director of Planning, they don't want a freeway, have never had one, and, if the present planning strategy and public mood holds, never will. Convinced that balanced development at high density works, his office is presently planning for 40,000 more people in the downtown.

The city has adopted a "special strategy to secure low-income housing, to foster housing for families with small children, and to ensure specialty housing for singles, mingles, seniors, extended families, alternative households and any other household formation that presents itself," including a growing houseboat community. "Vancouver is now looking at both commercial and industrial live-work forms," says Beasley. "Both the shop house and the industrial loft are appearing, as well as more multiuse, high-rise, high-ceiling loft spaces that are snapped up by buyers and put to many uses in connection with residences."[62] Vancouver's chief asset, says Beasley, is not any large global megacorporation hiring large numbers of people but "our good looks," meaning the mountains and the sea. To preserve those views while accommodating 2 million people, taller buildings are kept to a thin profile and spaced relatively far apart. The spacing also helps maintain a sense of privacy.

The planning department's major objectives for the city are "living closer to work, cutting commuting time, de-emphasizing the car, ... slashing capital spending on roads, bridges and the complex accommodations needed for mass auto commuting." Vancouver is building an advanced transit system and networks for bikeways, feet, ferries and greenways. A major goal is to "replicate the rich street life that is enjoyed in older traditional cities," creating an intimate egalitarian world on ground level, but in a high-rise mode supported by the economic engine of the larger buildings rising without much notice beyond.

According to Beasley, " 'Streetscaping' is the key design tool to tame the massive scale of the contemporary high-rise, high-density development that characterizes Vancouver and most modern cities." To heighten the intimacy at street level, a variety of plantings are encouraged along intentionally narrow and crowded sidewalks, often with double rows of trees on each side of the street. In many cases the sidewalk has been "expanded and enhanced by setback requirements that, in essence, reclaim a slice of private space for the public streetscape. Remaining private, however, these slices of streetscape have great agility as places for outdoor retailing, outdoor restaurant seating, townhouse stoops and landscaping to soften hard urban edges. ... Such setbacks have proven to not create economic hardship, yet dramatically improve the public realm."

Creating a pleasurable environment at the foot of the towers, Beasley tells, us "is first and foremost the art of creating the classic streetwall. First, the space of the street is fully enclosed; second, the enclosure is strongly corniced, with taller tower elements set generously back; third, the height of the resulting streetwall is carefully constrained at 3-6 stories to secure a comfortable human scale." In many cases the terrace rooftops of these lower buildings along the street are planted with trees, adding a second screen of foliage between the people in the street and the taller buildings in the background; the first screen is provided by the trees planted at street level. The resulting effect, says Beasley, " 'disembodies' the massive tower by screening its foundation and making it appear to float and then disappear beyond the immediate perception of bystanders."

Listening to Beasley characterize the streets as cozy and sociable, with the massive towers rising virtually unnoticed behind, it occurred to me that a great many of the same people ignoring the towers and delighting in the small-scale foreground live and work in the towers that this design concept treats as forbidding, massive and out of human scale. Were there two attitudes in each person, one elevated into the views of mountains and sea, remote from the ground, soaring like birds, and the other relishing a more terrestrial world as well? Despite the general reputation of towers around the world, are they really all that dehumanizing? Certainly nice folks capable of appreciating the finer ground-hugging details of life live and work in them, and that includes tens to hundreds of millions of people at this point in history.

STATE OF THE ART AND THEORY

The Kentucky architect Richard S. Levine has proposed that, while "sustainable development" delivered piecemeal may actually prevent "sustainable cities" from coming into being, building sustainable cities would produce sustainable development. It's a one-way street, he claims.[63]

> The dominant model of desired change advanced within the movement is that, if only we can build up the arguments, tools and resources in the sustainable direction, then at some point. ... the forces will shift and we will then be effectively on a sustainable path. ... These sustainable tendencies can at best provide certain necessary conditions for generating long term sustainability. Strategically, it cannot be the path itself. Sustainable development alone does not lead to sustainability. It may, in fact, by relieving some of the pressure, thus support the longevity of the unsustainable path. These many tendencies require synthesis and transformation into a new, dynamic process that overcomes the present system's tendency to produce and reproduce growth-oriented relations and processes of imbalance, instability and decay. Such a change from the old to the new can only come from a catalyst — specifically, the design and institution of sustainable cities. ...
>
> To the extent that sustainable development agents move from crisis to crisis, using technological fixes to patch up larger structural problems, they tend to strengthen the systematic relations supporting unsustainability — especially when such "band-aid" solutions lead to instances where these deeper problems fall below the threshold of public attention and the political momentum for more fundamental change dissipates.

The sustainable development path can actually be worse than that, since most of it is not to patch up larger structural problems but to ameliorate symptoms of structural problems that are not addressed at all. For example, converting Los Angeles's automobile fleet from gasoline to electricity would leave almost everything destructive about cars in place, while transferring energy generation and pollution abatement to power plants — many more of them — or require home power plants, which are expensive, in addition to the expensive car itself. Instead we could build communities that didn't require cars in the first place. Painting bike lane stripes on streets and posting "bike lane" signs as we do in Berkeley mildly encourages bicyclists, but does little to increase safety and nothing to change the city structure or the origins and destinations of bicycle trips. In fact, if bicyclists feel that they are doing about all that's possible by taking a little more time to bike rather than drive, and the city remains otherwise the same, the bicycle lane markings may actually stall or kill the decision to make more substantive changes. Thus the good sustainable development step can be, as Levine argues, destructive to healthy society and nature.

Scientists at the Lawrence Berkeley Laboratory who study energy conservation on generous federal grants have repeatedly proposed reducing the urban heat-island effect with strategies such as planting trees to shade parking lots and even painting parking lots white to reflect light rather than absorb heat. Again, why go to all that trouble greenwashing a parking lot and blinding drivers with glare from white paint when the problem could be far better addressed with urban design changes that make parking lots completely unnecessary. One LBL scientist has even proposed saving energy by taking down all the stop signs since they cause cars to stop and go and, therefore, use much more energy than cars cruising steadily along. Here the likelihood of enormously increased numbers of traffic accidents and pedestrian deaths are just swept under the rug for the sake of "sustainability." Experts, like fish in a small bowl, are failing to see the larger world around them. It's up to every-day citizens in large numbers to comprehend what needs to be done to reshape our cities, then educate, promote and politicize to that end.

Solutions based on understanding the city as a whole, living system exist now, and, if put in meaningful perspective, so do approaches to reshaping downtowns and even suburbs. If we know what we are looking for, we will find that the city today gives us magnificent opportunities for genuine progress — healthy, evolutionary progress.

When Cortez arrived in Mexico, the Aztecs had toy animals with wheels, but they had no carts, wagons or other useful objects equipped with wheels. The first they saw were the Spanish wagons hauling gunpowder, firearms, armor and supplies into their country. They had never extended the principle of the wheel beyond the toy. Similarly, the ecocity is represented in countless details functioning admirably and pleasurably in our world right under our noses, and even represented in places in its most fundamental land-use patterns. But we don't apply these features and basic principles to the whole society. Just as the Aztecs' toys were a source of pleasure, regarded as something special and enriching, ecocity features such as pedestrian areas, rooftop gardens and bridges between buildings are greatly enjoyed where they exist, but are thought of as playful, special things of not much utility. Instead, they should be seen for the much greater value they would have if generalized to the whole society — if applied in their full usefulness and as part of normal economics. We tend to be amused that the wheel was neglected in pre-Columbian North America but we are doing the same thing all over again — and regarding something even more important.

6

Access and Transportation

ACCESS AND ADVENTURE

The shortest distance between two points is moving those points closer together; every trip from then on is shorter. That's an efficiency multiplied thousands of times. Between cities and across long distances, approximating a straight line is a good idea, but within cities, access is most efficiently provided by proximity. You can travel there, or you can build for diversity of activities so that "there" is practically next door.

Animals move. When they cease living, they cease moving. In its poetic and darkly threatening tone, the Bible distinguishes between "the quick and the dead." If all else fails, we can at least have the illusion of being fully alive by moving about, the faster and farther, the more powerful the feeling. This is no small part of today's problems. The illusion is so pervasive that Mahatma Gandhi once felt moved to say, "There is more to life than increasing its speed." I think the only way to deal with this is to come up with an adventure that is as exciting or more: ecocity building.

Humanity's ancestors spent about 20 million years in the trees looking something like lemurs, leaping through the air in a three-dimensional, living jungle gym. In this environment we evolved our grasping, prehensile fingers with opposable thumb, and our front-facing eyes capable of precise, three-dimensional parallax vision. Deep genetic memories of this phase of our evolution bode well for a more three-dimensional life in the ecocities of the future. We are all gymnasts and trapeze artists to our double-helix cores. The forest environment helped launch us into a complex, exciting relationship with transportation: As we swung between and down from the trees and walked out onto the grassy surfaces of Gaia's broad tummy, we were as omnivorous for movement as we were for food.

It wasn't long before we started using our clever minds, tree-top-evolved hands and 3-D vision to extend our range, comfort and safety by fashioning moccasins, sandals, boots and shoes. We leapt onto horses, built boats, lifted sails into the ocean sky, zipped down hills on skis, built our first carts and wagons, and eventually took to flying through the air in mechanized birds. It was an exciting story of wind in the teeth, sweet cowboy loneliness as the unsung hero got up and moved on, the wonderful return to loved ones or the apprehensive reunion after a long voyage of exploration, the adventure of unknown lands delivered to us on this planet's amazingly varied surface by no other means than simply moving across it, and of ever increasing speed. And now that some of us have traveled in the neighborhood of 25,000 miles per hour to the moon and back, perhaps it is time to reconsider the point of it all. Now that we have spent about half of the planet's full endowment of petroleum resources in this racing about, perhaps we should entertain the notion of overmobility.

The sense of adventure, and that feeling of freedom it brings, is an important issue. If adventure is many things to many people, one of the few things practically everyone will agree upon is that being stuck in a traffic jam is not one of them. Ironically, beyond certain not so obvious limits, transportation destroys the potential for adventure. If everyone is traveling regularly back and forth across the city, the everydayness of the trip reduces its pleasure. Too much movement through one neighborhood after another as they lose their ethnic feel, sprout chain stores and franchise restaurants, post identical billboards, and adopt uniform if scrambled aesthetics, erodes the sense of excitement and alertness in the traveler. Excessive moving about crowds a place and, in the case of cars, contaminates the city with smog, noise, bad smells, inconvenience, irritation and danger — all of an accidental and pointless sort. No confrontations with ferocious animals, unpredictable tribesmen, or hazards of

Typical downtown of a "modern" city built around overmobility, mainly for cars.

avalanche and prairie fire, no tests of subtle cultural understanding, knowledge of nature's challenges, or requirements for well-tuned navigation skills as in past times of real adventure. Just remembering to turn at the same old freeway exit is about the most that the sad-eyed commuter on the ten-thousandth trip will be called upon to accomplish.

In the overly-mobile world of car culture the destination looks ever more like the source — roughly in proportion to mobility. Similarly, in the world of jet travel, cultures and languages, the physical features of geography and architecture, even clothes and tastes in food are becoming homogenized. *I Love Lucy* reruns from orbiting satellites reach dusty villages in Mongolia and Peru. The growing extinction of species is caused partially by expanded markets made available by cheap transportation. Don't forget the depressing feeling of finding a bottle cap on a remote mountain ridge, a cigarette package on what felt for a while like a lonely beach, or a vapor trail in what could have been a gorgeous sunset "hundreds of miles from anywhere." Transportation can go too far. It can change people's attitudes about travel and lower levels of respect for the

One of a thousand possible pedestrian city transformations, built around being there rather than getting there.

places and people visited. To preserve a beautiful world, we need to travel not only with more respect, but on the average, much less. When we arrive we need to stay a while, get to understand what's going on, become involved.

Inside cities, towns and villages, very different rules apply, just as the rules within an organism — respiration, metabolism, balance, coordination, contemplation — are different from the rules of intercourse with the world outside. Something happens at that skin, that edge, those city limits — something that changes everything. What happens is simply protective containment of integrally functioning systems, definition of a system with its own integrities, and the selective filtering of materials and influences so that the organism can benefit from exchanges and maintain health. In both the organism and the city, that whole system is a system of subsystems.

Inside the city, the best transportation is the least: Access by proximity should be the objective. The distances are potentially so miniaturized — "imploded," as some urban theorists would say — that within that semi-permeable skin, that social/ecological boundary, fifteen miles per hour — a fast running speed — should be the general upper limit. Any higher speeds should be reserved for special transit uses and longer-distance bicycle commuting and sports cycling. Any speed above about fifteen miles per hour becomes, on a geometric curve, more and more damaging as it increases. Below fifteen, even in a large vehicle, it is almost impossible to kill anything, even intentionally. Above that speed, safety erodes quickly. Speeding bicyclists occasionally cause serious accidents, though only rarely fatal ones, and when vehicles become motorized, pollution, noise and exhaustion of fossil fuels escalate while fatal accidents become commonplace.

There is a simple law of physics involved here: The forces increase by the square as speed goes up. A crash at twenty miles per hour involves four times, not two times, the force involved in an accident at ten miles per hour, and a crash at forty miles per hour involves not four but sixteen times the force. The qualitative differences are even more extreme as certain thresholds are passed. At ten miles per hour two people bumping into one another bounce off with almost no damage. (My daughter once asked me if anyone had ever been killed in a "people accident.") Somewhere around twenty-five or thirty miles per hour bones act brittle and snap or collapse, and at about twice that speed, grisly words reserved for insects hitting windshields apply to human beings, too.

When vehicles and their infrastructure (and we can include horses, wagons, stables, and so on, as well as cars, garages and gas stations) are present, the city is expanded by their physical size. When the city becomes motorized it is significantly expanded by public transportation vehicles and infrastructure. But when the automobile becomes the dominant transportation mode — move over people! The city blows out over vast areas, at extreme hazard to its citizens and nature alike. Ivan Illich says, "High speed is the critical factor which makes transportation socially destructive. The true choice among political systems and of desirable social relations is possible only where speed is restrained. Participatory democracy demands low energy technology, and free people must travel the road to productive social relations at the speed of a bicycle."[64]

The transportation system is much more than it seems. I have earlier described the role of the automobile in destroying the balance between the inward and outward forces of the city's growth and metabolism. I have portrayed the entire automobile transportation infrastructure — cars, sprawl, freeways and oil — as truly monstrous in its effects, dominating life on Earth by becoming the single largest agent of resource depletion, habitat destruction, climate change and species extinction. But this transportation infrastructure does not stand alone. It is supported by massive outlays of defense spending to keep cheap oil flowing our way.

Intimately connected with the car/sprawl/freeway/oil infrastructure is another of the more problematic technologies of our times: television. Television makes it much easier to combat what would otherwise be the loneliness of suburban isolation. It's a medium that tends to work best with constantly hyped-up, even furious change, and provides a visual format, at one end of the bedroom, living room, even kitchen, in which only a small number of objects work well at one time. A few fast moving cars are ideal; cars and television were made for each other.

Consequences of Car Addiction

The automobile touches all of our lives, whether we own one or not, whether we realize it or not. It's personal: We breathe its excrement in the form of air pollution. It's dramatic: Its alluring design details, its high speed and danger guarantee notice. It's sexy: Millions use it as a place to escape prying eyes, as an impressive lure for a big catch, as a portable bed failing more comfortable and convenient accommodations.

The car is probably second only to the house in status competitions the materialist world over, and often it occupies the largest room to boot. But the car is probably even more effective in this regard because most of us can't even afford to own a house, and, in addition, it can go out on the prowl gathering status anywhere while a house has to just sit there and wait for people to come to it. The car can announce who you are to hundreds, even thousands, of people every day and broadcast your opinions with bumperstickers. And if this were not enough, our very identity is dependent upon it. Who are you, after all? "May I see your ID? Your driver's license, please."

The car is omnipresent. From tall buildings, hills and airplanes people can't be seen, but the car is everywhere. The sprawling city layout indicates to the dispassionate eye that the city was built for cars, not people. If a Martian came to Earth and wanted to speak to someone in charge he would first speak to a car.

As Ivan Illich says, "The automobile has created more distances than it has bridged," and once created, rendered bridging those distances without the automobile virtually impossible. Thus we have become structurally addicted to cars. The structure of the city, even whole national transportation systems, have become thoroughly dependent upon them. Realizing there are 500 million cars in the world and about 50 million new ones arriving every year, then listing the resources destroyed or damaged makes the extent of the addiction evident:

1. About half a million human beings a year worldwide, and millions of mammals, reptiles, amphibians and birds of various descriptions are killed in accidents.
2. About a third of a million people die from air pollution, and cars are the largest single source of pollution worldwide.
3. Water is polluted by runoff from oily, sooty, sometimes salty roads, which, according to the Environmental Protection Agency, rivals sewage in water resource damage.
4. Precious time is spent commuting, sitting in traffic jams, waiting for car repairs, trying to sell or buy a car, changing tires, washing, polishing, trying to fix, dealing with traffic court, working to pay for the car, and visiting accident victims in the hospital or mortuary.
5. A great deal of money is wasted on the purchase of the car, insurance, upkeep, grooming, accident repair, parking space, home garages and driveways, taxes for highways, registration fees, drivers' licenses, fuel (about 500 gallons a year for the average American motorist), parking and moving violations, property damage in accidents, hospital bills for accidents, and income loss during disability. The total direct costs of operating a car in American cities according to Runzheimer International, the management and consulting firm, ran from $7,529 per car per year in Los Angeles to $4,626, or an average of about $6,075, which, multiplied by the number of cars in the country (140,000,000) comes to $634 billion.[65] The money that could go into building alternatives is

diverted into the manufacture and support of cars, buying off the creativity we need to solve our problems. Those who make cars know that the rest of us are addicted to and feel powerless without them and powerless to change our situation. Some people like to think that the manufacturers are being made to squirm when the Environmental Protection Agency forces them to install smog devices, but the apparent victory for consumers will surface as a defeat soon enough — when they foot the bill for the added technology and hardware.

6. Cars create noise with their engines, horns and obnoxious car alarms, and train whistles and emergency sirens would need not be so loud if people were not riding in cars with windows rolled up and producing so much competing noise.

7. Views are ruined by the car itself, its support systems of street lighting that blot out the stars, billboards designed very large to be seen from speeding cars, gas stations, junkyards, sales lots and freeways and their sound walls.

8. Cars cause frustration and hostility in traffic jams and cultivate interests in speed, power, violence, aggressiveness and "road rage."

9. Cars have separated people by scattering the city thinly and erecting walls of steel, glass and speed that breed isolation, alienation and loss of human contact in daily activity.

10. The military-industrial complex builds its power partially on the manufacture and sale of cars, highways and gasoline. Chrysler makes tanks, GM makes military trucks, oil companies make jet fuel. The interstate freeway system was originally named the National Defense Highway System in the 1950s. A highly mobile society is one easily mobilized for war (logistically, anyway), as the great freeway pioneer Adolf Hitler knew so well when he started building Germany's autobahns.

11. The automobile is a kind of weapon in a class war. When it's a Cadillac in the ghetto it's psychological warfare, blinding people and helping to keep them broke. Not being able to afford a considerable outlay of money — for Cadillac or rust bucket — makes you a member of a disadvantaged class created and maintained by the car.

12. Cars are so heavy that, in any relative sense, they average out close

to empty at any given time. In other words, mainly what they are moving is themselves. Cars are usually the heaviest things we own other than a house, which most of us can no longer afford. To keep the heaviest thing most of us own moving every day over large distances costs us enormously. And when they are not moving, typically from 95 percent to 99 percent of the time, they occupy enormous space: one of the largest rooms in the house, and outdoor space that could be shops, parks, playgrounds, natural areas or farmland.

If it seems a little absurd to think of cars as mainly self-justifying, it seems a lot absurd when we see how fast we are going. In 1972 Ivan Illich calculated that if the average American puts in 1,600 hours a year on behalf of, or in, his or her car (most of it work time for money to pay for the car) and gets 7,500 miles of transportation out of it, the car averages less than five miles per hour. Updating these figures to the turn of the millennium produces virtually the same speed.

13. Cars lend themselves to intentional use as a weapon, a kind of freelance, low-budget tank, in drive-by shootings and car bombings in Beirut, Bogota, Belfast, Bombay, New York and elsewhere.

14. And last on our list, enormous accidents plague the technology and its infrastructure. The *Exxon Valdez* spilled 11 million gallons of oil onto the coast of Alaska in 1989, and the wreck of the even larger tanker, the *Braer,* on the coast of the Shetland Islands in 1993 released 26 million gallons of oil. Car accidents can be truly catastrophic. On Interstate 5 in Fresno County, California, on November 29, 1992, a dust storm descended on the highway, and cars and trucks sailed into the swirling sand at seventy miles per hour. The accident went on for ninety minutes on a quarter-mile section of road. Drivers steered out into the fields to be out of the way of traffic only to be hit by other cars swerving to avoid burning wreckage. Some cars were hit as many as five times. The toll: seventeen killed, one hundred fifty-seven injured, two hundred cars and trucks wrecked. Drivers blamed the California Highway Patrol for failing to close the highway, and the Highway Patrol blamed the drivers for driving too fast. Everybody blamed the weather. Nobody blamed the sacred auto/sprawl/freeway/oil infrastructure.

An even more bizarre accident happened on April 22, 1992 — Earth Day, ironically enough — the twenty-second anniversary of the burial of a car to symbolically put an end to the automobile era. That morning, in a thirty-block area of downtown, the sewer system of Guadalajara, Mexico erupted in a colossal explosion. Three hundred bodies were identified and months later rescue agencies reported more than nine hundred people still missing. The Mexican government declared a national disaster. The sewer, electricity and telephone systems of the city of 3 million went down simultaneously. Dozens of buildings were flung from their foundations. As the smoke cleared, deep smoldering craters were slowly filling with sewage while cars and busses rested on nearby rooftops or hung from trees and drooping power lines. According to one reporter, "People were seen wandering aimlessly among the ruins, weeping, their clothing shredded." Automobile gasoline had leaked into the sewer system from facilities owned by Pemex, the Mexican government oil company. No one blamed the auto/highway/sprawl/oil system or suggest it might make sense to de-emphasize it as quickly as practical, but in a very meaningful way, it was an automobile accident.

In my own neighborhood, the role of the automobile in the 1989 Loma Prieta earthquake and the 1991 Oakland-Berkeley Hills firestorm got almost zero coverage. The earthquake brought down an elevated section of Interstate 880 crushing dozens of people and killing forty-two. Across the bay in San Francisco, three-story houses collapsed into their garages. Their first floors were homes for cars, not people, and the street-level garage doors created weak walls with no cross-bracing to resist sideways movement. With second and third stories sitting like big boxes on parallel stilts between garage doors, with a little back-and-forth, it was all over. The fires that erupted were fed by the gasoline that, in a more genteel fashion, pushes people by the many tens of thousands back and forth across San Francisco every day. The great majority of people who died in the Loma Prieta earthquake died because of the automobile infrastructure.

The Oakland-Berkeley Hills firestorm consumed 1,700 acres of landscape, destroying 3,375 homes and killing twenty-five people. Most of the people who died were trying to escape in automobiles and ended up killed in accidents at intersections or in traffic jams on narrow, winding, steep streets. The next morning the surrealistic landscape was littered with hundreds of burned out cars with glass headlight lenses melted like tears weeping down bumpers. Gasoline tanks became the obvious centers of intense conflagration, as garages frequently appeared as source points of extreme radiant heat. Asphalt around gas tanks was completely burned away, leaving grains of sand and crumbly pebbles.

Although 5,000 people were made temporarily homeless by the fire, not a single store was located in the fire zone. It was a single-use, residential area and thoroughly automobile-dependent — and so it remains after rebuilding. Speaking on Berkeley's listener-sponsored radio station two days later I was, as far as I know, the lone voice pointing out that we were dealing with two fires here. The one at hand, and an immensely larger if far more subtle one: the fire under the hoods of the Earth's half billion cars. Without that larger specter, a hillside fire would not have become a catastrophe. This unacknowledged fire, created by poor community planning and automobile addiction, is the much larger disaster.

Without success, I tried to cultivate community interest in rebuilding at least a small part of the firestorm area in a more compact, mixed-use, community-centered style of development connected to the rest of the town with regular bus service or perhaps a streetcar line. A dozen or so properties could have been assembled to create a neighborhood center somewhere in the burn area. Saving four or five properties to not build upon could have saved open space for a neighborhood plaza with magnificent views of San Franciso Bay from the hills. Two or three properties on the downhill side of the plaza could have been kept open to maintain the stunning view. Properties adjacent to the future plaza could have become mixed-use, with shops on the ground floor, offices on the second, condos and apartments on the third and fourth, and cafes with a view of the bay on the rooftops and around the plaza.

Two or three hundred units of housing in several attractive buildings could have been created on what used to be those dozen or so properties of the old, uniform, single-house lots. An equal number of residential units on the farthest, most dangerous and most automobile-dependent fringes could have been left unrebuilt and turned over to the regional park system. (Their owners could have had first option to move into the new housing.) A large swimming pool or two could have been placed on the side facing the fire winds — the hot dry winds always come from the same quarter there, the northeast — and the community could, by sharing its resources, have bought several pumps, hoses and nozzles to direct a curtain of water from the swimming pool on any future fire that might come bearing down on the neighborhood center.

Nobody interested. After about two months' effort I gave up and went on to other things. The lesson I failed to communicate at the time was that the car created and maintained that fire area and most of the people who died were in, or next to, their traffic-snarled cars, stuck in jams, trying to escape. It was a car accident. Now the area has been rebuilt on exactly the same land-use pattern, dependent as before upon gasoline for its very existence and for every day of its maintenance. It — and all of Car City — burns.

The only way around such accidents in the future is for people to have a much deeper understanding of what they are building and the roles transportation and access play in it. If plans are made in advance for rebuilding after disasters, informed by ecocity awareness, future disasters will be small in comparison. Funds need to be available for ecocity planning and rebuilding rather than as disaster grants and loans after the fact. Without such plans and funds, disasters caused by car-dependent design will not lead to ecologically-sane rebuilding.

To wind up this litany of problems and disasters, a sobering statistic: According to the respected Environment and Forecasting Institute of Heidelberg, Germany, "Each car [in Germany, but probably typical among wealthier countries] over its lifetime is responsible for 820 hours [34 days] of life lost through road traffic accident fatalities and 2,800 hours [117 days] of life damaged by road traffic accidents."[66] Poor countries have up to twenty-six times the fatality and injury accidents per mile traveled because of antiquated equipment, poor vehicle maintenance, bad roads, signs and safety programs, and sparsely spaced, poorly equipped hospitals and clinics. A closing oddity: Of the first five California Condors released into the wild by the captive-breeding program that is desperately trying to save the species from extinction, one of the five died from drinking automobile anti-freeze. A second was hit by a car.

BETTER CARS?

Of all the hundreds of charges against the car, only one would be lessened — and only partially — by a switch from gasoline to electricity:

There would probably be less air pollution. There is a law of physics that says that moving anything of a particular weight at a particular speed against a particular resistance of inertia and friction requires a particular amount of energy. In the case of the gasoline-engine car, fuel is burned and waste material is distributed as it moves. In case of the electric car, energy is stored in batteries that have to be recharged by plugging into a power plant, which has already burned the fuel and distributed the waste. Batteries don't create energy, they just store it. Essentially, they are gas tanks for electrons. If we put electric cars and trucks on the traffic grid, we will require staggering increases in electric generation capacity and this is energy that will most likely come from coal, oil, gas and nuclear energy. Mull that one over awhile, environmentalist electric car fans.

But what about solar- or wind-electric cars? We will get cleaner energy shipped in from desert locations or windy places on gorgeous new electric power lines draping the landscape with yet more metallic spider webs. (By the way, the other three condors in the first batch released into the wild died, too — hitting electric power lines.) What about generating the electricity yourself, if you live in an appropriate location? The price of gasoline will be subtracted from the cost of owning a car, but the cost of the electricity generating technology and its maintenance, battery replacement and disposal will be added. Gasoline costs, are, after all, only one-tenth the cost of car ownership in the United States. *The Utne Reader* says, "Gas guzzlers are harder on the environment than electric cars, right? Wrong! A conventional car creates 26 tons of hazardous waste for every ton the vehicle weighs. A battery-powered automobile produces twice as much, 52 tons, including a witches' brew of lead and toxic acids."[67] What about all those other problems: violent accidents, dismemberment of the city, alienation, full cost of ownership, paving paradise, destroying wildlife habitat, and so on? At least the electric car will be refreshingly quiet, but because of this pleasant development to the ears, it will kill and injure more pedestrians and more animals on the road — unless it is made to produce loud noises artificially and re-rendered obnoxious in that regard, too. What next?

War! According to Matthew Wald in his *New York Times* article entitled "A Military-Industrial Alliance Turns Plowshares to Swords," "The press to develop an electric car has become a holy quest for environmentalists, who seek an antidote for smog, traffic noise and the nation's reliance on oil. But lately, this peacenik technology has found an unlikely patron: the Pentagon, which sees battlefield uses for electric-vehicle systems." Wald says these will be, "scout vehicles that slip almost silently over enemy terrain and armored personnel carriers that have no exhaust pipes and so cannot be spotted by infrared detectors." Says Major Richard C. Cope of the Advance Research Projects Agency, the Marine in charge of electric vehicle development, "At night, they can't see you, they can't hear you, they don't know you're there."[68]

I am not saying that there should not be electric cars. There will probably always be specialty uses for some. Instead, I am saying that in view of what cars do physically and the role they play in society, ecology and urban structure and functioning, it is damaging to promote even the best of cars as if they were a major part of the solution. Car addicts welcome such excuses to continue their habit and avoid ecological city planning.

Defenders of cars have one last defense. "True, there are problems. But if there were just fewer cars, the problems would not amount to much. In that case, there would be nothing really wrong with cars."

What they are actually saying is, "It's okay if a lot of people don't have cars and a privileged elite do, including ourselves, of course." That's the undemocratic and unjust ancient city of hierarchy and strong separation of classes speaking. The disaster in Guadalajara is what happens when that small, car-driving elite fails to maintain the automobile technology. Those who do not contribute to the problem suffer. The smaller the number of cars permissible, the more privileged the few who retain their cars and thus the greater the injustice (assuming that owning a car in some final way does make life happy and full). Right now, among 6 billion humans, only one in twelve has a car, maybe one out of six in the age- and physical-capability group able to drive. So for reasons of social justice, seeing that cars are a good thing, should we multiply their numbers on Earth by six? It would be better to realize that we're doing something colossally destructive and start building the city for people, not cars.

There is another angle here, too. "If the total population were much smaller than it is today, everybody could have a car." I've heard this one a few times. Does the idea of trimming the population down to match the Earth's car-carrying capacity suggest that someone likes cars better than people? Even though I think population should be smaller myself, I find this people-phobic, auto-philiac attitude a bit hard to take.

The final excuse is the acts-of-God excuse — sweeping the problem under the rug because it's "just the way it is." The Hindus have gods for many inexorable forces of nature. One was specifically for smallpox, so unstoppable was that affliction — like hunger, poverty, storms, injustice and fate itself. So it is with the car. When a child, spouse, lover, friend, parent, co-worker or admired stranger is struck down, we act as if little could be done about it, as if it were an act of God. Former President Bill Clinton lost his father in a car crash and former Vice President Al Gore witnessed an automobile hit and almost kill his six-year-old son. But in March of 1992 Clinton and Gore sent U.S. trade representative Mickey Kantor to speak with leaders of GM, Ford, Chrysler and the United Auto Workers to assure them that the President's administration was a booster of their product. "I came here to Detroit because it's the number one priority not only on my list, but on the President's list."[69]

Senator Alan Cranston's son, Robin, was a friend of mine. He was killed in 1977 by a car before his father's eyes. A few years later I asked Alan if it had ever occurred to him that as Senator he should take serious steps against car dominance so they could be largely eliminated. He said he'd thought about it but it was just too big to tackle. Too big for the U.S. Senate! Our leaders promote the car as if helpless before the fates, incapable of doing anything else, but, in fact, many things can be done. Smallpox was eradicated, the dreaded god evaporated, the Earthly and cosmic landscape forever altered. Like the god of smallpox, the god of cars must be banished, too. We will be richer and happier without him.

FREEWAY BATTLES

Marshall Berman tells the following story:

> The South Bronx, where I spent my childhood and youth, is the site of one of the greatest recent ruins today outside Beirut. The physical and social destruction of the area began with the construction of the Cross-Bronx Expressway in the late 1950s and early 1960s spreading gradually southward from the highway and northward from the emerging Bruckner Expressway in the late sixties.
>
> Then in the early 1970s the disintegration began to spread at a spectacular pace, devouring house after house and block after

block, displacing thousands of people like some inexorable plague. ... In the South Bronx alone, more than 30,000 people fled in the 1970s as their homes were being destroyed. Many of these people were forced to run more than once, trying to stay ahead of the blight that kept catching up with them. Thousands more in Manhattan and in Brooklyn went through the same ordeal. In fact something similar was happening in working-class neighborhoods in older cities all over the US.[70]

The suburbanites not only fled the city, but destroyed much of it between their homes and downtown with their transportation system for commuting — that is, cars and freeways. Since Berman's words were written in the late 1980s, freeways have staged similar assaults in practically every corner of the world.

Rising to our defense we have such crusaders as Jeff Kenworthy and Peter Newman, introduced earlier in these pages, who studied thirty-two cities around the world and concluded:[71]

Traffic engineers still claim freeways are better for fuel emissions, but the results of our study do not. Economically, they also appear to have failed. Our data show that, instead of people in cities with freeways saving time, and hence being more productive, they just spend more time in their cars. Freeways space cities out and hence overall travel is increased. Those cities which do not go for freeways but instead build up transit and bicycle access have gained economically and environmentally. ... Some short-term pain will be experienced as businesses and developers adjust their plans to a more transit-oriented city, but experience shows that the transition is worthwhile.

They report a direct relationship between density and pedestrian amenities, bicycle use, and transit use and efficiency. Almost always the higher the density, the better for modes other than cars, and systems other than freeways. They also report statistically on the diversity of land uses. The closer together different functions congregate, the better for pedestrians, bicycles and transit. These are proportional relationships for city ecology of the same level of importance as the area-species diversity ratio is in island biogeography and evolution theory and law. In both cases, as far as I can tell, they are laws of order for living systems everywhere.

Kenworthy and Newman report that highway planners simply do not look at the most important information. I found this hard to believe until I attended the hearings on the replacement of Interstate 880, the elevated freeway that collapsed in Oakland during the Loma Prieta earthquake. I saw the immense pile of documents — several columns of paper three feet tall — generated by the California Department of Transportation (Caltrans), a monument to thoroughness, intimidating to any potential opponent. With this much information, the planners must have thought of everything. But not so. They turned out to have absolutely nothing to say about future impacts on land use in the suburbs.

Their argument was simply that expanded freeway capacity reduces congestion and increases automobile speeds, faster-moving automobiles burn fuel more efficiently and cleanly, and therefore widening freeways cleans up the air. End of argument.

The panel of men and women representing Caltrans sat at their table as straight-faced, intelligent and earnest-looking as parents and teachers at a PTA meeting. In the audience, the opponents of the plan were saying that, given a few years, the added freeway capacity would encourage further automobile-dependent sprawl development, and as more people moved into these areas and started using the freeways, the freeways would soon be as clogged as they were in the beginning, only with more cars. (This is exactly what happened.) This ancient and extraordinarily well-documented argument was clearly articulated by neighborhood activists, environmentalists, minority people, well-off and poor, transit users and even car users looking for something better. The members of the panel did not question this land use/transportation connection at all. They simply ignored it, pointed again to the towering wall of reports, and repeated that their studies indicated that making room for more cars allowed them to move faster and burn their gasoline more efficiently and cleanly and therefore cleaned up the air. Is this record stuck or what?

Another argument that the freeway planners brought forward was the cost to the city, the people, the whole region of not having a freeway "improvement" — the delays in delivery of products, the added time it takes to get people to work, and so on. In the case of the fallen Interstate 880, Caltrans compiled figures showing that companies were losing money because it took their trucks longer to deliver goods, and employees were losing money because their time was worth money and it was taking them longer to commute on surface streets or by transit than it would on a rebuilt freeway. These figures were tallied up at several million dollars a year and submitted as the added costs of not having the freeway replaced.

Meanwhile, however, thousands of commuters had switched to the local bus and light rail systems, and both the people and the system prospered. Some people were stuck on the opposite side of the bay from their families immediately after the earthquake and could not get back to them until the next day. They were suddenly shocked by their powerlessness to help their families — startled by their automobile vulnerability and their distance from loved ones. That night, profoundly shaken in more ways than one, some of them decided to find work closer to home, saving virtually all their commute money to spend in their own communities instead of sending it off to car manufacturers, oil companies and smog-device factories. The businesses they patronized close to home gained money by the freeway closure. None of this information was compiled by the Caltrans planners.

There are plenty of economic success stories about not expanding freeways. Toronto, Ontario, a city studied by Kenworthy and Newman, decided in the early 1970s to forgo further freeway development and no economic disasters materialized. Car dealers may have made less money over the years, though maybe people who otherwise would have become car dealers simply entered other lines of work and didn't come into competition with them as they otherwise would have. The city has prospered. It is among the cleanest cities of its size anywhere. Traffic jams did not become massive, and rather than having hundreds of miles of new crowded freeways and worse air pollution, Toronto's smaller highway system, expanded transit system and mixed-use development have significantly reduced the time residents spend in their cars.

For a long time, I couldn't understand how things so obvious could be missed by well-educated planners. Now I can. They don't miss the obvious. They simply bow to the pressure of a public caught up in its structural addiction to the automobile. Citizens put great pressure on politicians and planners alike to supply their habit. Planners know that there are plenty of statistics on the other side of the critical issues, and they are aware that today's decisions build tomorrow's dysfunctional or healthy environment, but they refuse to gather or think about information that would slow down or reverse freeway development. And their jobs depend on maintaining their apparent ignorance.

Kenworthy and Newman take these people on their own terms, assembling tall columns of data on the other side of the stage. They tell us to appeal not only to facts, but also to emotions and intuitions, since the ultimate decision is the result of a vague but powerful thing called public opinion, which touches politicians, planners, everybody. If Not-In-My-Back-Yard sentiment supports stopping freeways, as it often does, they recommend using NIMBYism along with more broad-minded arguments for conserving energy, fighting pollution and saving the planet.

David Engwicht provides a quick answer to a question he often hears. Is he anti-car? No, his family owns one, and he uses alternatives whenever possible. He is against "the inappropriate use of automobiles."

Am I anti-car? Absolutely! I owned one until recently, a small truck, which I used for work and occasional errands around this largely automobile-dependent, urban area known as the East Bay. And there will be appropriate uses for what we think of as automobiles today in the eventual ecological city — for about one car per 1,000 people, and serving specialty uses, I would guess. Something that deadly should be used most carefully and sparingly. But in the context of vast numbers of people using cars in everyday life, there is no "appropriate" use for cars unless simply as an acknowledged strategic compromise, making no excuses. Use it as little as you can. But if you need it, as you often will in cities built for cars, use it to make the contacts, run errands and do work to teach and plan for ecocity conversion. Don't feel guilty; be strategic. And if you own one, take full advantage of your first opportunity to get rid of it. The ultimate defense against freeways is building cities that make them useless.

FOR LOVE OF RAIL AND FERRY

By now you know that I think our love affair with the car is, in fact, a distorted dependency, an addiction based largely on the physical structure of the city. I will add that millions of people have loved taking the train.

When I was I teenager I found few things more exciting than waiting for the El Capitan or the Super Chief at Lamy station near Santa Fe, New Mexico, ready to head off down the tracks into the early morning or night, a cold wind bearing down over the dry plains or rolling off the snowy Sangre de Cristo Mountains, or at another season, watching tumbleweeds bounce along under a dusty sun. I'd be flattening pennies beneath freight train engines to give to friends, or saying good-bye before another trip to school or to visit distant friends in a different world.

The trains were beautiful in those days. They seemed to polish them up especially shiny, reflecting a fresh, clean sky. There were Fred Harvey Hotel-style Indian sand-painting motifs on the turquoise-accented walls and carpets of the trains and stations. There were romanticized images of handsome, implacable Indians in front of blue skies with pure, white thunderheads and zigzag lightning — which was exactly what you'd see from the observation car: a 360-degree panorama rolling by as the train slithered sensuously ahead and trailed behind like a great industrial snake.

Today's trains, the whole thing two levels high instead of one, with two or three observation cars, but lacking the front- and back-facing windshields of the old observation cars, completely miss the point. Inspirationally speaking, they are wimps. Whoever designed them? But from the old dome cars, at night the stars would come out, far away from the cities — billions of them overhead and all around, in winter sparkling over the wind burnished snow, in the summer between towering clouds which were flashing from the inside out, sometimes looming overhead, sometimes beyond an almost infinite horizon. I can't tell you how beautiful taking the train through the southwest was in those days. For a young person, wandering from seat to dining car to observation car, feeling the adventure of the unknown, meeting new people — it was absolutely wonderful. And in those long trips, as if that kind of spectacle were not enough, you'd roll back into a blanket rocked and soothed by that clickity-clack and slide off into real dreamland, too.

And then there are the wonders of the ferry. When the Loma Prieta earthquake closed the Bay Bridge for a month, suddenly Berkeley got back its beloved ferry to San Francisco. Just for fun I took it with my friend, Nancy, to San Francisco to have clam chowder, and to look at this beautiful bay we share with 6 million other people and countless fish, cormorants, sea gulls, crustaceans, sea lions, cord grasses and seaweeds. The ferries between the East Bay and San Francisco used to have full bars and famous dinner menus, the world's best corned beef and Irish coffee. When was the last time you took a dusting of salt spray whipping through a door suddenly thrown open while eating dinner, laughing with friends, and getting just a little tipsy — driving a car?

One image I will never forget: Walking down the stairs from the upper deck of the ferry I looked over at the table next to the big parallelogram window — one of those design elements angling into the direction of the machine. There sat or, rather, unconsciously posed a man in a gray, three-piece suit reading the paper. While people wandered from table to table eating hot dogs and sipping beer, wine and soft drinks, while a volunteer band played music to help raise money for the Ferry Committee, nobody could have been more placid before a newspaper, unruffled by his surroundings. On this distinguished commuter's table was a cup of coffee, steam rising in lazy curls, and in his hands a copy of the *San Francisco Examiner* as he leaned back, lost in thought, and behind him the most furious crashing and bursting of waves imaginable, smooth slices of water cut by the prow of the vessel, leaping and exploding into foam and careening by on the far side of the glass as the little ship leaned into the night. Now where on Earth can you see that if you don't have the right kind of transportation machine?

Public transportation in the San Francisco Bay Area was once rail- and ferry-based. One of our local, East Bay writers, Dashka Slater, writes about the pleasures of commuting on ferries and trains:[72]

> It's hard to imagine how chummy the world must have seemed back then before the building of the Bay Bridge. Transportation was a social occasion. Americans, in contrast to the more reticent Europeans, were notorious for chatting it up with strangers on boats and trains. Both the Red Trains and the Key System had a commuting ridership that was so regular that commuter clubs formed on the San Francisco-bound ferries. Some commuter clubs held on-board parties as often as once a month, and just about every club gave a Christmas party on the morning of the last working day before Christmas. The car by contrast is the world's most antisocial invention. People are at their worst in cars — I know I am. ... If the metaphor of the train is, "We're all in this together," the motto of the car is, "Me first."

You might as well be somewhere interesting while en route. Cars are made more interesting with tape decks, CD players, radios, cell phones, drink holders and ego-inflating design features. But being in what solar train promoter Christopher Swan calls "rolling architecture" is really being someplace while going someplace, too. The cyclist or pedestrian in the town, city or country is completely enveloped by the experience of that place. By the time a vehicle has developed a speed greater than the cyclist's and become as big as a streetcar, train, ferry or large airplane, the vehicle has become an environment in its own right. It becomes a designed place akin to architecture moving through a larger place, an environment within an environment. It sprouts all the special appendages that fit its circumstances, from loops hanging from the ceiling to grab hold of to advertisements over the windows, from dining tables and bars to magazine racks and cork life-rings lashed to the walls. The car is a neither here nor there world, sealing out the natural and the built environment while being too small to be an environment of consequence in its own right. As suburbia is neither here nor there in the sense of being neither city nor country, the car itself is neither a real environment nor a means to experience the larger environment. If larger vehicles are something like rolling architecture, cars are more like expanded, high-powered, wheel-supported, steel-clad clothing, and probably, being so personal and so strongly tied to identity, they function psychologically like clothing — and armor, too.

Why not invest real care and love in the public transportation vehicle? Why do we build freeway interchanges for hundreds of millions of dollars and shortchange the environments that are public transportation vehicles, especially considering that public transportation is far kinder on nature and society than the car system? If, in the ecological city, the city and neighborhood centers were intensively lived in, the nature areas, corridors and creeks treated like places of real value, and the vehicles that connected people were designed, used and enjoyed in the same spirit, then in both being someplace and in going someplace, we'd always be someplace.

PERSONAL TRANSPORTATION — BICYCLES, CARTS, SHOES

Planners call cars "personal transportation," since one individual owns and controls the vehicle and is the only occupant of the vehicle or has a relatively small number of riders. Bicycles are personal transportation, too. The world has more than a billion bicycles — twice as many as cars.

According to Ed Ayres, bicycle production worldwide surged in 1970 and has been, by units produced, pulling out beyond automobiles ever since. By 1990 bicycles were being produced at a rate almost three times that of cars.[73]

These figures are encouraging but a little deceptive — like saying that Howard has more because he has twice as many coins as Lucinda, ten copper pennies to her five silver dollars. Bicycles weigh about one one-hundredth as much as cars, so in terms of weight of materials used in construction, one car outdoes one bicycle about one hundred to one. Twice as many bicycles, then, is still only one fiftieth as many cars. How about the energy required to accelerate and decelerate a vehicle weighing one hundred times as much as another — up to and back down from four times the speed? That would be fifty times four equals two-hundred times the energy, but not really. We need other multipliers, too: one because the energy required for acceleration and deceleration increases with speed; another to factor in air resistance; and one more expressing how often the vehicles are accelerating and decelerating and how long they stay at their speeds. All in all, I'd guess about four times again, or eight hundred times more energy for cars than bicycles on a typical trip. How about the fact that one is powered by a finite resource that damages the world profoundly and is used in enormous quantity and the other is powered by breakfast and lunch? How about the death rate in crashes, the full cost of the vehicle, pollution? You get the idea. Cars have thousands of times the negative impact of bicycles, even if there are half as many.

Declaring the impending victory of the bicycle thus seems a bit premature. Declaring we need to radically reduce car numbers is far more important, and to do that, redesigning the city for pedestrians and the people-powered machine bicycle is the big step.

But the bicycle-to-car ratio is encouraging in this way: The fact that twice as many people are getting service out of bikes than out of cars is hopeful. What if we had an intelligent world democracy and decided to vote between bicycles and cars? We could get rid of cars today and begin building ecocities as early as tomorrow. That only one out of twelve people on the planet owns a car shows the democratic potential here. The trend is especially hopeful because the city of walkable centers and the bicycle are best of friends. They support one another. For short-range commuting from the edges of these centers and mid-range commuting from one walkable center to another not far away, bicycles are the perfect vehicle. They do take up about two-and-a-half times more space than pedestrians and they do inflate the horizontal scale of the city slightly, but they require only about one-tenth to one-fifteenth the parking space of a car and an even smaller percentage of maneuvering space. If they are used as a means to get to, rather than through and inside of the centers, their impacts on the pedestrian city will be virtually nonexistent — except in the positive sense of bringing a greater diversity of people together from the new urban fringes, in distances measured in a few minutes a day rather than a few hours. And they are incredibly efficient, about eight times more energy-efficient than walking because, in walking, a considerable amount of energy goes into muscle action simply to keep the body erect. The bicycle and the reshaped, ecologically-healthy city were made for each other.

V. Setty Pendakur of the University of British Columbia points out that the bicycle is the major or only vehicle for hundreds of millions of people around the developing world. "While 40 percent of the driving-age people in developed countries own cars, only 1 percent of those in developing countries do. North America, Europe and Japan have 16 percent of the world's people, while owning 81 percent and producing 90 percent of the world's cars."[74] India has a seven to one ratio of bicycles to cars. Pendakur points out that in India and other developing countries, the bicycle and its three-wheeled pedal-powered equivalent serve both as personal transportation and as a way of making a living — in delivery, carrying passengers, or used as an open-air market stall. In India, the average bicycle occupancy is 1.4 people, higher than automobile occupancy on the Oakland-San Francisco Bay Bridge. And yet, despite the utility of bicycles to so many people in poor countries, policies are being adopted to motorize transportation and penalize bicycles and their owners. "In Jakarta," Pendakur points out, "the government has announced a total ban on bicycle rickshaws. Yet 100,000 licensed and 50,000 illegal bicycle rickshaws ... help support the livelihood of 1,000,000 people." In Singapore, bicycles and rickshaws are dumped into the ocean by a government oblivious to the interests of very small entrepreneurs and those conserving energy.

This massive subsidy to the automobile and penalty to the bicycle come about for several reasons, Pendakur says. In an effort to attract wealthy investors and expanding business, developing countries believe in "modernizing" by motorizing, acquiring status and higher money flows at the same time.

> Aid practices of western countries are being used to distort the transportation attitudes of people in third-world countries. For example, $10 billion in aid given by the U.S. to China will be used on car-related projects in Shanghai in the next ten years. However, only 2 percent of all trips in Shanghai are made by car, while 43 percent of trips are made by bicycle. This aid will be spent on improving roads, and as a result, bikes will be taken off the main roads in Shanghai. ... A total of 83 percent of the World Bank's urban transportation lending is for car-oriented facilities. ... [Another reason for this bias against bicycles is that] planners are middle- or upper-income bureaucrats with access to use of private or government vehicles.[75]

Why, then, would I agree with Ayres conclusion that, "In the human habitations of the twenty-first century, there will be no place for death-dealing vehicles powered by exploding gasoline. In thousands of cities ... the bicycle will be riding high long after the internal combustion engine is gone."?[76] First of all, the automobile's absurdity grows more conspicuous every day — its "death-dealing" being only the tip of that iceberg. Transportation violence would virtually disappear if we simply built ecocities. Ayres cites, in addition to economy and kindness to the environment, mobility. In an urban context, bicycles work far better than cars. In heavy traffic, police on bikes are frequently successful in apprehending lawbreakers when police cars are stuck in the jam. Also, "The bicycle shows more potential for improvement — and consequently, for expanded markets — than the gasoline-powered car."

Recent advances in mountain bikes lead the way toward sturdier, more comfortable, and more reliable bikes for varied terrain, *World Watch* says. I would add that in connection with redesigning cities and towns, bicycles have enormous flexibility, fitting into a radically rethought infrastructure. This might include bicycle streets, elevated bicycle trails, bicycle parking structures taking up one-fiftieth the volume of car parking structures, folding bicycles that can be carried onto elevators and transit vehicles, and banks of three-wheelers for fast hauling and for disabled and seniors. "Green roads" made of a dense covering of plant growth instead of pavement have great potential in a shift away from cars and toward bicycles. Ayres cites an example from Nepal. Such roads are very inexpensive compared with highways, soak up rather than flash off water in heavy rains, and exclude the use of automobiles. The biggest reason that bicycles will eventually supplant cars is, however, simply that the anatomy of the ecological civilization will match bicycles and not cars. Walkable centers and small, narrow, cheap, even living roads are supported by, and in turn support, bicycles. Those walkable centers will also work well with transit. "Green roads," rails, bicycles and walkable centers will all gang up against cars.

Ayres says that perhaps some cars in the future could be competitive with the bicycle. "If the internal combustion engine is replaced with a radically less-damaging power plant, and if other major changes are made in the size and intrusiveness of cars, that would be a whole new story." It would *not* be if the car was conceived of as essentially what it is now: a vehicle traveling far above Ivan Illich's optimum of fifteen miles per hour, carrying a private person and a few items or friends long distances in spacious comfort. But what about electric carts?

When we in Urban Ecology were planning the first Slow Street for Berkeley there were many people on Berkeley roads in small electric golf carts. We thought of such very small vehicles as substitutes for bicycles for in-town travel for the disabled and the aged and for dealing with the heavy loads of family shopping. We investigated these carts with great caution, being more than a little skeptical of the "better" car, but were encouraged to find them radically less damaging. Their small electric motors were about one-tenth as energy-consuming per mile as the automobile and, since trips are much shorter in the neighborhood and in-city context, used one-thirtieth to one-fiftieth as much energy per trip. We noticed that the electric cart occupied about 20 percent of the room required for parking and maneuvering a car, and at fifteen miles per hour, it was also radically less intrusive socially and ecologically. The small, slow, weak, clean, energy-conserving cart is Ayres's radically altered car — altered so much so that it is no longer a car at all. It's a cart, and it fits well with both Slow Streets and the walkable centers of the future ecocity.

ACCESS: BEING THERE INSTEAD OF GETTING THERE

While attempting to stop the rebuilding of Interstate 880 after it collapsed in the Loma Prieta earthquake, I came up with the slogan "Build community, not freeway." The freeway was rebuilt, but building the community will emerge victorious in the long run. That one-and-a-half-mile strip of freeway cost over one billion dollars, an expenditure that would have solved most transportation problems even if we ignored transportation altogether and just solved access problems by building right in the first place. In the low-income neighborhood of West Oakland where the old freeway on stilts swayed and then caved in, people could use jobs and workplaces, shops and far better services.

Out in the suburbs, from which commuters poured over Interstate 880, poisoning the low-income minority residents and pounding their ears with noise until that final grisly, deafening crash, they could use a little community-supporting development, too. Some of the money could have leveraged new mixed-use development in future suburban walkable centers, restored natural features, or helped social service organizations. Some could even have gone to ecologically-imaginative buildings, providing jobs during their construction and enduring workplaces after their completion. It would all have been based on what I call "proximity consciousness" — awareness that access can be delivered by building close to a diversity of experiences, services, products, environments, people and natural features.

Michael David Lipkan of Albuquerque, New Mexico, put proper emphasis on the concept in invoking the slogan, "Proximity Power!"[77]

> When you think of power to build a new future, what do you think of? Nuclear? Oil? Hydroelectric? What about Proximity Power?. ... Proximity Power is the power of choice, the power of convenience. It reduces our need for energy resources while it saves us time and frustration. It is the power of complexity. It is the richness of being close to opportunities. Proximity power lets us spend less time getting to our lives and more time living them. It is a survival necessity.

How do we apply proximity power? By establishing proximity policies:

1. Hire locally. Whether as official or personal policy, other things being equal, if several people are suitable for the job, hire the one who lives closest to the job.
2. In seeking jobs, try to find one close to home.
3. If you are a landlord, rent preferentially to people who work close to home or don't have a car, or both.
4. Try to find a home to rent or buy, even if it costs a bit more, close to work, unless this would disrupt the pattern of the rest of your life — seeing friends, shopping, taking classes, recreating, and so on.
5. Shop Locally. Don't drive to the big-box regional mall. In fact, don't shop there even if you live next door, since it promotes other people's Earth-damaging shopping habits. The sooner the automobile-oriented malls are replaced by locally-oriented shops tuned to the fine grain of pedestrian town centers, the better for us all. Buy books at locally-based bookstores and food from farmers markets. Circulate your money at close proximity where it can work other pleasant changes in addition to the ones created by your initial purchase.
6. Use delivery services. Communities with diversity at close proximity and modest levels of population support delivery services, and delivery services in turn make it easier for walkable centers to function. For the disabled, delivery services are crucial, and in many cities they are not uncommon already. If the centers are compact enough, delivery can be by pedal power. In Berkeley we have a great delivery service called Pedal Express founded by the teacher and local energy and transport historian Dave Cohen. It uses cargo bikes to deliver messages and mailings, lightweight and high-value breads and vegetables. In Arcata, California, the Alliance for a Paving Moratorium picks up organic food at a farm outside town and pedals it to the weekly farmer's market. Ever imaginative, the alliance's founder, Jan Lundberg, has added sail power to the delivery of food and other items up and down a river in the state of Washington. These delivery systems work magnificently at relatively close proximity.

Shoes are not exactly vehicles, but skates and roller blades begin the transition that becomes vehicular with skateboards and bicycles. Shoes, bicycles and a few electric carts, supported by rail transit and by ferries for fun and utility, are the transportation devices that will assist pedestrian centers. The present hierarchy of transportation modes needs to be completely reversed: Feet first. Now it is cars first, then transit, then bicycles, then, lastly, access by foot. It will be the opposite order when we build healthy cities. Then we will be designing to empower foot-power transport.

If the first rule for supporting pedestrian access is to plan and design for mixed-use neighborhoods and buildings, then the second rule is to make such places and buildings enjoyable. Cars and clothing are not sold on the basis of utility and modesty alone, and buildings have to be exciting and expressive, too. Public squares and greens, complete with shops appealing to a variety of people, need to be close to residences and workplaces. Seattle has an arts in public places program in which 1 percent of the cost of new development is required to go to public art. Among many other intriguing things, the program has paid for cast-iron manhole covers in beautiful designs of the local Indian tribes. One look at a manhole cover with a relief map of downtown and you know where you are — and enjoy it. The opportunity to sit in a puddle of sunshine on a step, short wall, or bench is a pedestrian-friendly feature helpful in luring the would-be driver into a different pace of life. Berkeley has a "Peace Wall" covered with bright-colored ceramic tiles from around the world, mostly made by children and representing their ideas about peace with flowers, suns, rainbows, people of every color, doves, peace symbols, crossed-out atomic bomb clouds, broken swords and a chip of the Berlin Wall. People love looking at it, contemplating it, sitting on it.

Buildings themselves can be helpful in weaning people from their cars, not only by their location in areas of great diversity at walkable distances, but by their not providing or not allowing parking. Car-free apartments and condominiums by this definition are ones with lease agreements or deed restrictions that forbid residents to own cars. Millions of people live happily without cars even in the United States. The developer's or owner's job is to find and recruit these people. Car-free apartments and condos can be built more cheaply than urban residences with parking provided — for about $15,000 to $25,000 less per parking place eliminated — and therefore can be sold or rented at a lower price than apartments or condos in a building with parking provided. The owner of such a building will pay lower city taxes, since the building places less stress on the streets and city services than one housing car drivers. If, in addition, some or all of the units are smaller than conventional housing, the prices can be reduced even more. This will allow people who do not need many possessions or tools for their work to live inexpensively. For people who participate actively in the community, whose dining room is often a local restaurant, whose living room is mostly the plaza, cafe, theater, classroom, park, museum, gallery, whose garden is a community garden with a toolshed shared with others, car-free apartments and condos are appropriate and potentially very inexpensive.

Presently most cities require that parking be built for new housing in higher-density areas so streets will not be jammed with parked cars. Instead, governments should give tax breaks to building owners for guaranteeing that their buildings' residents will not own cars. Laws can be written to ensure that a car-free apartment or condo will house only car-free people. Tenants who have a change of mind and just have to have a car can always buy or rent one of the millions of car-oriented houses, condos or apartments. The car-free arrangement simply provides another choice — a good deal for people whose very-low-impact lifestyles are a good deal for the rest of us.

In some places, even more effective than building new car-free apartments and condos is converting buildings that now provide parking into car-free buildings. As people gradually move out in the usual turnover, new people are recruited to sign the car-free agreement. As more and more ground-floor and basement space is made available in this process, former interior parking can be remodeled into shops of all sorts, new car-free residential space, or storage space. Parking spaces once reserved for residents in open-air lots can become parks, gardens, farmers markets, playgrounds or new car-free buildings. City, state and federal governments can subsidize such conversions from their transportation budgets because they provide access by remodeling for diversity at close proximity and save the expense of providing more roads, traffic services and the like. Car-free conversions provide, by design, planning and major remodeling, the access that transportation is suppose to deliver.

Passageways like those promoted by Jane Jacobs in *Life and Death of Great American Cities* that pierce buildings or go between them in the middle of blocks add enormously to the pedestrian environment, as do beautiful hallways in public buildings such as libraries, government buildings, museums, post offices and train stations. Streets and sidewalks can feature beautiful tile work or inset stonework. The details here, too, can be just wonderful. In 1976 I discovered a "time line" about a hundred feet long painted on the sidewalk in front of the small public library of Prescott, Arizona, taking in all of evolution from "The Beginning," replete with clouds, light beams and angelic cherubs, through the crescendo of recent history in the last few feet before the library's main entrance. Other elements of connection, such as exterior transparent elevators with views, escalators and bridges between buildings can be part of a lively pedestrian transportation system. From Minneapolis and Cincinnati to Adelaide and Melbourne, there are bridges and walkways between buildings, some sealed and some open. Nine bridges, one above the other, soar between the two towers of the forty-two story California Center Building in downtown San Francisco. People movers — the conveyor belts in air terminals that help get people and bags from garage to service counter to gate — could be used in larger, more three-dimensional downtowns.

Features that protect in harsh weather, such as shade trees or cloth stretched over marketplaces, broad porches and verandahs in hot climates, wide eaves on buildings and arcades over sidewalks in wet climates, all make the pedestrian environment work better. In British Columbia roofs are built over walkways that traverse long distances between university buildings. In Hilo, Hawaii, I walked hundreds of feet one night between several buildings of the university campus with dense sheets of water roaring down inches from me on both sides, not getting wet. Whole pedestrian streets or special intersections can be seasonally covered. Awnings attached to the sides of buildings serve this function fairly well today. Bernard Rudolfsky [78] takes us on

> a leisurely walk under Bologna's famous portici to the mountain
> sanctuary of the Madonna di San Luca. The distance is about four
> miles, the last part leading through rural country to a height of
> eight hundred feet above the plain, with fine views of the
> Apennines, the Adriatic Sea, and with luck, the Alps. The point is
> that one walks, first through the town, and then up the mountain,
> under a continuous stone canopy, an astonishing piece of
> architectural extravaganza, even to the blasé.

In winter snow or blasting summer sun, this structure with its roof and marching arches lavishes kindnesses on the pedestrian, providing a means of access almost unbelievably extravagant to today's mind, but only because we forget how much more expensive and extravagant freeways for drivers are than pedestrian amenities for people on foot.

All of these pedestrian-pampering features are integral parts of the urban transportation system of the future, but there is more. Good bus stops, with posted schedules and maps, help support walkable centers. Covered and wind-screened bus benches make a big difference. On a cold night in Stockholm in 1972 I sat down on a bus bench — and reflexively popped right back up. It was warm! Comfortable and attractive public benches in streets and parks make a town pleasurable and lure people away from cars.

Urban features that do not at first glance seem related to transportation and access can inspire, even enchant, the citizen moving about walkable centers. Such pedestrian features deflate the allure of the automobile by outdoing it. The water art of Herbert Dreiseitl takes streams — artificial and real — down stair cases, through swirling "flow forms," and into ponds for biological purification or puddles for city kids to splash in. In Freiburg, Germany, air-freshening channels of water about eight-inches wide and four-inches deep called *bachle* course through pedestrian streets. Step in one, goes the local legend, and you will fall in love and marry in Freiburg. The spectacular six-story waterfall inside the big atrium of San Francisco's Rincon Center also functions as part of the cooling system, and when viewed from the right angle, creates rainbows inside the building. I haven't heard of these yet, but they could be built: giant hanging planter pots hovering over a public square moving in the breezes like Alexander Calder mobiles, holding bushes and flowering vines, turning in the wind, butterflies and birds following their movements.

Terracing of buildings with the use of rooftops for planting, as in the Austrian artist Friedensreich Hundertwasser's colorful, eleven-story low income housing project in Vienna, and the new Gaia Building in Downtown Berkeley, are recent expressions of features found in older resort hotels. Pedestrian bridges linking similar pleasant rooftops are scattered here and there around the world. Kathmandu, Pokhara and Darjeeling, facing the great Himalayan range, have a great number of rooftop restaurants, picnic tables and informal work and leisure places under the sun, sporting colorful umbrellas, prayer flags and drying laundry. Rooftops there are used by locals and tourists alike and sometimes connected by bridges. The rooftops with bridges become a transportation system in their own right, and at the same time a place like no other from which to contemplate and comprehend the city and its environs. Some buildings incorporate bridges not just as links to other buildings but as the building itself. Seven exist on the University of California campus in Berkeley; part of the City Hall complex of Palermo, Italy is one; Frank Lloyd Wright's Marin County Civic Center Building is, in fact, a triple bridge over wide driveways. I have a dozen more represented in slides that I use in my public talks..

Although aqueduct-like structures for streetcars in hilly cities like the one flying through the air on stone arches high above downtown Rio de Janeiro are rare today, they can link the ecocity's parts in a wholeness experienced in natural environments but seldom sensed in today's cities. Utility aqueducts, taking their hint from Roman water aqueducts, have recently been built in Malagueria, Portugal where they carry water — but this time in pipes — electricity, phone and shade in the form of shadows cast into the streets in the hot climate. Everyone in a built environment like this can sense that someone knows and very likely loves the place and encourages that feeling in others.

"Intelligent" Highways, Cars and Buildings

Advocates of the wired village of the future tell us to move electrons, not people — to wire the ten-lane freeways, make them "intelligent," and build "smart cars." Intelligent buildings, they say, will have energy conservation systems that take care of themselves.

Intelligent highways inform the driver of conditions ahead by radio alert or expensive electronic signs. Electronic toll plazas collect tolls by reading a signal transmitted by the car as it passes, automatically transferring money from the driver's bank account to the bridge authority's. Someday they might even move the car forward by pumping electricity into the car's electric motor with a magnetic induction field created by wires buried in the highway itself, while, once again, simultaneously draining the driver's bank account and shifting money to the highway owner's.

The intelligent highway can let drivers know there is a wreck in the left lane three miles ahead so that they can get off the freeway and clog up the local streets. Often what it can tell drivers is something he or she can see anyway. In other words, this kind of "intelligence" can add counterproductive or superfluous information at high cost to a polluting, energy-squandering transportation system while victimizing people living nearby, who may not even own cars.

Telecommuting, another electronic "solution," promises contradictions, too. It could simply reinforce suburban isolationism and preserve or even extend sprawl. The vision of everyone alone in the suburbs united by electronics is fundamentally different from the vision of people in face-to-face communities. Just as cheaper, more "efficient" automobile transportation gave people access to ever more distant and cheaper land, thus expanding sprawl development, so the computer makes it possible to travel to the job site less frequently.

Not all that tingles with electrons is dubious or damaging, however. In the service of intelligent ways of building, computers could figure in reshaping cities and suburbs around walkable centers. Large corporations could use computers to help break up their mega-offices and centralized functions and scatter them to satellite offices in the suburbs and small cities where they could form the nucleus of ecotowns and even villages, drawing in more density around public plazas and pedestrian areas that the corporations could help capitalize. They could invest in the long term by designing and building passive energy-conserving buildings and installing solar technology. These centers could attract a variety of services to revitalized centers or new ones. Housing could be built near jobs, shops and services to rebalance development. Efficient transit service and stations could serve these new centers.

In a different means to a similar physical arrangement, large companies could be replaced by smaller companies located in future small ecotowns, ecovillages and neighborhood centers. Customers could switch from large companies to small, shifting economic investments and habits closer to home. Smaller companies could be encouraged — through loans and other assistance to small businesses of the sort provided by local economic development offices and federal Small Business Administrations, and through changes in zoning regulations — to set up operations in small centers with supplies, services, shops, homes, education for the kids, parks and nature all within walking distance. Electronic technology would seem to make this alternative more practical than ever by helping to create more diverse business cores for vital, real community centers. Most of the profits in this model would circulate inside the community.

DEPAVING WHILE REBUILDING

The inescapable conclusion about access and transportation is that we have built an immensely destructive transportation infrastructure and need to create access in a different way. What this implies is tearing up the asphalt and rolling back sprawl — organizing the community, buying the seedlings, breaking out the sledge hammers, warming up the muscles, and firing up the bulldozers — on our side this time.

Nature depaves. Why don't we? My favorite depaving *cum* restoration project is one that must have been completely accidental. On the freeway from Santa Fe to Pecos, New Mexico, traces of the old road are still visible. The new highway cuts a swath through the landscape, while the older road weaves in and out of the line of the new highway. The old road goes up and down and snakes about from side to side considerably more than the modern wonder, sometimes higher, sometimes lower, looking like the oxbows of a meandering river. It appears that the state didn't have enough money in the budget for the new highway to grind the old highway into dust and gravel. It just let weather and time take care of it, and weather and time are doing a good job.

The old highway's asphalt has partially dissolved and washed away under forty or fifty years of intense New Mexico sun, occasional cloudbursts and the action of water freezing and expanding, melting and evaporating, many dozens of times each year, year after year. The old, dotted white line and yellow line are still there in thick paint holding pebbles and grains of sand together where the long-departed petroleum bonding material has washed away. Chamisa, a powder-blue bush with bright yellow flowers in the spring, has sprouted there, though it usually lives exclusively in the wet valley bottoms. On the moldering old road its seeds have found the cracks and enjoy the increased runoff concentrated by the road surface there. The crumbling road actually adds a bit to the hilltop biodiversity. Whole trees, looking extraordinarily healthy, now ten and fifteen feet tall, grow right out of the middle of the road, prying open the pavement like wedges. The forty or fifty years represented on this humble piece of highway with its sun-basking lizards and cicada-buzzing piñons is a very small slice of evolution. Given half a chance, nature recovers.

Jan Lundberg, founder of the Alliance for a Paving Moratorium (a project of his Sustainable Energy Institute), was once co-editor and publisher, with his father, of the *Lundberg Letter*, the influential oil industry journal. He often asked oil industry executives what they expected would happen when oil ran out, and they always said, "It won't run out. We'll find more." Jan considered this answer absurd and dangerous, so he quit the *Lundberg Letter* and organized the Alliance for a Paving Moratorium, reasoning that calling for a halt to paving would be a shocking notion that could alert people to the destructive effects of the car/sprawl/highway/oil civilization. I told him that he was getting close, but we needed not only to stop new paving, but begin depaving what should never have been paved in the first place. If we could be vigorously building ecocity centers, at the same time we could be building bicycle and transit systems. In no time we could be happily bulldozing large tracts of suburban sprawl. Employing the powers of nature and time in the way of the under-funded highway department of New Mexico — by benign neglect — would be the low-budget approach to depaving. We could let derelict shopping center parking lots turn into weeds first, then bushes, then trees all by themselves — or buy the real estate and really do the job right.

A major motorway was recently removed from the side of the Willamette River in Portland, Oregon, and replaced with a riverside walk and park. A marsh full of native plants and wildlife has been reestablished where the airport runway of Crissy Field used to be in San Francisco's Presidio. In the suburbs of St. Paul, Minnesota, a failed shopping center and its enormous parking lot have been bulldozed to restore a lake filled forty years ago. According to St. Paul city staff planner, Al Torstenson, it was a Master's student at the university named Sherri Buss who proposed opening the lake again, adding new development that would define a vibrant neighborhood center. To everyone's surprise, the idea was large enough to intrigue the neighbors, and Harrison Fraker, then at the University of Minnesota and now dean of the School of Environmental Design at the University of California at Berkeley, helped secure the funding for a planning process that produced a convincing plan for Phalen Village. Says Torstenson:[79]

> It always wanted to be a lake, even after it was paved. Water collected in the parking lot during rains and stayed for days, and by the end a few cattails were pushing through the asphalt even before the bulldozers came back. One day last fall I saw ducks floating in the rain puddle in the middle of the parking lot near those reeds. The lake was insisting on coming back.

One old-timer told him, "I was there fishing when the first dump truck arrived. Never should have filled that lake in the first place." Most of the shopping center is gone now, down to 40,000 square feet from 260,000 square feet, and new construction and remodeling are adding to the housing and creating a small commercial center along a new transit line and a new bicycle path beside the restored lake.

Around the United States a few other old shopping centers gone belly up are being bought up by developers and transformed to new housing developments. Many are utilizing the New Urbanists medium-density housing formula. The Crossings in Palo Alto, California, a project by architect Peter Calthorpe's Berkeley-based firm, has accomplished this next to a railroad crossing and commuter stop. Small plazas and greens have been created as part of these projects, but they are not enough in number to make a dent on trends in the opposite direction — pedal to the metal sprawl. But they do constitute an important step in the right direction.

Depaving strategy needs to make freeways smaller, reducing them from six to four lanes, for example, then two, as demand shrinks because of ecocity building and the rebuilding of railroads and humble, inexpensive, two-lane roads. We would be downsizing, not destroying transportation utterly, perhaps adding small roads while removing big ones. Just as the biosphere needs corridors for migration, ranging and habitat continuity, so society needs social-ecological links with itself and nature. These are the bicycle and footpaths that meander out from cities and towns into natural and agricultural land and off to other cities. They would pass under or over intersections with wildlife corridors. They could be greenways like the ones in Nepal, which help prevent rather than increase erosion — roads of firm, crabgrass-like plants that can give support to people on foot, bicycles and even light vehicles like electric carts, but do not interrupt the natural order. Similar small roads, though hard-surfaced, are being built along city waterfronts: around San Francisco Bay — the Bayshore Trail — and in an ambitious effort in Scotland, England and Wales called the "Sustrans [for Sustainable transportation] Traffic-Free Network." This is a system of country paths for bicycle and foot traffic, not for cars, and it is over 300 miles long and growing. The organizers, based in Bristol, England, are working to consolidate a number of routes from one end of the island to the other.

This is how most of the surface transportation of the ecocity civilization should be. Like most other "radical" features of our future ecocity civilization, it actually exists, like a humble but intelligent creature poised in an obscure niche, mostly unnoticed among the dinosaurs, ready, with just a little encouragement, to replicate and spread over the world.

It's time to depave, withdraw from sprawl and rebuild the cities. Time to move on.

7

What To Build

In 1990, as keynote speaker at the First International Ecocity Conference, Denis Hayes asked how it was environmentalists could be making such progress in so many areas and still be falling behind regarding "the really big issues": climate change, habitat loss and species extinction. He suggested that we need more vision. Ten years later, at another event, he said the same thing in slightly different words. I was in the audience and asked him, "What is your vision? Do you have a strategy to provide that vision, to solve that problem?" If he didn't, as past director of the Solar Research Institute, organizer of Earth Day, and now head of a large foundation, who did? What's the answer? To which he replied, "Richard, I don't have a strategy. I try to support whatever seems to help."

Shortly after, an analogy came to mind: You can't build a house starting with the roof shingles or the baseboards. It can't be done randomly. Building a house — any complex project — needs a strategy to realize the vision. There is a natural sequence to follow. If a fleet of trucks dumps a pile of building materials on your construction site and you start nailing the roofing shingles to the plywood, painting the sheetrock and sanding the floorboards, you're going to have terrible chaos, and an immense waste of time, energy and materials. In short order you are going to have a pile of mangled, moldering building materials rather than a house. To build a house you have to start by laying out and building the foundation.

With cities, the natural order of things starts with land uses. The analogy that compares constructing houses and constructing cities is so simple, logical and even conspicuous in everyday life that it may, in its own right, ultimately lead to addressing "the big issues." How could we imagine restructuring society for a healthy Earth without a reasonable approach to rebuilding the largest things we build, our cities and towns? And how could it make sense to structure cities on vehicles on rubber tires that have no loyalty to any place at all instead of on people who plant and nurture things in the soil? And if rebuilding is in order, doesn't it make sense to follow a logical sequence?

We need a strategy if we want to make real progress on the big issues, and part of that strategy is simply to get the sequence right. Foundation first, land uses first. If the vision is the ecocity, the strategy is the builders' sequence. That has a real chance of solving the larger problems.

ECOCITY PRINCIPLES

What are the principles for building ecocities? To begin, we might try the Ecological Golden Rule: Do unto others — including plants, animals and the Earth, herself — as you would have others do unto you. Dividing the Golden Rule into two, we might embrace the social-ecological commandments taught to every pre-kindergarten child: Be nice to others and clean up after yourself. Refining a bit more, we could say that there are three major environmental prescriptions into which most others fit: Conserve, recycle and preserve biodiversity. This is still a bit broad, but specific examples immediately come to mind. We are off to a good start, and people are beginning to get comfortable with what these three things mean. Then there are the "four pillars" of the Green Party of Germany: ecology, social responsibility, grassroots democracy and nonviolence.

So far, there is little here that prescribes how to build and live in a healthy physical structure, a built community, much less a whole functioning civilization. Without expressing the ecocity insight and actual design principles for ecocity building, we can't make much improvement in our built habitat. Much more is needed, and a few good people are in the process of thinking it through. There are the five principles of permaculture of Bill Mollison; the six "guiding principles" of "social-eco-nomic-natural complex ecosystems" of systems thinker Rusong Wang of Beijing, China; the eight planning and design principles of the developer Joseph Smyth and Citizen Planners of Ventura County, California; the nine design principles of William McDonough Associates for the 2000 World's Fair in Hanover, Germany; the ten "guidelines for re-building the eco-city" of the Australian planner/activist David Engwicht; and the twelve "Ecopolis design principles" of the architect, Paul Downton, the activist, Cherie Hoyle, and the other leading lights of Urban Ecology Australia.

Without dissecting all the above, and for getting a sense of the think-ing on the subject, here are the "Ecopolis Design Principles," as written in 1993:

1. Restore degraded land.
2. Fit the bioregion.
3. Balance development.
4. Halt urban sprawl.
5. Optimize energy performance.
6. Contribute to the economy.
7. Provide health and security.
8. Encourage community.
9. Promote social equity.
10. Respect history.
11. Enrich the cultural landscape.
12. Heal the biosphere.

One can extract several major principles from Paolo Soleri's work and Ian McHarg's, while architect Christopher Alexander of Berkeley, Cali-fornia, offers no fewer than 253 "patterns" in his book, *A Pattern Lan-guage,* ranging from pleasing ways of arranging furniture and lighting to grand principles arranging urban patterns, from tentatively recommended prescriptions to virtual holy commandments: "Thou must build thus."

Struggling with all this I've come up with lists of from twenty to forty "principles," and here I'll just mention the few I think are most im-portant:

1. Build the city like the living system it is, that is, on a basically three-dimensional, integral, complex model, not flat, random, and largely uniform and simple. Like any living system, the city should be compact, and it should be designed primarily for a population of living things, mostly people, rather than for machines like cars or even busses. Its physical body and logistics must be based on the needs of flesh and blood, not steel and gasoline. It must be a pedestrian city. Paolo Soleri got it right about that shape and function, and for doing virtually nothing to explore his discovery we have been suffering every day for four decades. The "organic city" is a term some people are beginning to use, and so it must be.

2. Make the city's function fit with the patterns of evolution. Not only must it not destroy its sources of sustenance — be "sustainable" in the current language — but it must support and express creativity and compassion. As the universe evolves, its entities like stars and planets spawn beings like animals and plants, and some of these invent wings like those of insects, birds and bats, that never were before. And so people invent, among other things, Justice, Truth, Beauty, and the techniques of law, philosophy and art to embody them. These and future inventions not yet imagined are what cities should support.

3. Follow the builder's sequence — start with the foundation. This means starting with a land use pattern that supports the healthy anatomy of the whole city. The land use/infrastructure, or "landustructure" as I sometimes call it, has to be ecologically tuned from the start, either the start of a new town or the start of reconceptualizing and remodeling an existing city. The ecocity map, which we will explore in some detail later, is the tool to get the foundation right.

4. Reverse the transportation hierarchy. Transportation is so important in working with or against land uses and thus supporting or subverting practically everything else that could be healthy about cities, that it is important to plan for pedestrians first, bicycles next, rail transit next, "flexible" (on-the-road busses) transit next and, lastly, cars and trucks.

5. Build soils and enhance biodiversity.

Beyond this, I can support the ecopolis development principles (I would change the fourth to read, "Halt sprawl and roll it back."), and add a last proviso, a principle of sorts: Ecocities are not everything virtuous. I just don't think anything, even the best things, can be all things good and nothing bad. But ecocities can define a new game board, much healthier for nature and society, which will define a new panorama of problems while solving many old ones. With ecocities, at least the field of action is likely to be far more relevant and peaceful in terms of human cultural product and effect upon the Earth. As we build ecocities we should at least be able to greatly reduce our "collateral damage" to nature, and that is more than is promised by any other strategy I've yet heard of.

BIKE TOUR

With principles in hand, what to build?

The ecologically-healthy community, of course, from land uses on up, from small-scale villages to radically-reshaped metropolitan areas and the whole ecocity civilization of the Ecozoic era. Let's say we've landed about 100 years from now and we're looking around.

By now, ecocities are common. They are sparkling outposts in the deep green forests, oases on the desert, frontier towns in oceans of grain, islands on salty waters lost in clouds of sea birds as ferries push through the waves and fishermen come home. There are hundreds of them on every continent and dozens on offshore islands where people don't worry that bridges don't connect them to the mainland.

So here we are, down on the ground approaching one right now. Forget that rent-a-car, even though it is an electric. They won't let you past the dinky parking lot behind the pharmacy anyway. We're taking bikes.

It will be a leisurely cruise, much calmer than driving a car, and you can be especially relaxed because in this town you're not going to be hit by a car. Despite our slow speed, we will be experiencing enormous change in short periods of time. In typical car-dependent cities, miles and many minutes can go by on the freeway or main streets with little change in that monotonous repetition so prized by billboard advertisers and graffiti scribblers who capitalize on the nothing-much-worth-looking-at situation. Not so in the ecocity. We round a bend from our country origins and leave grainy fields, shimmering summer deserts, or secretive forests behind us. Suddenly we pop into a neighborhood center, one of a few scattered around a major ecocity downtown. Look over your shoulder — it's still there, the fluffy summer clouds, birds, breezes, loamy earth smells. But blink your eyes and you are also inside something that looks like a larger country village.

In just three or four blocks, this neighborhood center changes scale and character dramatically. Two- and three-story houses and other buildings on the edge quickly give way to five- and six-story structures and bustling street life. The taller buildings step back in rows of balconies and terraces. It's a three-dimensional, adult jungle gym. People are leaning over the railings of both balconies and pedestrian bridges to talk to other people two or three stories below in the street or on other balconies and bridges. They can hear each other, too. No cars rumbling through to drown out human voices.

Design motifs and local styles and materials, as well as actual bridges, link the buildings with consistency of style, echoes of traditions. The people here may love wood and detail, in other places, simple whitewashed stucco on adobe or perhaps stately old brick or stone. Consistency in design is suggested by locally available materials and — a felt presence in all ecocities — the sense that the whole thing is built on the human measure. In some places traditional design motifs may be interrupted by a modern insert of startling contrast, but the counterpoint is exciting, and these buildings, too, are linked functionally, often with bridges to the others.

In this neighborhood center, the one through which we are bicycling, there are varied roof lines, small towers and planting everywhere on porches and balconies and in window boxes. Fruits, berries and flowers attract bees, butterflies and an assortment of birds. It's a bit like a multispecies Mardi Gras, with windmills cartwheeling above the rooftop trees, and shimmering light reflected off solar collectors and greenhouses passing through the moving branches of trees, bushes and vines. Nodding sunflowers look down at us from several stories up. The neighborhood seemed sleepy at first glance, at the edge of town, but it buzzes with activity for its central two or three blocks.

In the neighborhood center, we glide to a stop in a small plaza. Looking around, we see handrails, trellises, stairs, ramps for the handicapped, cafes on street and roof level, an atrium movie lobby, a sculpture garden with panoramic views. At first it's a jumble, but soon enough things begin to make sense, continuities are established, linkages unite, cycles close, consistent design elements begin to be evident. It is almost as if people had created small, built hills to bring people up to higher vantage points with beautiful views, while at the same time creating a fascinating thing to look at: the neighborhood center itself.

Leaving the neighborhood center, in only two or three blocks we are cycling through what's left of the old suburban belt of homes that in the twentieth century went on for dozens of blocks in all directions. Now, garages have been converted to second units and houses raised a story or two, making way for third and fourth units. Then, quite suddenly, we are in open space, on a rural road — and it only took us six or seven blocks to move through the entire neighborhood area from open agricultural space on one side to restored natural land on the other.

Cycling from the neighborhood center to the city center amounts to a four or five block length of country trail built for foot and bicycle. Motor vehicles — trucks mostly — in very small numbers, are on another two-lane route, mostly underground. On both sides as we pedal along, we see the natural landscape as it might have been 500 years ago, but with the addition of a cluster of farms with their associated ecovillages in one curving valley about a half-mile to three miles away. Each ecovillage is like a small neighborhood center in its own right, a traditional compact village that, unlike the neighborhood center, works the land and secures the convoluted greenbelt. The closest village was once a neighborhood center and now works a community supported agriculture project (CSA). Its subscription customers participate in the farming from time to time. Not surprisingly, this increases the city and neighborhood folks' understanding and enthusiasm for local agriculture and, they all say, makes the food taste better. From a porch or terrace in town, you can occasionally see your friends across the open fields working the farm.

Midway between the neighborhood center and the city center, the edge of the downtown is only two or three blocks away on the far side of a bridge. That span carries us over a local creek in its shallow valley, with native vegetation on one bank and an orchard of fruit and nut trees and a bicycle trail on the other. Then, where a small hill rises, we dive into a tunnel for one more former city block, now open space. Inside the tun-

Keyhole plazas bring nature into towns cities and villages by framing views by specially-designed buildings.

nel, large open skylights illuminate most of our path, with two or three fiber optic lights connected to the day's sunshine on the ceiling between the skylights. Solar-powered, electric battery lights, along with bicycle lights, are sufficient at night. Inside the passageway we are under a nature corridor that deer and, even recently, antelope have begun to use in passing between the neighborhood and city centers.

In just another few blocks our small road enters a kind of "gates to the city," with special buildings facing one another where the road becomes the city-center street. From these gate buildings or, when they are especially formidable, "ramparts," the burghers hang out their banners announcing and celebrating civic events. Here we find ourselves entering one of the downtown city center's "keyhole plazas." From above, the plan of one of these public squares looks something like an old-style keyhole, open in the middle with a slot on one side. Around the plaza, larger buildings surround a public space filled with people, plants, art and water works. The plaza and associated buildings generously frame a cherished local view. The sky is crystal clear — no pollution. Sun and wind power the place, and there is practically no motorized transportation.

In the distance the area's tallest mountain is silhouetted against the sky, framed by the town's most celebrated tall buildings. The buildings themselves rise up like the cathedrals of a religion of reverence for life on Earth, carrying trees and bushes up to high crags and crests and cascading vines and flowers down into the canyons. Butterflies and falcons live up top. Swifts and swallows slice the air at ninety miles per hour, missing residents, office workers, lunchers and rooftop joggers by inches as they hiss by and break right or left, plunge, or shoot straight up almost out of sight.

From the street we can see people walking and biking over the bridges between public areas on the fifth floor. Pedestrians — no cyclists — are way up there on bridges between the tenth floors of buildings, emerging high overhead, crossing over streets, boulevards and alleys and disappearing again. In really large ecocity centers there is often a set of bridges at twenty or twenty-five stories. Some have sets of bridges every five stories with express elevators set for stops on these floors — the idea is that nobody has to walk vertically more than two stories up or down, getting very fast access and some modest exercise on the stairs. Slower elevators hit every floor. In our particular downtown, artificial waterfalls cascade down six, seven or eight stories into small ponds, breaking up into mists that cool the surrounding buildings. Where the sun pours in, these practical flourishes introduce interior rainbows to the city canyons. All this is paid for with assessment-district funds that replace the air conditioning expenses formerly paid by each building owner. Now, windows are thrown open to the fresh air.

The towers and domes of the city center are oriented toward the sun in cooler climates, collecting energy and good intentions. Where it's hot and humid, patches of parachute cloth are stretched out horizontally and ripple on cables between large rooftop trees and metal or wooden poles. These urban "garments," as Paolo Soleri calls them, cast moving pools of shade into the light breezes of the streets below, saving millions of dollars in cooling machinery and energy.

Our bicycles glide by notches in the variegated walls of buildings that offer glimpses of bays, rivers, distant hills and broad horizons. We bicycle over bridges spanning local watercourses right in the middle of town. There are ancient rock outcroppings and magnificent trees in settings that make them the focus of special attention. We move along orchard-lined streets on bicycle paths marked by different colored brick or tile. There are no curbs here to help separate cars from pedestrians because there are no cars. We stop to pick a fruit or two and pass street cafes, hardware stores, dentists' offices, banks, bookstores, entrances to underground warehouses, main-street movie theaters, pedestrian-mall computer shops, alleyway bird-watchers' suppliers, side-street food stores and galleria fabric outlets.

Police use bicycles and operate out of closet-sized "neighborhood stations" on the fifth and tenth floors, as well as on the street level, apprehending their suspects by darting across bridges, up and down ramps and elevators, and through streets and alleys, often radioing ahead for assistance or locating the rare fleeing suspect by looking down or up from a bridge or rooftop railing. Jane Jacobs' famous statement about the safety of streets with people in them — "The streets have eyes." — adds, here, that the rooftops and bridges have eyes, too. Ambulances are well-outfitted gurneys pushed quickly by strong paramedics on roller skates to the scene of necessity in less time than it used to take in any vehicle — traveling about eight times the distance. There are no screaming sirens through the streets but rather a modestly loud bicycle bell. "Ching-ching, ching-ching. Coming through now, 'Scuse us. Ching, ching."

These would-be ambulance drivers in other times wear the sporty "lock and roll" skate-shoes, popular among ambitious business people, athletic types and teenagers who call them "skoos." Flip a lever and they roll free; flip it back and the wheels lock tight for walking. With four or five small wheels per axle, and five or six axles set in flexible plastic, they are so comfortable many people wear them all day in "lock" position at work, in classes, around the house. Then, for doing errands, they flip the lever to "roll" and take to the streets and bridges at twice walking speed.

As we pedal along we have pedestrians, lock-and-rollers, bikes, occasional streetcars, street musicians, playing children and songbirds for company. The intricate weaving together of ecology and society is a pervasive impression. This New Synthesis Architecture rises to an unavoidable level of consciousness. Its purposes can't be missed in an environment with this many parts assembled, each integral to the fullness of the whole. Hummingbirds pollinate the flowers and delight people. People plant the flowers and the fruit and nut trees, which give birds food and shelter. Salmon jump, snap and wriggle their way up the fish ladder in the

Birds flying through an ecological town with buildings that maximize useable rooftop space on terraces.

city center, eating the insects that eat the leaves of trees and bushes. The salmon's relatives at sea provide dinner for people in the restaurants. Dragonflies drink from side pools, eat occasional pesky mosquitoes and gnats, and inspire five-year-old future hang-glider pilots who, with their parents, plant fuschias and trumpetvines for the hummingbirds.

In the middle of the city center, we decide to take one of the oversized elevators, folding bicycle and all, to the fifth-level bicycle and pedestrian network. As we are about to enter the glass elevator attached to the outside of a building, a strangely shimmering shadow spreads over the streets. People by the hundreds stop and look up. An enormous cloud of seabirds is passing over the city, and we fall into a hush to listen to the breathy sound of millions of wings. In patches and waves, the flood of primordial life flows over the roofs of buildings and pours between the taller ones like waters around boulders in a mountain stream. The birds are on their way to the great wetlands that have been reestablished just two miles outside of town. They take fully ten minutes to pass over and through town as we take the elevator to the tenth floor, folded bicycles in hand, and into the midst of the birds.

The people in our rooftop cafe have carried their refreshments to the railings to look down upon this stately flood of living creatures and up at the few birds taking higher paths. Some birds come within two or three feet, and a few stragglers alight on the railings and tables for snacks as the flock begins settling down on the marsh in the distance. "Never fails to take my breath away," says one patron, replacing one of the cafe's pair of loaner binoculars. As people drift back to their tables, the conversations turn to the spectacular air shows produced for free by various species of migratory bird. Each species comes in its proper season. Great flocks dive, turn, split and explode apart and swirl together out over the bay and marsh, turning swaths of sky from coal black to shimmering silver and back again, all reflected in the waters below.

Back with our bicycles on the fifth floor, we take a brief ride around the downtown on rooftop streets and bridges among the gardens, benches, mini-parks. The usual crowd is flying kites and radio-controlled gliders. Continuing on the elevated bicycle-pedestrian street toward the far edge of the city, we emerge from the city center in another three or four blocks, the density dropping rapidly as we descend gradually toward terra firma — or, more correctly, as terra firma rises toward us, since there is a hill on that side of town and our rooftop street/bridge heads horizontally straight for it.

City-life excitement is quickly replaced by an almost village calm in three blocks, and in one more block we pop out into the magnificent views of the countryside where the elevated bike and pedestrian route finishes its trajectory through the canopy, branches and tree trunks, touches down and winds off into the countryside. Soon the path plunges under a close-in wildlife corridor. Not far away to one side, so does the main rail line. The bicycle path emerges a couple miles farther away, and the railroad tracks reappear far in the distance as they begin their stitching in and out of the landscape toward the distant mountains. There the tracks wind part-way up, then burrow under the granite into the next bioregion while the bicycle road makes switchbacks up the slopes, passing through a few more tunnels, visiting a few ecovillages, and finally running up and over a pass.

We have now experienced many of the major features of the ecocity in a matter of, say, a lazy thirty-minute bicycle ride, with a fifteen minute stop to watch the birds. At sixty miles per hour on the freeway bypass, we'd shoot around the whole thing in just three minutes or glimpse it stop-and-go through the billboards, sound-wall gaps and obscuring smog. We'd miss it all. Instead, staying within Ivan Illich's fifteen mile-per-hour maximum convivial speed limit, we saw a walkable neighborhood center, a pedestrian downtown and open land between and around them, and we enjoyed the views from the keyhole plaza and a spectacular panorama from the tenth level. In fact, a route through the whole city was walkable in perhaps twice the time it took us to bike it. We crossed restored creeks, dove under nature corridors, and returned to the wide open spaces.

Ecocity Layout

Let's look more closely at some of the features of ecocities. In contrast to the general urban pattern today — skyscrapers in the middle with tens of thousands of acres of ground-scrapers all around — the general pattern of ecocity development is much more fine-grained. The center is still tall and dense, but reorganized in an enormous complexity of uses, while the area around this will, in most cases, be new belts of nature and agriculture. Islands of civilization in the form of dense subcenters and compact neighborhood centers are situated fairly close to the major city hub, and farther out, at a distance seldom traversed by daily commuters, there are real towns of some scale. Neighborhoods turning into villages and hamlets reach out, scattering ever more sparsely across agricultural and natural country into the hinterlands. Probably most of these outlying communities will be agricultural villages producing most of their own food and selling farm produce to the more centrally-located towns and cities. Of course, real geology, topography and ecology will modify this pattern from place to place. To this general urban anatomy all other ecocity features and technologies are attached and thus empowered to function fully.

Streets are the main circulation systems of the ecocity as they are in the conventional city. However, since they are designed for humans rather than cars they can, in many cases, be relatively narrow. Still, for variety, wide boulevards here and there provide real urban/bioregional views worth celebrating as well passage for streetcars.

The layout of streets in today's cities is a topic of lively discussion among planners and architects, with some championing the right-angle gridiron pattern, others the meandering curving lines conforming to contours of topography. Still others champion cul-de-sacs and dead-end streets on the suburban theory that the only good street is one with almost no traffic. Grid advocates derisively refer to the squiggly lines on many suburban development maps as "dead worms," and squiggly-line fans refer to the grid pattern as "rectilinear," as if it were a long version of a four letter word. Some insist on streets radiating out from center points, parks or circles, and still others like the ordered power of broad boulevards arbitrarily pushing their way through the urban fabric, usually connecting major centers. They like the light and air provided by these grand swaths of open views — boulevards like those of Paris and Washington.

But if we imagine cities with precious little automobility and near total human mobility, street layout becomes less important. Since pedestrians make fewer demands on the infrastructure, there is less pressure to accommodate transportation with wide streets. With footpaths cutting through blocks and no fear of being run over crossing the street, the whole town becomes permeable and pleasantly accessible whatever the street arrangement. The sightlines of the grid are fine for a sense of location and for aesthetic appreciation of distances. Curved streets create a close-in intimacy that can have its value. But the straight lines of San Francisco's hilly landscape create their own excitement and offer distant views of bay, ocean and hills that would be lost with curved streets.

Higher buildings with elevated public access also provide the kind of grand views that boulevards provide and, if beautiful, are great views in their own right. The supposedly democratic opinion that building heights should be limited to a consistent two, three or four stories so that views can be maintained makes no sense. If all the buildings are the same height, everyone's view is more buildings of the same height next door or across the street; I have to walk blocks from my house to see beyond the two-story houses and three-story trees to the mountains across San Francisco Bay or to glimpse a sunset. Uniform height limits guarantee that no one can see beyond near-in neighborhood blinders. The solution is to have public access to high places: terrace and rooftop restaurants, miniparks and promenades. All that is a design challenge to be worked with and one with endless excellent solutions.

WALKABLE CENTERS

Downtown is already seen as the heart of almost any city and could be seen as the heart of the concept of a vibrant culture in tune with nature. Downtown and neighborhood centers in larger ecocities will constitute a whole new urban reality, complete with clusters of dwellings nestled into terraces on the upper reaches of tall buildings, as replete with natural life as many places on ground level. Co-housing arrangements — a form of cooperative housing mentioned earlier in which residents, usually ten to thirty households, share some facilities but have small-scale, private living spaces — could be worked into larger clusters of buildings, for example, being built around a large rooftop garden or plaza.

In the highest-density parts of these ecocities, uses that need artificial light or function well with controlled reflected light could be placed in the lowest floors or basements of buildings, lifting other uses higher into the air. These uses include certain kinds of laboratories, semi-automated clean industries, theaters, warehouses, rental storage space, mechanical and electrical systems for heating and cooling, and the like. Storage will often be just a few feet below or immediately beside the citizens going about their business rather than accessible only by automobiles and trucks.

Centers have traditionally been the cultural hubs of art, entertainment, civic education and political discourse. In the ecocity, what I think of as the *agora futura* is here, not in the television studio. It's that wide place in the street or sidewalk or small open-air gathering place available for debating and sharing news. The city centers, large and small, are for moving from one activity to another, for just hanging out, for sidewalk cafes and delis, for benches and walls at the right height to sit on, for trees for a little streetside fruit picking. In larger scale centers, intensity of use by large numbers of people justifies the channeling of money and imagination into special civic features. Investment potential is very high where many people congregate. More people per square foot equals more money per square foot, and this is where money should be lavished on public art.

The land area of neighborhood and city centers is a topic of debate. The New Urbanists say that people are only willing to traverse centers of activity one-quarter-mile wide, and their various plans show uniform circles of that size spaced along transit lines centering on rail stations.

The planner, Dirk Bolt, studied cities in Thailand and discovered that one kilometer, or closer to a half-mile, worked for Thais on foot. Joel Crawford [80] agrees substantially with Bolt, and imagines clusters of car-free cities surrounded by nature or agriculture along convoluted loop transit systems with each center having a diameter of a half-mile.

My own guess is that a variety of sizes of centers from fifty yards in a small village or neighborhood to about three-quarters of a mile, or even a mile in an ecologically-healthy downtown, makes sense for lively mixed-use pedestrian centers. Ecosystems are generally healthiest in great diversity, and hence one might think that diversity of city center, district and neighborhood sizes would tend to be healthy for similar reasons. An odd thing to my way of thinking is not only the uniformity of the diameter of the New Urbanists' and Joel Crawford's city centers, but the fact that they generally set a four-story height limit as well. The size of the center is the horizontal multiplied by the vertical, and so a four-story height limit, though more dense than one or two, still forces horizontal development out several times over relative to a cluster of, say, ten- to twenty-story buildings, and eliminates the kind of civic focus that can produce grand plazas, parks, settings for sculptures and other special features. The vertical dimension can multiply the center's size several times without affecting whatever horizontal distance is being considered. Tall centers are thus far richer culturally and economically than low rise ones. Crawford and the New Urbanists seem oblivious to the realities of the centers of thousands of everyday downtowns in practically every country in the world and what makes them "work."

Given the world's population, the efficiencies of three-dimensional organization of urban activities and the disasters of sprawl, it seems eminently appropriate to create higher density centers than a four-story maximum allows. In fact, given that building materials and construction techniques are easily able to support much taller buildings and that tens of millions of people are living or working at the fifth story or higher already and appreciating its benefits, it strikes me as nothing less than perverse for architects and theorists to refuse to explore the possibilities. Some of the most beautiful buildings on Earth are taller than four stories. Elevated gardens, art and public spaces on rooftops, terracing that could take rooftops up four stories at a step, bridges and rooftop streets that could make a real adventure of the third dimension — almost none of these are seeing serious experimentation. What glimpses we do have into this elevated realm are very promising and inspiring. To refuse to even experiment and to actually promote not making such explorations is limited in architectural imagination to say the least. In addition it is just plain damaging to efforts to solve our urban ecological, economic and social problems.

There is a reason that millions of people in the low consumption world live in concrete-block or concrete and steel buildings five- to twenty-stories high: the low per-person costs permit decent shelter near jobs and transit, whereas waiting for more luxurious one- to four-story arrangements could sideline millions of people for their entire lives from any but shantytown shelter and grueling commutes. Sitting in a friend's cozy one-story house in Oakland, California, a couple I recently met from Belo Horizonte, Brazil's third largest city, were almost apologetic in telling me that they lived on the sixteenth floor, explaining, "It's just the way millions of us live in our country. Not many people can afford to live in houses." They considered themselves environmentalists and much looked forward to their occasional trips out into the countryside. When people like this are put into smaller buildings scattered over ten times the land area, transit no longer works for them — they need to buy a car, and they can't afford it.

People will put a little more effort into crossing larger centers if the centers are diverse in uses and higher in density. Different districts and centers have very different moods and human energy levels. The sturdiness of the people and their particular traditions figure in. Bicycles add to the diameter of centers, as do people-moving conveyor belts and escalators. Such mechanical devices as elevators in intense city centers function at efficiencies easily justifying their construction as public works. The oldest set of movie films ever made, by the Lumiere brothers of Lyon, France, from 1895 through the turn of the century, shows, among the many mechanical devices of the day, parallel moving sidewalks — conveyor belts sliding along side by side that increase in speed as the pedestrian steps from the slower to the faster track. Such devices could likely magnify city centers by two or three times the population with decreased energy requirements per person. Considerations like these seem abstract now, but as we delve into ecocity studies and experiments they will come to seem quite practical and common.

Extremely cold and hot climates tend to compact centers, and so do waters surrounding the community. Mild weather and open flat land have the opposite effect. Elevators and bridges between buildings add to the vertical dimension and total population. Banning the car for all but emergency use and planning for diverse uses at close proximity will create a new condition. Then we can begin to refine our knowledge about the "natural" size and shape of a wide range of types of centers.

COMPLEX BUILDINGS AND NEW SYNTHESIS ARCHITECTURE

The mixed-use buildings traditional in many cities before automobile domination still remain in some places, with shops on ground floors and apartments above. James Kunstler, somewhat tongue in cheek, calls this "low-cost housing" as he describes the smells of the pizza shop below lowering rents for the tenants above. [81] Typically this kind of building will be located in, and immediately adjacent to, ecocity downtowns, transit villages and neighborhood centers, but it will have new ecocity features built in, such as multi-story greenhouses and rooftop and terrace public spaces. In the area immediately adjacent to the denser centers, one zone out, predominantly residential "zero lot line" development will be typical, with each building touching the building next door. Row houses, Indian pueblos, ancient Middle Eastern towns and many two- to four-story Victorian houses from San Francisco to Melbourne exemplify this pattern. Adding additional uses to this arrangement of buildings will produce a mixed-use block. It will look fairly dense from the street, but the style can be quite beautiful, and back yards will be peaceful pockets of green and private retreat because the buildings themselves will create, as they do presently in cities like San Francisco, a thick wall separating back yards from the street.

The complexity of the ecocity goes deeper yet. Buildings seem intuitively simpler to us than machines. It has something to do with identity. We animals believe that we are in many ways more complex than plants, and, unlike plants, we move around. Our houses remind us more of plants. They don't move around. In fact, many of them are made of plants — usually wood, sometimes of bamboo, with thatched roofs, with mud blocks held together with straw or other plant fiber. Others are made of stone, the very archetype of immobility, or stone-derived materials.

Though doors and windows swing and slide, the whole thing doesn't up and locomote, and neither do most buildings.

This simplicity is changing, however, as houses are increasingly outfitted with all sorts of complex tools, from dishwashers to computers, and timing switches to control sprinkler systems, alarm systems, lights, thermostats and garage door openers. Some buildings already regulate blinds and even the opacity of windows to conserve energy for heating and for balanced natural lighting. Someday, we are told, we will have intelligent houses that will be programmed to take care of their own cleaning, provisioning and bill paying, maybe even repair.

When biological systems are let in through the window box, rooftop garden and solar greenhouse; when recycling chutes and compost systems are designed to be integral to the building; when collection, storage and distribution of rainwater are built-in; when buildings become co-op, co-housing, multi-generational family residences; when the building becomes mixed use in itself, with jobs, shops, education, entertainment, grocery stores and banks, and then is linked to other buildings with bridges, elevators and bicycle skyways; when urban orchards, creeks and prevailing winds come flowing through semi-interior atriums and corridors; and, finally, when the entire city becomes essentially a single structure, tempting poets and mechanics alike to an analogy with living organisms, then we will have complex buildings.

We are talking about New Synthesis Architecture here, but focusing on a synthesis of ecology and society, not of the individual or the family with nature. When diverse community activities are gathered together in one physical container and that built community is harmonious with nature, we have the synthesis of the social and the ecological, and a special kind of architecture deserving the name. New Synthesis architecture is just beginning to appear in some places with the shift toward "balanced development" and the more mixed-use buildings that are part of that shift. Hundertwasser Haus in Vienna, with its trees planted on terrace roofs and brought right into some of the rooms and growing out the windows, is an example — a clear symbol of, and an actual living example of, bringing nature into city structure.

Traditional villages and towns focused on compact centers, and sometimes those centers constituted the whole town. This traditional village structure featured buildings close together, often joined together side-

Bridge buildings over streets intensify and diversify city centers and enrich the pedestrian environment. Here dashed lines indicate buildings replaced by larger ones.

by-side, demarking streets and public plazas. Residences over shops, next door to pubs and across the street from the post office with church a block or two from school were typical, and so were relatively high buildings. In many parts of the world, for conserving heat and village land, few buildings in this mode were one-story except in the smallest, poorest of hamlets. The Southern California contractor Michael Hoag has recently been campaigning to create traditional pedestrian villages copied directly from northern Italian rural towns as an alternative to urban sprawl. His idea, supplemented with ecocity structure and technologies, could result in strings of rail-connected towns and small cities.

Oddly, though, the new ecovillages, for which there is a worldwide movement of support, are not adopting this traditional village pattern. Findhorn Foundation of Findhorn, Scotland, the site of the first international conference on the subject in 1995, is a scattering of trailers and one-story buildings, with only a handful of two-story houses with solar greenhouses and productive gardens. There are two major community buildings, one of them a beautiful meeting hall about three stories high. The other thirty-some ecovillages represented at the conference are made up mainly of scattered individual buildings with little sense of arrangement around streets and plazas and no zero-lot-line buildings at all. Their most common ecological features amount to solar design and equipment, windmills, permaculture gardens and beautiful craft work in local and recycled materials. Four miles away from Findhorn is Forres, a traditional, old, Scottish small town with solid, dignified, three-story buildings of many uses around narrow streets and cozy wide spots something like small plazas. Our host community had real ecological conscience and consciousness, but its planners were taken aback by my suggestion that they might consider adapting the traditional structure of the communities all around them. They had never thought of it quite that way. I proposed that those traditional towns and villages exemplified a profound structural response to social cohesion and cooperation and some aspects of ecology, in particular access by proximity and responsiveness to local climate conditions and building materials.

Meanwhile, the dedicated and hardworking people at Findhorn are making impressive progress in restoring the nearly destroyed Caledonian forest of Scotland, but they and the other ecovillage dwellers and promoters are not alone in overlooking the virtues of the traditional village. The town I live in, Berkeley, California, with its world-class university, has no plaza or town square, no pedestrian street and no clear policies to stem its growing domination by cars. A few neighborhood centers have a bit of the feel of a traditional village, but none have a small plaza, none approach the vertical ratio of height to width of traditional villages, and all lack relief from cars pushing in from all sides. Santa Fe, with more solar houses than any city I know of, which is proud of this accomplishment, has developed a sprawl pattern that would make citizens of Dallas-Fort Worth feel right at home — and this with the model of the pueblos and even its own deep history as a pedestrian city right under its shoes. Our communities all have their histories and patterns of learning — and forgetting. The traditional village structure is one of the most profound inventions in history, and it applies to cities as well as villages. For this reason, the village can save the city and then the city the world.

In ecocity transformations there is a direction, scale and form seen here: toward the centers, and smaller and taller. According to Peter Van Dresser, New Mexican solar innovator, one-time rocket scientist, science fiction writer and author of *A Landscape for Humans,* the time has come for "small scale recentralization."[82] The ecovillage pioneers could just be the ones to lead the way for cities, too, if they adopted traditional village form. But, city folks, no need to wait.

Water

Our cities should use water conservatively and interfere minimally with the intricate patterns of the water cycle. This is yet another reason for the compact, three-dimensional city-building prescription: Do not block the soil's permeability, and do not dump storm waters off streets and parking lots at the wrong time, that is, when rain is heavy and water courses are swelling. Berkeley is about 35 percent streets, parking lots and sidewalks, 25 percent rooftops, and 40 percent "open space," mostly marginally-permeable lawns. The sealed 60 percent and semi-sealed 40 percent send rain rushing off to scour out the plants we ecocity builders have carefully dug into the restored creek banks. The runoff grinds away most of the insect and fish eggs and flushes them out into the salty San Francisco Bay. Then, in the summertime, most of the creeks dry up because too little of the runoff has soaked into the soil to join the waters of our small, local aquifer, which otherwise would ooze its groundwater into the creeks all year round.

In times of flood, as became obvious in the Mississippi and Missouri flood of 1993, building sprawling cities out over flood plains is a literal disaster. The larger the land area diked and sandbagged, the more the rivers are pinched and their flood levels raised. Instead, cities and towns can sit as smaller elevated islands in or next to the flood plain, rising above the calamity, letting the flood cover larger acreage with shallower waters, as happens in Curitiba, causing little damage and often some benefit through fertilizing stream-side parks.

We should lay down our cities on a much smaller footprint on the soil, catching and releasing water at rates similar to the landscape around those cities. There are places on which to avoid building altogether, and there are places to which we might want to introduce water for reasons both traditional — in fountains, say — and new — in interior waterfall mobiles or sculptural prismatic fish ladders, for example. In all cases, what we do with water is important.

In water, as on land, it is possible to add to biodiversity in the way we build our cities. Oceans just off sand beaches are often far less biologically diverse than along rocky coasts and coral reefs, especially if those rocks and reefs provide tide pools and convoluted, protected areas at many levels relative to the tides. A city that is built to become an artificial island or archipelago can act like this to increase biodiversity and productivity of many species if its wastes are carefully limited and recycled, and if its people take responsibility for building in imitation of tide pool coastlines and brackish estuaries, providing canals, marshes, calm waters and mixes of fresh and salt water.

On low-lying coastal lands, aquatic environments can be created by digging canals into the land for salt water circulation. Interior canals and lakes can be excavated and kept clean by two artificial creeks or rivers with locks that open and close so that the rising tide fills the inland waterways with ocean or bay water through one "creek" or "river" and the ebbing tide draws the inland water out through the other. On a larger scale, these tide-pumped waters could carry boats into and out of the new water system as the tides rise and fall twice a day. In Venice, California, a system of inland canals like this was built in imitation of Venice, Italy, but doesn't have the benefit of tidal locks and circulation of water. The result is a colorful but smelly set of residential islands, with dead fish floating and being deposited on scummy backwater shorelines. Nobody swims or fishes there. The building of timed tidal locks on two entrances to such a system could turn a set of sterile canals into a thriving ecosystem serving fish, bird and animal, as well as human populations.

There was a time, before television made entertainment passive and cars scattered people to the boondocks, when cities had fabulous pools for the enjoyment of citizens. With a growing interest in ecology and larger populations concentrated in walkable centers, such pools can be designed back into cities and linked with existing rivers, streams, lakes and bays. There is no reason we could not, in less than a generation, be swimming playfully with giant sea turtles, sliding down water chutes on the coast with sea otters, joining in the activities of porpoises and dozens of other sociable species once we have allowed their populations to rebound. We can design cities in close association with, and awareness of, the needs of life in the water.

On a more prosaic level, we can catch rainwater for our own uses in cisterns, temporary ponds and temporary lakes to gather water in dry areas and prevent flooding in wetter regions. Thus we can also store close to home some of the water that is typically impounded by the flooding of distant valleys behind dams. Such seasonal or periodic bodies of storm water in and around cities, which are described in some detail in Anne Whiston Spirn's book *The Granite Garden*,[83] can create beautiful scenes, reflecting city and sky, mountains and stars in these ephemeral waters. Sprawl provides parking lots that can double as holding ponds in this manner, she says, but with open space replacing parking space come fleeting scenes of paradise already glimpsed in Curitiba. In cities meeting most of their water needs through conservation and capture of local precipitation, and by reducing their land areas greatly through ecocity restructuring, local water tables could be recharged and dried-up springs brought back to life. Adding this to energy generation by the Sun would allow the removal of many dams and let rivers run free again.

NATURAL FEATURES AND BIODIVERSITY

The bottom line in evolution is the survival or extinction of species as they go about transforming themselves and their environments over tens of thousands to tens of millions of years. Humanity's confrontation with other species has been a growing disaster since even before cities appeared, but has accelerated with the advent of urbanism. It is now careening out of control. Yet cities could be places where biodiversity outstrips almost anything in nature. Already cities are botanical gardens of ornamental and food plants, complete with human pets and pests, imported from around the world intentionally and accidentally, bred and fed. But urban biodiversity can be deceptive, trading higher local diversity for lower worldwide diversity. When an introduced plant or animal drives indigenous ones to extinction we may not be conscious of the loss. Our environment may appear lush with variety, but all those introduced species live somewhere else, too. Their addition in the new place is not an addition to the world, and the extinctions they cause are a subtraction from it.

With deeper understanding of the ecocity vision, however, there is no reason that biodiversity cannot be preserved at almost today's levels. The naturalist, Sterling Bunnell, points out that, ironically, cities serve well as places for reintroducing certain endangered species back into the wild. Animals that have been carefully bred in captivity sometimes find predation, severe weather, starvation and agricultural insecticides in the country far more dangerous than problems in the cities. Some animals are protected by the oddest of habitats in cities, such as the least tern, a rare colony of which lives between runways on Alameda Naval Air Station in San Francisco Bay. When the airfield was operating, the birds were protected from feral cats by — of all things — taking off and landing jet bombers and fighters. Since the base closed, sympathetic humans take care to fence and patrol the colony for its preservation. Cities can be good halfway houses *en route* to some species' reestablishing themselves in nature.

ARCOLOGIES, ARMATURES AND IMPLANTATIONS

Earlier we took a bicycle ride through a "conventional" city transformed into an ecocity. There is another type of ecological city possible, a "new town" built on ground unoccupied by previous urban development. It starts as small as the aspiring ecovillage, and could include modified New Urbanist developments and whatever descendants of the Garden City might come next, as well as the single-building arcologies proposed by Soleri.

Imagining the ecocity on the arcology model takes the idea of three-dimensionality and organic compactness to a hypothetical zenith. The intensely three-dimensional arcology could be envisioned as a space city on the land, open to its environment instead of closed like the completely sealed Biosphere Two experiment near Oracle, Arizona. It would be one-thousandth as expensive per person as an orbiting space city and 1,000 times more relevant. We could build several such Earth-bound, sci-fi cities for a few tens of thousands of people for the price of a nuclear submarine or two, with far better results for future security. Some single buildings have more than 25,000 occupants right now without being anything close to ecocities.

In an arcology, some plazas, large and small, might be more like enormous rooms — maybe the John Portman hotels around America, with their big public interiors, are hints of things to come, though I see no reason not to open up his designs in various places to sun, wind and weather. Jon Jerde's shopping and entertainment complexes are something like single-use versions of the kinds of spaces we could expect of arcological interiors. In both the reshaped city and the essentially single-structure new town, beams of sunlight will project down and slowly move their spotlights from west to east through the quiet interiors all day, and stars will sparkle through the openings at night. Birds will fly through, and some will nest in these large, semi-open rooms. The NMB Bank Building in Amsterdam lets water run down grooves in the banisters; the Memorial Publico Building of Curitiba where the Fourth International Ecocity Conference was held takes a small, artificial creek through its towering glass foyer; the Scandinavian Air System headquarters building outside of Stockholm has a small artificial cataract running down the staircase on one side; the foyer of San Francisco's Rincon Center, mentioned earlier, has a waterfall/sculpture with rainbows in the swirling water droplets. These could be more grand and more numerous in future arcologies.

Recyclables will be gathered by gravity via spiral chutes of the sort we saw in Oakland's Montgomery Ward Building. Warm air will rise in vertical shafts by its own natural convection from the large solar greenhouses on the sunny side of the city. "Waste" heat from industry down in the basement will be directed up on cold days to the different neighborhoods nestled into a three-dimensional latticework, or used to preheat industrial processes.

An arcology will take far less land, less energy to operate, less connecting materials such as pipes and wires, and less surface coverings and paint per person than any other building type. The building materials will be substantial, as enormous strength will be required. The arcology will not, however, need to be as strong per story as a conventional tall building since it will be thoroughly tied together, resisting lateral forces, and "base-isolated" against earthquakes, floating like a rock or a strong ship on softer soils.

The distances to be traversed to lead full economic, social and civic lives in an arcological city will be extremely short, and preserved nature and agriculture will be just outside the city gates, as well as invited into the city itself in small pockets and passages. Life will be maintained here with great frugality (one of Soleri's key terms) — with great efficiency and enormous cultural richness but little waste — in fact, with almost all waste folding into new resources.

From the top of such a city/building the views will be — obviously — breathtaking. Looking over your shoulder as you leave it, you will see the city rising out of the landscape like an ancient castle, perhaps, or a strange immense sculpture or small mountain, but with a skin almost translucent with life. All around, in sharp contrast, there will be nature, agriculture, forest, water or desert, as appropriate to the city's particular location. Only if we build structures like this will we be able to actually comprehend and assess such intense experiences of compactness, on one hand, and openness on the other; of remoteness from the land's surface below, while nature remains instantly accessible by simply stepping out the door.

Other new town approaches building on the Garden City movement and the recent ecovillage movement could carve out communities where giant industrial farms should be breaking up. Michael Hoag's imported Italian villages could be built in California's Central Valley, for example, and connected with major cities by rail. Grasslands and forests could be rescued from desertification, and in these spaces new, town-style projects could be created to serve human purposes with little or no damage to natural systems. In such country, a city could be home to a College of Wildlands and Agricultural Restoration, engaged in training while experimenting in the field. In industrial rust belts, "brown fields" could be recovered for ecologically-tuned development where integral neighborhoods, in-town ecovillages and major developments like Australia's Halifax project proposed for Adelaide could be built.

A proposal of architect Herb Greene gives us an intriguing way of visualizing some larger patterns in a city being transformed into an ecocity. He has proposed that we build "armatures." He and a number of other observers of buildings over the ages have noted that new buildings are occasionally built on top of, or added to, the walls of much older buildings. In fact, it has only been with the excess of energy and wealth prevailing in rich countries today that we have gotten into the habit of expunging the ruins of older buildings before building anew on the same site. Çatal Hüyük was built one floor upon the ruins of another for 850 years. A compacted hill six-stories high stood as foundation for the last generation of buildings there. Solidly-built Roman coliseums and aqueducts have ended up as foundations for medieval and recent apartment houses in this mode. Greene proposes intentionally building such immensely enduring spinal structures — big decorative walls, really — on which future buildings could be added and existing ones subtracted as the needs of times change.

In Italy the ancient armatures were made of stone. They could be again today as well, but could be stronger yet if made of concrete and steel. Holes could be left in them for expansion-bolt attachments for changing new structures. Keeping such an armature dry and sealed with paint or other sealant would make much of the skeleton of the city virtually eternal. Using near-permanent materials adds great efficiency over long periods of time, minimizing building material requirements deep into the future and saving enormous amounts of money for other of society's investments. Armatures amortize.

Stewart Brand has written a book called *How Buildings Learn*[84] about the transformation of buildings by remodeling over the decades. Greene takes the idea to cities that are transformed over centuries, accommodating the same kind of flexibility on a larger and longer scale of space and time. In addition to their economic efficiencies his armatures would contribute considerable aesthetic interest to ecocities.

"Implantations," an idea of architect Richard S. Levine, amount to larger scale integral neighborhoods becoming in-city towns or even arcology-like structures. Levine believes that the larger neighborhood is the smallest scale at which the solutions to ecological, social and economic problems can be addressed. The most promising sites for implantations are those that have been abandoned because of major economic dislocations, such as the cleared former industrial areas of rust-belt cities. Levine has proposed to the city of Vienna that an implantation over a major railroad station be constructed which would be shaped something like — again — an Italian hill town. The streets and small parks and plazas of such a structure would provide views of the mountains and woods, the Danube, and the ancient cathedrals of the town center. Vienna, in fact, is used to burying transportation infrastructure. It has bridged and buried under a city park two-and-a-half miles of the freeway that runs down the far side of the Danube from the city center. Something I thought was just an ecocity fantasy when I was writing *Ecocity Berkeley* in 1986[85] is thus built and operating in Vienna.

Each new implantation would amount to a car-free, walkable center, a fully functioning community, but one located close to a previously existing center — for the economic benefit of both. The implantation itself would be a kind of instant ecological neighborhood or town center and could be a powerful model of the benefits of this kind of building, influencing the whole larger city and other cities everywhere.

Arcologies could be seen as large-scale implantations. They could also be seen as the ultimate armatures, with not only solid walls but also permanent floors, something like artificial land stacked in layers, open for light, air and circulation, and staying in place for generations. Imagine an arcology's vertical framework and suspended platforms, with twenty or thirty feet between ceiling and open buildable floor surface as the basic structure. The circulation system would include elevators, walkways and bridges at many levels, spiral gravity chutes for recycling, and large tubes, sometimes made of colorful cloth, for air circulation. Utility cores would carry water, "gray water," sewage, electric and fiber-optic channels, and so on. Into these basic "city infrastructure services," private or corporate divider walls and two or three stories of inside mezzanines and whole floors can be built, rearranged and remodeled on a time scale of decades or generations, while the whole arcology superstructure would last 1,000 years or more.

Here we have a picture of both permanence and flexibility — a construction project that is expensive up front but, amortized over the lifetime of the whole built community, many times more economical than the conventional city. Today's car city is endlessly demolishing and rebuilding itself while supporting systems like automobiles, freeways and oil technologies that not only waste energy, land and life profligately, but produce corrosive pollution that attacks and greatly shortens the life of building materials. With arcological armatures such afflictions would whither away.

8

Plunge On In: Economics and Politics

Economics and politics are actually one seamless continuum — the engine of productivity together with the rules of its functioning, including who benefits and who pays. Those rules include natural laws and human policies. This whole system is made up of plants and animals recycling and rearranging the raw elements of solar and mineral wealth, eating one another and evolving on behalf of each individual, each species and all of life. As if this weren't complicated enough, human beings work on behalf of families, religions, ethnic groups, professions, cities, nations, alliances of nations and the United Nations, as well as self, species, and the one and all of life in the universe. We seem to be so diverse in our deeper selves that each of us works for a different mix of those constituencies, sometimes forgetting one or more altogether. Yet we are always building that edifice that supports us all, our civilization, which is made up of all our cities and physical systems functioning according to rules we made up ourselves, based in turn on the rules of nature. Given the order, with the human edifice built upon the natural one, it is clear that if our rules differ markedly from nature's we are likely to run into problems.

Therefore, some basics prevail. As Thomas Berry says, nature's eco-

Ecocity activism office. Plunge on in!

nomics are primary, humanity's economics derivative. Chérie Hoyle of Urban Ecology Australia puts it tersely, "No ecology, no economy. No planet, no profit." According to Hazel Henderson, the pioneering economist and futurist, the economy can be graphically represented by what she calls her "cake chart," a take-off on the pie charts economists use tirelessly to express percentages of this and that.[86] The top layer of the cake is the "private" sector: production, employment, consumption, investment, savings. The next layer is the "public" sector: infrastructure, schools, municipal government and various services. The third layer down is the underground economy including tax dodges, black market exchange, and the like. Beneath these three "monetized" layers, in which cash is used as a means of valuation and exchange, is the non-monetized layer, based on bartering, home-based production, "sweat equity," and what she calls the "love economy" of volunteerism: working to support family and friends with vegetables, cleaning, baby sitting, medical advice, and so on. In turn, this base layer of the human economy rests on the bottom layer of the cake, nature's economy: the natural "resource base," which not only ultimately provides everything basic to the human need for sustenance, but also serves to clean up our messes if we don't get too far out of hand.

Since economics deals in proportional valuation of resources, goods and services it is inevitably based on numbers. The most basic of numbers essential to the economy are the following: Humans appropriate about 25 percent of all solar energy collected by all life on the Earth and about 40 percent of all solar energy collected by life on the land. Only 3 percent of all mammals, birds, reptiles and amphibians on Earth's surface (in terms of biomass) are wild; the other 97 percent are here solely to serve us. In biomass, we humans are about a hundred times the size of the runner-up species in our size range. These are the basics about the foundation layer of the economic cake.

Turning now to how things are distributed within our species, about 20 percent of us have about 80 percent of the resources at our disposal and the other 80 percent about 20 percent. Things are a bit out of balance among us humans, as well as between us and the other species. If we believe in democracy and justice, then we need a frontal assault on cold and heartless values. Though ecocity building can't solve these problems in itself, it can help by giving us a means to run the whole society on a small fraction of today's demand for land, materials, energy and other living creatures. Perhaps, then, being frugal and considerate in its very conception, structure and functioning, the ecocity can help create a climate of frugality and respect for life processes.

The clearest expression of a strategy to build ecocities and the kind of society they would enable, and at the same time one of the best descriptions of how such an economics would work, is contained in what I call "Four Steps to an Ecology of the Economy."

First, we need to determine what goes where. We need to draw up an ecocity zoning map — a map of the city's anatomy, its land use and infrastructure. We need to plot the areas to be developed for density and diversity and the areas in which to restore nature and agriculture. We can undertake this mapping exercise knowing full well that it will need revision and refinement as we consider the many variables of any town. As Jaime Lerner counsels us, we can't wait until we have all the answers, because if we do that we will wait forever. Waiting for perfection or certainty is an excuse for inaction. We have to plunge in and expect to make adjustments along the way. Once we have a good map, we will have a much clearer idea of all the details that follow. This map is the indispensable first step in "the builder's sequence." True, we can say to ourselves, "Reinforce the centers with higher-density, pedestrian-balanced development and withdraw from automobile dependent areas and areas with important natural features." But it's much clearer to have it on paper.

Second, we need to develop a list of technologies, businesses and jobs that will contribute to a vital economy based on the ecocity zoning map — those required for constructing mixed-use buildings and solar technologies; for producing bicycles, streetcars and rail stations; for building greenhouses and rooftop and organic gardens, and so on. Not taking this crucial step helps explain why we have been winning so many battles and still losing the war.

With the map and the list of technologies, businesses and jobs, a vision and how to build it are coming into focus. They give us some clarity about what we need to educate for if we are going to have a healthy future. They create a context and a means for evolution toward a more creative, compassionate relationship between society and nature. True, there are many things that don't relate directly to building. A second category on our list, "Part B," we might say, contains all those technologies, businesses and jobs that create products and services that are not particularly related to city structure but that are relatively healthy in their own right — recyclable or biodegradable, energy conserving, non-toxic. These serve us in providing healthy food, clothing, medicine, information products and services.

Third, we need to rewrite the "incentives package." The present car/sprawl/freeway/oil system is viable only because a long list of incentives, including enormous subsidies, supports it. It is regulated into existence. We need a new set of incentives to make it profitable to build a society at peace with nature. Developing the laws and policies, the ordinances, codes, regulations, taxes, fines, grants, contracts, loans and leases to support the community defined by the ecocity maps and animated by the businesses that build and maintain the ecocity civilization will make it so. Without the proper incentives it can't happen. A whole culture of support needs to be created and expressed in such incentives. An ecocity civilization ultimately needs the imagination and support of people everywhere creating the incentives that make it possible to switch from one list of technologies and jobs to the other.

Fourth, we need to gather the people. They are everywhere. In Berkeley, for example, there are hundreds of students and retired people who would love to live in reasonably-priced housing downtown. The location is ecologically-appropriate according to our ecocity zoning map of Berkeley. All sorts of functions and services are there — jobs, food, arts, entertainment, the university campus, good transit to the whole San Francisco Bay Area. Downtown Berkeley is a perfect place for car-free housing. Developers should build it and go out and recruit these key people, who are ready and willing to sign car-free leases. A local developer named Avi Nevo recently offered to build a new, car-free apartment house a half-block from the downtown rapid transit station and do just that: recruit tenants who would do very little environmental damage while bringing new customers — themselves — to the downtown. His tenants would sign a lease agreement to not own a car and Nevo would make his building's operation legally contingent upon that agreement. He sought a use permit from the city to that effect.

To my amazement the "progressives" on the Berkeley City Council, usually ecocity allies, voted the project down, saying they wanted the parking. The real reason, since they all claim to be ardent environmentalists, is more likely the reflexive opposition several of them have toward developers who, from time to time, they feel obligated to cast as greedy exploiters of their constituents, thus maintaining clear, party-line fights. The height of the building was cut down, too, making room for fewer people near transit and eliminating a rooftop garden that we in Ecocity Builders had been promoting and Nevo wanted to build. But tomorrow is another day. Claiming to support the citizens while voting against housing and claiming to support transit, energy conservation and pollution reduction in the atmosphere while voting against placing housing near transit gets more obviously inconsistent by the day.

Chambers of Commerce in most cities vigorously promote their towns, looking for conferences, tourists, companies to relocate, and so on. Cities with the ambition to lead society into a prosperous green future will need to adopt some of these boosterist techniques to seek out and round up talented people who are ready to relocate and carve out conscientious careers. People are needed for the technologies, businesses and jobs on the list, and if there are incentives and if the people are invited, they will come.

I grew up in Santa Fe, New Mexico and across the Rio Grande valley was Los Alamos, the "Atomic City" constructed to save the world from the Nazis. There the atomic bomb was designed and the first several constructed, including the two used against Japan. Whatever we may think of the use of the atomic bomb or its influence upon human events, the city itself had an *esprit de corps* based on its mission to defend the country and the "Free World." Today we could similarly use larger-scale community building projects with a mission — for example converting military bases to ecological towns. We could populate these transforming communities with citizens who want to lend their talents and dedication to building a better world — to achieving peace between people and the rest of the biosphere. I know that such people exist, because every year a hundred or more find Ecocity Builders, coming to us from all over the world. They ask me if I can steer them toward exactly that kind of experience. They want to build educations and careers around ecological city building, and many of them want to live it. I am constantly frustrated by having to tell them there is no place where such work is being done in anything close to its wholeness. If an economy were being built around the four steps there would be many.

Berkeley promotes "green" businesses. If it put "green infrastructure" under those businesses as proposed by the four steps, the pieces would come together. Jerry Brown established a military academy for Oakland. If instead he established an academy to explore the Four Steps, an economic strategy would find its physical and theoretical foundations.

THE FOUR STEPS EXEMPLIFIED: IDEAS FOR ITHACA

Joan Bokaer is not only building EcoVillage in Ithaca, New York, one and a half bicycling miles from downtown, but proposing to transform the city of Ithaca itself. She has an economic strategy that, first, assumes the reinforcing of centers and the withdrawal from sprawl pictured on the ecocity zoning map (Step 1). Next, she defines the particular kinds of work needed for such a city (Step 2), and resolutely confronts the need for incentives to make the first two steps profitable to investors and the whole community (Step 3). Then she lays out an investment strategy based on what she calls the Green Fund. Watching it unfold, we are reminded of Jane Jacobs' "Engine of Prosperity" (the city) finding its optimal relationship with its hinterlands, and thus becoming capable of assuming its unique place in the larger world economy. Gathering the people (Step 4) is where Bokaer started — by inspiring and helping to organize the thirty-five families now living at EcoVillage at Ithaca.

Bokaer points to the cycles of money that typically circulate in an economy, being reinvested and accruing to owners of businesses while workers are being replaced by new technology. A relatively small number of owners benefit disproportionately while a larger number of workers set out to find new work, retrain, attempt to start their own businesses or go on unemployment or welfare. Why not encourage them to get ready to build the ecocity? Why not actually help them by investing in businesses that contribute to that effort? She suggests that the city could be an active investor and thus join those who generally benefit the most in any economy: the owners.[87]

> I propose that each city create a Green Fund in which the city itself invests in numerous local entrepreneurs and holds a percentage of stocks in those investments, and its citizens become partial beneficiaries of the enterprises that succeed. The investments will stimulate economic growth by supporting local entrepreneurs, and it will foster a diversified economy by continuously investing in more of its citizens. The returns on the investments should be used to promote an ecological rebuilding program.

A city government embarking on such a strategy could count on itself for the zoning changes and ordinances beneficial to those it invests in and to itself — that is, to the citizens of the city.

The city government could start small, with a modest-sized one like Ithaca setting aside, say, $2 million the first year. It could invest in a hundred of its businesses, choosing to fund the ones that are on the list. Some cities offer loans and technical assistance to recycling businesses. In Berkeley, the program dispensing such funds and services is called the "Recycling Market Development Zone," and it's part of an overall program called "Green Valley," a conscious attempt to compete with Silicon Valley across San Francisco Bay. Says Bokaer, instead of loans these funds should be investment stakes and should be extended far beyond recycling to support a much wider range of businesses for ecocity rebuilding — with top priority assigned to businesses that will flourish with changes in the land use and infrastructure in the direction of walkable centers and restored natural and agricultural areas.

> The city, working in cooperation with the surrounding towns and the county (which should eventually become one government, city and bioregion together) need to draw up an Urban Growth Boundary (UGB) to define its edge. ... The outside of the UGB should be zoned for a variety of forms of agriculture including agricultural ecovillages, and for the protection or restoration of natural areas. Future development would take place within the UGB along transit lines, filling in much of the area presently used for cars. Since the surface space of about one third to two thirds of most U.S. cities is devoted to the automobile, that leaves a lot of room to fill in. As the population grows along public transit lines, there will be more people paying taxes and shopping in the city — without requiring auto commutes and parking — thereby stimulating the local economy without creating traffic problems.[88]

Bokaer makes the point that house-moving and construction material recycling businesses should be among those most favored with Green Fund investments. The Green Fund itself could be seeded by a mere .5 percent to 2 percent allocation of the city's general fund every year, supplemented each year by profits from its investments. It would be a growing revolving fund, the profits of which would pay for its administration and for helping more businesses until the city was thoroughly transformed. Increases in tax revenues due to rebuilding could be spent on furthering the ecocity transformation process, "turning life in the centers and along the transit corridors into a true paradise," as the city invests in beautiful downtown pools, fruit trees in the streets, ecological restoration and arts programs, and so on.

Consistent with the Green Fund, she also proposes a voluntary membership ecological rebuilding program administered by the city that directly addresses withdrawal from sprawl. The citizen freely chooses to join that program by "living within the urban growth boundary or, for those outside the boundary, participating in agriculture and giving up the privately-owned automobile." Pasadena once examined what might be called its "automobile balance of trade" and found it was losing $6 million a year in costs to the city that were not recouped in parking fees, fines, state gasoline taxes transferred to the city and other car-generated revenues. Since members of the ecological rebuilding program would be saving the city money by not owning cars, they would qualify for free transit passes, coupons for taxi rides, no-charge swims at city pools, subsidized medical coverage — whatever the city decided was appropriate for the citizen who saves them so much money — in addition to enjoying benefits available to everybody, such as tree-lined bicycle paths safe from automobile traffic along newly opened watercourses.

This ecocity restructuring strategy could be implemented anywhere. Rust Belt cities need to reinvigorate their inner neighborhoods, and many of them already have derelict open space that could be the beginning of great new walkable centers and restored agriculture and nature corridors as well. Depressed lumber towns could use more diversified economies based on reduced logging and increased other uses of land, from restoration and fishing to herb and mushroom cultivation, from tourism and college campuses to high-tech research think-tanking, as well as practical services to any community: food, clothing, hardware, repair, banking. Loggers recast as carpenters would feel more at home taking dangerous risks in building tall buildings than retraining for desk jobs. I know the style and feel of those two kinds of physical and practical work and that they are similar because I have worked at both.

Economically "successful" suburbs cranking out dollars but suffocating in asphalt could find their centers and begin the transition. As we have seen, it was an incentives package, complete with GI loans for new houses in the suburbs, tax dollars for freeways to get there, and student loans to learn how to build and run cities like that, that helped create sprawl. If we add the "ecocity insight" to the impulse to have both culture and nature, which helped fuel sprawl, and if we adopt an economic strategy like Joan Bokaer's, we might just get what we plan — just as we did when we planned sprawl and freeways.

ECOCITIES AND RETHINKING ECONOMIC IDEAS

Are we in a Post-Industrial World or does the notion simply indicate a blind spot? The United States, northwestern Europe, Japan and a few city regions in the developing world are becoming office to the world. From inside these places it may appear that we are in a Post-Industrial World, in the Information Age. That world is an information world, as are all business administration worlds, but it is not the whole world. Post industrial? Never before has the planet been more industrialized, more ravenous in its consumption of energy, resources and low-cost labor. Never have we taken more from the soil, waters and atmosphere. We are isolated in our cities and suburbs from actual remnants of nature and vast tracts of poverty and resource exploitation around the Earth, cut off from firsthand experience by that weird, one-way communications filter called "television." Frugality, as Soleri advocates, has to be designed into economic systems with the honesty and imagination to do, as Buckminster Fuller advised, more with less — the specialty of ecocities.

"Shrink for Prosperity" might be a slogan to help establish a better founded set of economic premises. This notion has several dimensions. On its face it looks contradictory, since we are so used to growth appearing to be the very basis of prosperity. Our economists tell us this over and over. But they neglect to discuss the exploited peoples in the world who often see no real gains from economic growth and many terrible losses. Are the rich getting richer and the poor getting poorer, or not? History is the record written mainly by the victors. Winston Churchill is said to have assured his colleagues that, "History will be kind to us, gentlemen, for I plan to write it,"[89] and after making a fair share of it he did "write it" in his study of World War II. Economics is the record written mainly by those with the money and directing the exploitation. Both records, historic and economic, tend to bolster the interests of their authors and their patrons, and the illusion that the world can be an office oblivious of the effects of the productivity it manages is comforting because guilt for overexploitation is assuaged. But it is a false construct based on denial and with dire results. By any normal understanding of it, growth simply can't be sustainable on a finite planet. Long-term prosperity will require very judicious "shrink."

Then there are people who are doing well enough who would rather buy something handmade even if a little more expensive, and shop at the corner store rather than Wal-Mart because they want to see their money circulate in the community rather than go to owners out of town. They want to free themselves of time-consuming email and junk mail and sorting coupons because they'd rather relax in the garden. In reality, there is nothing "simple" about living in a close-knit community or close to nature. Pursuing organic agriculture or permaculture? Very complex worlds are those. The ecocity makes it possible to greatly reduce the physical impacts of complex cultural involvements. It facilitates many forms of complexity, providing interconnections and high levels of efficiency honoring their foundation in nature. The ecocity is in itself a miniaturization of the city, in keeping with the dynamics of evolution.

The whole city, shrinking from the sprawled giants of today with their contradictory internal functions to complex three-dimensional structures, integrally-tuned, should produce complexities linked to one another so efficiently as to produce enormous prosperity relative to resources consumed. We may discover that the kind of prosperity that enriches life the most is a prosperity of opportunity for untold enjoyment of time, creativity and nature.

Buy and boycott lists are crucial. Why so many people assume that giant corporations have all the power mystifies me. The attitude gives up our democratic powers without a fight or even a conscious whimper. We can disempower the giant corporations immediately just by not buying their products. We can use boycott and buy lists that reflect our values relatively easily with great effect and there are organizations that provide such lists and ratings. So far there are no real lists available for supporting ecocity building with our dollars. But starting your own list is not that hard. No shopping at any place that has a gigantic parking lot or is served by freeway off-ramps. No shopping on-line for what you could buy in a walkable neighborhood. No more new cars, and as soon as possible no old ones either. No buying into gated, suburban communities with three-car garages, and so on. From many different angles, thinking through our four steps is a start in buying like a conscious and conscientious ecocity/bioregional citizen would.

Ethical investing is another approach. The investor might begin by asking questions that lead to supporting companies that should be on the positive list. No investing in car/sprawl/freeway/oil companies. No investing in companies with headquarters in car-dependent suburban office parks. Buy and avoid lists could be developed for municipal bonds. A city with a General Plan and zoning friendly to ecocity development and restoration would rate high and one unfriendly would rate low.

Cheap energy has been regarded as an economic boon. It's a problem. We are accustomed to thinking the cheaper the energy the better. It doesn't work like that anymore. Oil is amazingly powerful relative to its cost, but from its origins at extraction sites in the Ogoni territory in Nigeria or the U'wa lands of Colombia and Venezuela, to the building of sprawl on its basis, to the reservoir of its CO_2 wastes in the atmosphere and accidentally dispersed oil in the oceans, everywhere cheap energy comes from and everywhere it goes it causes damage. Cheap energy means we don't have to think through ecological design and building. We can ignore the virtues of "access by proximity" and simply ship in our "solutions," paying as little as possible, thinking as little as possible. We've substituted savings in the cost of BTUs for clear thinking. Solar energy, thoughtful architectural design, carefully-placed insulation and lifestyle adjustments to respect the seasonal and daily cycles, all look expensive compared with simply blasting in some more heat or air conditioning when fuel is cheap. If energy were expensive we would almost assuredly discover genuine efficiency on the larger scale. To help rebuild the city, then, we should consciously, as part of the strategy, increase energy prices by taxing fossil fuels while we still have the time, shifting resources toward renewable energy.

We should also be conscious of the simple weight of shipped goods and the basic physics that says it takes energy to bridge long distances. Frequently used and relatively heavy materials should come from relatively nearby. Using lumber coming from Southeast Asia and bottles of wine from Chile in the United States, for example, other things being even close to even, does much more damage ultimately than buying these products from close to home. Shipping lighter weight items from great distances and things purchased infrequently is generally less of a problem.

We also have to get over the voting threshold to ecocity building. A solar-based town with many of the ecocity features described in this book was proposed for an old military base north of San Francisco in 1979. There was a clear strategy behind it, but politics defined the threshold for decision, commitment, investment, designing, planning and building. What promoters of Marin Solar Village envisioned for the decommissioned Hamilton Air Force Base would have been both a community of solar homes and a manufacturing and solar services town, a whole mixed-use community large enough to justify reestablishing an abandoned rail link that ran through the area. The Air Force sold the base to the county for a dollar, but the project lost in a countywide vote 49 percent to 51 percent. Jerry Brown was Governor then and trying out all sorts of new ideas, and friends of ecocity work were in high places, but what should have been an enormously influential project at a crucial time just dissolved into oblivion.

Getting over the threshold could have opened up new worlds. Only one out of twelve people on this planet own a car. It is in the great self-interest of the very large majority to adopt the ecocity economic strategy and get the appropriate land-use patterns established literally underneath the products and services of the green economy. On behalf of ecocities, many such thresholds of the sort that blocked Marin Solar Village have to be crossed. The capitalist dream that we can all get rich contaminates reasonable voting for the public good, as millions of voters vote for privilege, hoping that one day they will be able to take advantage of it. On the lower rungs of the economic ladder, people who can't afford to own cars vote supports for cars never even thinking about the possibility of ecological land-use changes. We need to begin voting what's best for the great majority, realizing that we are part of it. When that majority includes the other species and the people of the deep future — the true Great Majority — and we vote on its behalf, we will have a political/economic solution of profoundly creative and healthy power.

Third parties in the United States take votes away from one major party or the other. As we know so well after the 2000 national elections, the third-party role is too often the role of the spoiler. The two major parties are considered the only viable ones, and they steal the ideas generated by third parties when they appear to be on their way to becoming popular. This is a great way of taking away from creative people the opportunity of applying and refining their ideas in the crucible of practice and preventing them from having a voice in decision making. Thus the big parties are the real spoilers. The third parties seldom elect anyone and tend to fade out as their best and brightest turn cynical.

An ecocity political strategy with greater potential would seem to be closer to that of the German Greens of the 1980s, rethought in the ecocity context. "We're neither right nor left. We're ahead," they said. The strategic alliance here is between the environmentalist and the developer. Traditionally seen as archenemies, if they could get together they could solve an enormous range of problems. The objective is to build a new infrastructure for humans, not cars; for health, not just for whatever we happen to be able to do with some technical ability backed by a few dollars. The present system promises profits to those who build and big profit to those who build big. What we need to do, therefore, is design a political/economic approach that rewards builders for building the right thing.

Environmentalists should understand what needs to be built and support the builders of just that with public education and political backing, and builders should support environmentalists by helping pay for their work with the profits from the development that environmentalists help make politically possible. Specifically, environmentalists and developers should work together to pass General Plans and zoning codes that make it possible for developers to make money building ecological features into their buildings and opening up landscapes. If the balance of wealth shifts too far toward the developer, those concerned about this inequity should pass higher taxes and use these moneys, too, to help restore nature and rebuild cities.

An ecocity environmentalist/developer alliance would have an interesting effect on the spoiler status of a green third party. With voter support coming from both the traditional left/environmentalist and the right/business community, it would be far less clear which of the two major parties would have its dreams spoiled by the green or ecological party candidate. Third-party voters could vote their consciences without fear that doing so would shift the balance much between the two larger parties. Whether it would hasten an ecological restructuring of society best to build a third party largely around an ecological rebuilding program or to influence society enough that the major parties would champion ecocity policies, doesn't really matter; we just need to get on with it. At the moment environmentalists are not much wiser than many developers when it comes to knowing what to build. The Green Party in my home town is promoting low density development with all the enthusiasm of a loyal citizen of Dallas or Phoenix. As it becomes ever more conspicuous just how destructive the car/sprawl/freeway/oil syndrome is, and how sensible the ecocity alternative, perhaps everyone will be more willing to acknowledge the power of environmentalists and developers working together.

PERSONAL ODYSSEY

As far back as I can remember, I've had an urge to do something about the problems I see, to work with other people and organize. Meanwhile I have also been an artist — sculpture and drawing — trying to create a more personal expression of what makes sense to me. It has been a difficult juggling act, but it has helped me discover, and sometimes invent, a few things about ecological city design and planning.

My father, Phil Register, is an architect and my mother, Jean, an enthusiastic supporter of the arts, sciences and the garden. Many of my earliest memories are of tagging along with my father as he surveyed the bunch grass, cholla, piñon and juniper-dappled New Mexico sites of future buildings, and of digging in the garden, or drawing pictures of houses, plants, bugs and birds. As a child I loved the countryside, the strongly punctuated seasons of the region around Santa Fe, the sunsets. I still see distant thunderclouds hurling purple lightning bolts ten or twenty miles across mountain ranges, across the face of the low orange sun, or between me and the crescent moon. I can't forget the lightning's metallic ozone smell on the breeze, the smell of rain on dust before it arrives. I remember the clean, open sky, so rarefied and clear that the setting stars would hit the distant horizon and suddenly and silently disappear — blink. That almost surrealistic clarity and lack of pollution on a geophysical, even celestial, scale is gone now, but perhaps we can bring it back in a few decades. If Jamie Lerner can improve the sunsets in Curitiba, maybe the rest of us can elsewhere.

The year I was twenty-one was a big year for me in many ways. I left college to do my art work, moved from New Mexico to Venice, California, and started an organization called "No War Toys," which was part of the peace movement and focused on the attitudes promoted by toys and entertainment. That was the year I began making sculpture for the sense of touch and the year I met the person — Paolo Soleri — who launched me into ecocity thinking. As chance would have it, the mother of a friend offered me a ride across Arizona and asked if I would mind if we visited a famous architect on our way, in Scottsdale. Of course, I did not. It was her car, after all, and my fascinating, if ever after difficult, fortune.

I didn't grasp what Soleri was up to right away. It was maybe 105 degrees when we arrived just after sunset and Soleri, lean, wiry and browner than the Arizona dirt, was scampering over a large mound of earth, cutting it with patterns in fine silt, using a trowel, working late to finish the job. Concrete would be poured over the mound tomorrow, I was told, and the shape, patterns and colors of the fine clay would be transferred to the inside surface of the concrete. The concrete would set and the mound of earth under it would be dug away, and thus a half-dome shell would be created for the roof of a new building at his Cosanti Foundation.

That first evening Soleri talked with my driver about his search for land to build "the new city." She wanted to help. New city? What new city? "Arcology," he called it, a combination of architecture and ecology. It would be the city to demonstrate his new ideas about ecologically-fit architecture and whole-city design. I wasn't clear what that was, but I did pick up some of his papers and took them back to Venice.

They were stunning. It was hard work deciphering the language he was inventing as he went about exploring his idea of arcology and its place in the evolving universe. But once I'd made the effort and sorted out the terminology, the clarity of thinking and its implications for change struck me as one of those keys to the secrets of the universe, a revelation of how things work and what can be. Though I was swamped with work for No War Toys and busy making my tactile sculptures, I wanted to do what I could to help Soleri and better understand the issues he was working with. On the simplest level, he was talking about a single-structure city, like an Indian pueblo, but completely rethought and updated — a city that would occupy a small fraction of the land consumed by a conventional city or town, rising much higher, linked together physically as a real unity, conserving energy and natural and agricultural landscapes and providing a container extremely good at firing the human imagination and making it real. On a deeper level, arcology promised nothing less than an instrumentality for the healthy evolution of life and consciousness far into the future.

Over the next five years I kept in touch and wrote three or four feature articles on Soleri and arcology for the underground papers in Los Angeles and one for the *Los Angeles Times' West* Magazine. Meanwhile Soleri found and bought the land he had been looking for when I met him. Five years and one month after that meeting he started construction at Arcosanti, the first arcology of his Cosanti Foundation. I was among

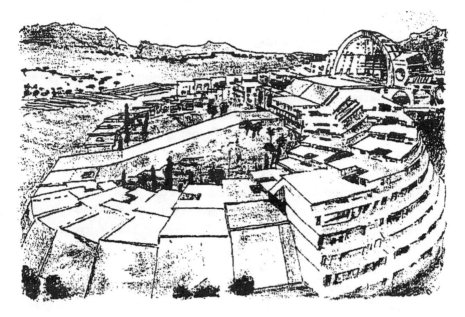

A small arcology for a dry region with solar greenhouses providing heat, food and other agriculture. The whole town is accessible by foot or bicycle.

the twenty people that day, July 23, 1970, and with one other student of the budding ecological city raised the first structure: a shelter of two-by-fours and polyethylene film to protect boxes of nails and bags of cement from the rain. A cloudburst hit almost immediately, complete with lightning and thunder, and filled the sagging plastic roof with icy water. We scooped out a few glasses full and drank a toast to the project, and right on cue a rainbow appeared. We were off to a good start.

Three years later I had moved to the San Francisco Bay Area and decided to see if I could help spread the word about arcologies. In a haphazard way I began making slide presentations to friends in my Berkeley apartment, at coffeehouses in San Francisco, for classes and conferences at Stanford and Berkeley and other schools, for civic and fraternal groups, and so on. I sold bronze and ceramic wind bells manufactured at Arcosanti and Cosanti to help defray costs and passed out brochures on workshops at Arcosanti after my talks.

By 1975 I had met a number of others interested in getting organized and perhaps building an arcology or beginning the transformation of an existing city somewhere in or near the San Francisco Bay Area.

We decided to start an organization. Our mission was to explore and educate about ecological city planning by building new towns or parts of an ecological city, and by other more conventional means. Most of our members were architects, engineers, contractors, carpenters, city planners and technical tinkers enthusiastic about solar and wind energy. There were all sorts of other people, too, and we had one thing in common: We thought that cities were great places but needed lots of work, and we all considered the idea of ecologically-healthy cities magnificent, creative and positive in difficult times. Some of us wanted to help save the world, while others just wanted to build something better: Everybody thought Soleri's ideas were a good point of departure for such explorations and deserved serious experimental effort and experiential immersion. Most of us wanted to live in such a place and work intensively with one another to build it.

We initially called the organization "Arcology Circle," and set it up as a California educational nonprofit, tax-deductible organization. We took the name "Circle" because we considered ourselves rigorously democratic. Each of our directors had to be a representative of an active committee: Land Search, Public Education and Outreach, Newsletter and Publications, Study Group, Design and Model Building, Financial and Fundraising, and the like. We wanted no armchair philosophers, resumé padders or power-crazed bureaucrats telling the workers what to do. We were all workers. One of the things we did well was publicize Arcosanti and recruit people to lend their bodies to the cause by going there for workshops. These participants actually helped build the place. The workshops are ongoing to this day.

It became all too clear by the end of the second year, however, that we were not going to be building a whole, new city anytime soon. We'd gotten excellent publicity for the concept, but no one of means or connections was joining in. Our membership had leveled off at around 250, and the really active members numbered eight or nine. We planted street trees, got to know the neighbors, started working out a notion called an "integral neighborhood," spread the word through our newsletters, and began looking for a house we might buy to serve as an office. We went to Arcosanti twice for seminars on our aspiring arcology project (not shaping up) and our integral neighborhood project (with real possibilities). Another year or two later we dropped the arcological new town project, and Soleri was telling us that he simply couldn't endorse the piecemeal transformation of existing cities as arcology. "Arcology" meant single-structure city and we just were not building that.

We agreed that the term, by his definition, didn't really fit what we were doing, but we felt that we could explore the basic principles — three-dimensionality, relationship to ecology and evolution, mixed uses and pedestrian environments — in existing cities. We were beginning to use the words "ecological city," and "ecocity," and saw what we were doing as a kind of urban ecology, at least for the time being. And so we changed our name to Urban Ecology.

At that point, 1980, we began to focus on our integral neighborhood project. The Farallones Institute, whose founding president was Sim Van der Ryn, had purchased and renovated a building in West Berkeley they called the Integral Urban House. The prime movers of that project were Bill and Helga Olkowski, who went on to become pioneers of integrated pest management. The Integral Urban House featured systems "integral" to one another. It had a passive solar greenhouse on its south side and solar hot water panels on the roof. Human waste was composted in a Clivus Multrum™ dry toilet, added to kitchen and yard compost and used as fertilizer in the garden. Lots of food came out of the ground there — and out of the air, too, since they had bees that collected honey flying from neighborhood flower to flower. Classes were held at the Integral House on dozens of subjects related to recycling, ecological building and technology, and there were offices and residential spaces for students and staff. Our first Urban Ecology conference, "The City, the Garden and the Future," a small one with about 45 people, was held there and featured Paolo Soleri, Huey Johnson, *Ecotopia* author Ernest Callenbach, and bio-dynamic gardener and philosopher Alan Chadwick.

We in Urban Ecology were great admirers of the Integral Urban House. We proposed to take the next step with the Olkowskis and others by creating an "integral neighborhood." It happened that just one block south of the Integral House was a two-block area fiercely contested by the neighborhood and the city's Redevelopment Agency, which had been buying and tearing down houses for an industrial park. By the mid 1970s the industrial park was highly unpopular, dead in the water, but what was to happen to the site hadn't been decided. About 80 percent of those two blocks was *tabula rasa*, weeds and sand.

With our friends in high places (Huey Johnson and Sim Van der Ryn) and a number of local allies, including the Farallones Institute, two churches, several businesses, several restorationists, and the recently founded Berkeley Architectural Heritage Association, we thought we had a very good chance. What we worked for was a cluster of apartments at the north end of the two blocks sloping up to six stories and flanked on the south with solar greenhouses and terrace gardens. Active solar hot water was sketched into our drawings, and we included several electric and water pumping windmills for show and fun as well as utility. (Six or seven ancient windmills with their water tanks still existed in the neighborhood then. Only one remains as I write.). We advocated restoration of a historic street with mixed uses — that was the historic pattern there.

On the theory that variety is the spice of life as well as the health of ecology, we planned to restore many of the old houses that still remained, as well as move some other old ones onto the site and build new apartments. The scheme was to use open space made available by the clustering of housing in apartments for both community and private gardens. We had drawn up an internal, rather European-looking street system in the higher-density area complete with laundromat, corner food store, small movie theater, and shops on ground floor. It would be a neighborhood center for that area of town. One version of the project was a poster drawn by Bill Mastin, an architect who has worked with me ever since. His integral neighborhood became a near-archetype appearing in four or five books and dozens of magazine articles.

But we learned a few nasty lessons about non-ecological citizen planning. A number of low-income advocates we had originally thought of as our allies started circulating the thoroughly fabricated story that we were in bed with big developers planning a large shopping center. Fresh from the battle with the Redevelopment Agency over the proposed industrial park, their strategy was to promote housing only. According to one of our friends who, for a while, was in planning sessions with our new "opposition," they said, "The people won't understand mixed uses anyway." Their strategy was to keep it simplistic, keep it polarized, make it a fight and win it. Keep the industrial park out and go "back" to housing. Never mind that the original uses there were not "housing only," but mixed uses with shops, small manufacturing, a lumber yard, fish market, candle factory, shoe factory, laundry, a kind of general store and a bar that once served temporarily as a grade school by day. Talk about mixed-uses. We were the ones with a sense of time, looking to both the past and the future. Our opponents claimed to be working for the people — narrowly focused on right now.

They defeated us and built a pleasant but relatively nondescript one- and two-story all-housing project for low-to-moderate income people. No progress, no city planning history, no story worth telling in it. Of course, an integral neighborhood is an equal-opportunity employer and housing provider. It can serve anyone very well, including low-income people, and, in addition, provide jobs that are so close you don't need a car, plus community gardens, energy conservation, and so on. Not only that, but our plan would have produced 50 percent more housing.

Thus the next step up from the integral house to the integral city in West Berkeley was never taken. It would have been an "in-city village" as one of our friends called it, an in-city ecovillage ten years ahead of the rural version, but with traditional village structure as its basic form, though none of us were consciously thinking about "traditional village structure" at the time.

Failing that we decided to settle into an existing neighborhood and see if we could transform it piecemeal. Several of us bought a house to serve as home and headquarters for our work. We designed and built a solar greenhouse shaped like a big bay window so that it would fit into the architectural styles of the neighborhood. To build a greenhouse we had to first pass an ordinance making it legal, since such greenhouses invariably protrude beyond the imaginary line called a "setback line" that prevents people from building out into their lawns and blocking the views of their neighbors. Our rationale for the ordinance was that the attached greenhouse constituted an energy-saving device, it was mostly transparent glass so you could see through it, and it helped with gardening, providing an early-season nursery for plants. The City Council liked the idea and voted it in.

Once built, our greenhouse generated temperatures up to 107 degrees on sunny winter days. We'd just open our windows to the greenhouse and the house was adequately warmed deep into the night. Two tomato plants grew up to the twelve-foot-high ceiling and back down to the ground and produced almost all our household's tomatoes for two years. We planted fruit trees in the front yard and along the planter strip between the sidewalk and curb, and, of course, set up recycling and composting.

We designed a Slow Street for six blocks, terminating three doors from our house at one end and in the downtown at the other, and got it built. It is free of parking on one side, and the parking shifts from one side to the other about mid-block, causing the traffic to shift, too. Trees were planted behind curbs that extend out a short distance into the street, obstructing views a bit, and low-profile speed bumps were built that are inconsequential at fifteen miles per hour to help slow traffic. We also brought a bus to our street, Cedar Street, the only bus connecting the east and west sides of Berkeley through the middle of the twelve blocks of the northern half of the city. The bus filled up and took a fair number of cars off the street.

Our opponents in the case of the bus were owner-neighbors who were securely established and had no interest in helping the bus riders or getting cars off the streets. They didn't like the noise and pollution of the busses. I largely agreed with them, but with high-density destinations at both ends of the line, evidence of a fair number of potential riders between, and a bus replacing five to thirty car trips on our busy street, our organization and our household felt that the balance tipped toward the busses. With the Slow Street, the bus line, the solar greenhouse, the fruit trees and the composting system falling into place around and in our house and neighborhood we had the feeling we were about 20 percent of the way to an integral neighborhood. It wasn't much, and had no jobs, shops or community gardens involved, but it was something.

One of our most enjoyable projects was a sort of street theater piece we called the "Vegetable Car." It was an attention-getting device for our Car Wars campaign, which hung out the dirty laundry on the car/sprawl/freeway/oil syndrome. We took a baby-blue, candy-apple, metal-flake, 260-horsepower, 1969 Pontiac GTO, cut its roof off with an acetylene torch and turned it into a vegetable garden. It was a monument to the first automobile fatality in America, the death of one Henry H. Bliss, killed by the best of all possible cars — an electric taxi — in New York City, September 13, 1899. For three years it attracted photographers and tourists to our house or one of the street and "energy fairs" that were popular at the beginning of the 1980s, with the memory of two oil crises fresh in the mind. What it meant exactly even I wasn't sure, though it was my project. Said one foreigner, "What if everybody did that to their cars?" It seemed to be working.

Our biggest success was convening the First International Ecocity Conference, attended by 775 people, 153 of them speakers — not only some of the best-known, but many of the relatively obscure real pioneers in ecocity design and building, planning and activism. The conference was held in six separate buildings near Berkeley's Civic Center park. The city itself was the conference center. The conferees were there between sessions out on the streets with everybody else in town, running into each other, smiling, waving, having lunch in the park. We had big flags in bright colors on light poles welcoming our guests with silhouettes of creek animals representing the city's twelve creeks. Beautiful!

After the conference, however, there was a sea change in attitude inside Urban Ecology, and I found myself in a minority wanting to carry on with the actual buying and building of real physical projects. We had done very well with the house we had bought earlier, our headquarters for eight years, in which the organization was one of seven partners, but members of the board majority were not interested in that approach any more. They preferred a strategy of supporting transit over cars, infill and transit village over sprawl, and allying themselves with greenbelt advocates — all worthy as far as it went. Thereafter they made *pro bono* support of low-income people in rather conventional projects their highest priority. They proved very successful in securing funding, and when I left the organization their primary preoccupation was trying to determine how to create projects that funders considered stylish. "This is 'in' among foundations these days," they'd say. "That's not. Be sure to use this key word; they'll really go for it." I found this distracting from the things I felt needed to be explored.

I wanted to continue doing the projects I thought were most important and participate much more directly in actually building things. I wanted to celebrate, not bury, our history. Even if it didn't seem popular with foundations, community groups and local politicians, explaining it would be educational and education was the requirement for non-profit status. I felt we were dealing with a real science that had to be truthfully portrayed, like a mathematician saying two plus two equals four. If foundations and others in the community wanted to hear two plus two equals five, I wasn't going to agree.

By setting up a new organization, Ecocity Builders, I was able to go on dealing with issues on a very fundamental level. At about the time I left Urban Ecology I was drawing an ecocity zoning map for Berkeley. From developing the map and thinking through exactly where we thought some city infrastructure should be removed, we evolved our "de-paving" projects. We silk screened T-shirts with the slogan (paraphrasing Joni Mitchell), "Save paradise. Tear up a parking lot," and managed to accomplish half a dozen small projects: depaving planter strips around the city, removing concrete from between sidewalk and curb and planting a hundred donated fruit trees.

One of the largest depaving projects took place at University Avenue Homes, an old, four-story hotel that had been converted to housing for the formerly homeless. Low-income and cooperative housing builder Susan Felix got permission from the city of Berkeley to remove about five parking spaces for a garden. After all, as she pointed out, of the seventy-five very low-income residents, only three owned cars and only two of them worked. A local activist and mentor to several adolescent boys, David Eifler, wrote me about an encounter on the way to this depaving event. The boys with him suddenly darted across the street to look at something a friend seemed to be hiding in his shirt, and, after furtive glances and excited whispering, returned to his side. When he asked, "What's your friend got?" it turned out to be a gun. "Thanks for giving the kids something else to think about," he wrote. "They talk about this as their garden now." I noticed that they worked over that asphalt with sledge hammers and crowbars with real relish and then helped mix in the horse manure and finally plant and water the trees, vines, bushes and seeds.

The largest depaving project yet was a satisfying collaboration with Urban Creeks Council. Urban Creeks Council co-founder Carole Schemmerling did most of the negotiating with one private landowner, two cities, the University of California, and several other agencies to get permission to open a block of buried creek on Berkeley's border with Albany. Before we started working on this section of Codornices Creek it was in a concrete pipe under a little-used parking lot, a street that had been closed, a sidewalk, and a flat, earth-filled area covered by almost nothing but fennel. Urban Creeks Council applied for and got $25,000 from the State Water Resources Board and hired a semi-volunteer bulldozer operator — he worked for half his usual wages. With the creek continuing to run through its culvert a few feet to the south, he carved out a rough cut about 80 percent the depth of the eventual creek canyon. Then for the next two years of Saturdays with 375 volunteers, most of them only working a day or two, but about a dozen working once a month, we carved out a pleasant small valley and hilly area with picks, shovels and wheelbarrows. Ecocity Builders' main role has been coordination of the volunteers and stewards of the land, then and since.

This was a very low-budget project in a mainly warehouse-district neighborhood without landed gentry to protest or tell us with fifty conflicting voices what to do. The result was a great opportunity for innovation. Since funds were very limited, the landscape architect never specified what plants should go where. Our philosophy was to plant natives, but since we had a fairly large area we decided to have an orchard as well. Within a few months we had accumulated donations of twenty-five fruit trees of all sorts — apples, plums, apricots, figs, oranges, lemons, nectarines, peaches, cherries, persimmons, Asian pears. The place is a wonderful little paradise, home to a dozen types of butterflies and birds, steelhead trout, sticklebacks, crawdads, water snails, frogs, garter snakes, water striders and lots of other insects, including sulfur-blue damselflies and vermilion dragonflies as brilliantly colored as tiny red neon lights. There are not many mammals yet: pocket gophers, raccoons and, unfortunately, stalking cats.

The place is amazing. We took cuttings from willow trees, carved them into stakes about an inch or two thick, cut the trunk side of the branch at a sharp angle and the end toward the leaves square, and drove them with a hammer into the banks of the creek. Within days roots were shooting out from the lower parts and branches popping out of the sides and beginning to reach for the sun. Now we have four-year-old, thirty-foot-high willows and alders. Watercress, cattails, horsetails and bulrushes showed up on their own in our micro-wetlands, and along the banks nasturtiums, wild grapes, mint, chicory and plantain. Volunteers planted dozens of local native flowers, grasses and bushes — nine bark, silver tassel, monkey flower, lupine, manzanita and ceonothis — and trees — madrone, buckeye, bay laurel, California glory and two kinds of oak. Anyone may come down on Sunday, midday, and help us water, weed, prune, harvest and, occasionally, plant.

ASSESSMENTS

In my thirty-five years on this personal odyssey through ecocity terri-tory, I've come to see the economics and politics of sprawl development something like this: Historically towns have grown up around fairly high-density centers of work, commerce and social life, with some people liv-ing in them but many more close by in lower-density housing. As towns have grown into cities, the close-in residents in low-density areas have resisted growth in their neighborhoods, forcing development farther and farther out. That next ring of low density development, once established, forces development even farther out, and so on. Richer people have bet-ter economic and political resources to resist growth in their neighbor-hoods, so pockets of higher density for jobs and commerce have been carved out of lower-income neighborhoods or placed far out on the fringe near major arterials, highway strips, or freeway off-ramps, where land is cheap and political resistance is as low as the population. Downtowns have been remodeled with high-density, single-use commercial build-ings and large areas of space dedicated to parking. Motorized traffic domi-nates the streets. Then, finally, vast low-density "centers" of business, iso-lated by immense parking lots, have been established on the fringe, and everybody in the megalopolis is expected to commute endless distances, mostly in cars. Thus, as in the San Francisco Bay Area, we have put up gigantic parking lots to collect suburban residents, knowing that their triple garages at home are what we are really designing for.

Why is sprawl being relayed outward virtually forever? At the start of our cause and effect chain it's because people relatively near the cen-ters are used to what they have and want to keep it that way. Some consci-entious people, aware of the costs of sprawl, and some who actually like the company of other people in real urban neighborhoods near real city centers, see cars as a major problem and vote for greenbelts surrounding cities — cinching development in, in theory, slowing sprawl development. But just punching a hole through the greenbelt with a major transit line or a freeway has allowed sprawl development to pop up another ten or twenty miles out. Slowing sprawl with greenbelts in many cases begets an even larger sprawl called leapfrog development. Due largely to the fears of suburbanites and their political influence, what infill that does go on is mid-range density — and often located where it would be ecologically more sensible to unfill for restoration rather than infill for development. The whole pattern presently lacks a system, a vision and a means both political and economic to reshape a healthy environment.

In my city, neighborhood activists and architectural conservatives fight against new housing and especially higher-density housing in and near centers, as well as in the lowest-density areas. They have made their emotional and financial investments and have become comfortable in their immediate environment. Higher density, they believe, would mean more shadows from taller buildings and many more cars on the street. The real problem is that there are well-established people working against growth even where it makes sense. Some of them deride opening creeks and expanding community gardens as silly, but never giving reasons why. Just to condemn something makes people uncomfortable, gives it "bad press" and raises the fear that supports no change at all.

Preservationists tend to share this anti-growth and anti-restorationist-anywhere point of view — but not always. Some want to freeze the whole town as it was at some point in time determined by a favored personal aesthetic. Others, however, want to preserve just particularly worthy buildings and sometimes extraordinary clusters of buildings or districts. Some who really love architecture want to save special buildings, but also want to see what can be built that addresses present and future realities and expresses the best, most creative designs the present generation can contribute to the next. Needless to say, I'm in the latter camp, and there is a lot to work with there.

One important force is conscience. Sprawl is an injustice against other species and the struggling classes. Some people not only respond to that idea, they are aghast at how damaging sprawl is turning out to be and they want to do something about it. They already vote for greenbelts and transit stations, as well as pay dues to the Sierra Club and ecocity organizations. We can also work with the disenfranchised — the students without housing, the elderly, some types of professionals and artists —who would all be happy with car-free accommodations downtown near transit. Those who oppose higher density in these locations are quite simply denying housing to thousands of such people in city after city.

The no-growth-anywhere people often claim the moral high road, saying that it is a grave injustice to force a change in the lives of people living in an area of proposed higher density. The reality is that these few already there are up against several times as many who often have only modest amounts of property and seldom any real estate in the community affected, but may be local citizens nonetheless — or would be if they could find housing. The numbers game of democracy would seem to favor providing housing for them, but money and established connections, not to mention deeds to real estate, work against them. Meanwhile it is seldom mentioned that the already established residents could move into the new development itself, or sell their present real estate, often at a very big profit, and move to another pleasant neighborhood. Many of them have great flexibility, but believe or claim they don't.

Then, too, circumstances change for all of us. Children grow up and move away, which means that both those children and their parents could be ready for a change, often a smaller place. Some of them do, in fact, end up interested in higher-density, pedestrian-environment living. What if nearby natural watercourses were available? What if they could get up into buildings easily for local distant views? What if there were sunny public plazas and shady trees and pedestrian streets to stroll without threat to life and limb from hurtling motor vehicles? We who would change the city toward the ecologically healthy have a very full deck of cards. We should be resourceful about playing them. Bringing this kind of argument to bear on the resistance I see in my city, which claims to cherish the poor and downtrodden while opposing the housing that could actually allow some of them to live here, would help us begin building something that works both ecologically and socially.

Some politicians have told me that theirs is the art of the possible, meaning that unless an idea is already popular, they will not represent it. They play the representative in this case, not the leader, much less the educator. But all the features of the ecocity exist — if scattered only very thinly around the world — and whatever exists is possible. We have that foot in the door, too. We can tell the story of the Aztec toy with wheels. The reality is that politicians who don't help us identify those ecocity features and help assemble them are simply failing their duty as people who should professionally be concerned with change toward a healthy future. For thirty-five years I've been doing just a little of what is "possible," making some progress. But being "visionary" and courageous is required of all of us if we want to bring our cities into balance with nature. My best offering: Try those four steps to an ecology of the economy.

9
Tools to Fit the Task

Tools suited to the task of reshaping cities for a healthier future have existed for a long time and will remain important far into the future. Some of them are being used effectively in many places, but should be used much more widely and may require redesigning to work better and replicate themselves more quickly. In addition, completely new tools need to be designed to fill out a whole tool box for ecocities. When Jaime Lerner told the people of Curitiba that environmentally-healthy policy and practice were important and they, the people, were important, he helped create a culture of support for very substantial urban transformations from the foundation in land uses on up. Given a culture of support in which people take problems and solutions of the sort addressed in this book seriously, these tools can be used to change the world profoundly. Some of them, in fact, can be used effectively by a small number of people right away, and this can build momentum toward more general public support. Then healthy future cities and a vital biosphere become possible.

ECOCITY ZONING: MAPPING THE FUTURE

Many planners consider zoning a great invention, lending structure and order to city building. A vocal minority says, in contrast, that zoning has divided the city and precluded the natural development of land uses in complementary relationship with one another. The anti-zoning camp suggests that destructive segregation is intrinsic to all zoning. I am not so sure. The problem, I think, is with the kind of zoning and the purposes it is designed to serve, and it can be largely solved by reshaping zoning itself — on the human measure. How, after all, will we talk about these complex things without a language, visualize them without images such as maps and graphically represented plans? Zoning provides these things, if not in an aesthetically beautiful language, at least in words and images that can carry important meanings. Without words and pictures to represent human anatomy, it would be hard to understand and repair our flesh and blood physical equipment. So, too, for ecocities.

In support of zoning, it may be said that it does have a certain fairness, in the sense that anyone who wants to play the real estate development game knows generally what to expect. Zoning is simply a means of letting people know what they can build and where and what sorts of activities are allowed there. Many of the ecological and social disasters of ill-conceived and poorly-applied zoning can be corrected simply by planning for the city, town and village of walkable distances and inspiring pedestrian environments, thinking three-dimensional instead of flat, and insisting on looking at whole-systems patterns and long term results. When these four major ideas have been added to zoning, it becomes ecocity zoning.

To create such ecocity zoning, first we have to acknowledge that the forces that gave us our present zoning are vested in the present system. They are personified, too. They include living, breathing people who are afraid of change in their neighborhoods, business people worried that customers might go away, people who just happen to like the way things are now, and people who know little or care little about ecological collapse. Mostly, however, people just haven't heard about ecological planning, much less ecocity zoning. Many would see it as a good idea, including people who can make money on ecocity zoning — among them developers and merchants in centers where density and activity increases.

There are people likely to be interested in the greater cultural diversity possible with a shift of densities toward pedestrian/transit centers, and environmentalists these days understand that density and transit go well together and that restoration of nature is very important. The next step in their thinking is to realize that ecocity zoning makes their dreams

Basic toolkit of the ecocity builder.

possible as does nothing else. There are those who are unable to find housing near the centers who want such housing — often, as in Berkeley, desperately. It is difficult to gather support from this diverse crowd to out-
number those afraid of the kind of changes represented by ecocity zoning, but it can — and must — be done. In any case, we have to start work
on ecocity zoning by simply doing it ourselves as concerned citizens. If it
has the value I think it has, it can then be held up to public scrutiny and
found to be a powerful and positive tool.

The objective of an ecocity zoning map is to open up landscapes
covered by car-dependent development and recover agricultural and natural landscapes while shifting density toward centers. The new density
should be in buildings with the ecological features described here and
others not yet invented. At the same time, the objective is to move toward
a far more balanced set of land uses with most aspects of life provided for
in a small area. This means, generally, mixed-use development and very
little commuting. It means creating the physical structure of the city so
that architecture, technologies, nature and healthy lifeways can harmo-
nize. It represents — it is — the first step in the four steps to an ecology
of the economy and shows how we can put a green infrastructure under
a green economy.

With basic ideas from this book and your own knowledge of the

231

place in which you live, you have enough to get started on an ecocity zoning map. If you consult aware ecologists and concerned citizens en route, and then revise, you will produce a good preliminary document. Then you can take a break for a week or two — visit a place that is mostly natural and similar to what your town's location looked like 100 or 1,000 years ago and wander around your town a little to see what attracts your attention. Then return to refine the map. If you want it to look more professional or attractive, you can find a local geographer, cartographer or artist to help. Then you can put a date on it and start using it. It will never be finished and final; such is the way of all maps.

These are the essential steps:

1. Produce a local natural history map. Visit your library, local college or historical society to locate the earliest available maps of your town and learn about its natural history — native plant and animal species, weather, climate, soils — and its cultural history. Features from these old maps may include creeks, original marshes, seasonal ponds, springs, shorelines, outcroppings of rock, ridge lines, major animal migratory routes, types of plant cover, areas of steep slope, sunny and shady slopes, archeological sites, old historic buildings, neighborhoods that may now be gone, and so on. Put this information on paper. Call it "Map #1." It prepares you to assess the priorities for restoration development and where these activities should take place. You may be going back thousands of years; the exercise will be fascinating. You might generate several: #1 a, #1 b, #1 c. ...

2. Establish walkable centers. On an up-to-date map of your town, which will be Map #2, locate the present city, town and neighborhood centers and draw concentric circles indicating distances from these centers. On about one fifth to one third of the land area of the town, in the zones closest to the centers, the density of development should be greater than elsewhere. On about half to three-quarters of the land area of the town, in the zones farthest from the centers and most dependent upon automobiles, there should be less density of development and, ultimately, natural or agricultural land uses. The lower the density of the whole town the smaller should be the percentage in the increasing density area and the larger the

percentage in the decreasing density area. Everywhere the mix of uses should become far more complex, even in the restoration areas on the future fringe. All sorts of diverse agriculture and patches of nature can be established in time.

How many concentric circular zones you choose to draw and their width depends upon your own intuitions and, as you develop it, experience. It also depends on the particular centers in question. Five to nine concentric circles give enough definition to different areas to make it clear where more or less development will be happening. Using five zones, for instance, will mean highest density in the centers, second-highest density just outside that zone, a minimal-change area next, an area of reduced density outside that, and finally, farthest from the center, the areas of highest priority for "de-development," that is, depaving, removal of buildings, walls, streets, creek culverts and other structures so that nature or agriculture can be reintroduced.

The concentric zones should be generally larger for the larger centers and smaller for the smaller ones, and these sizes will also relate to the total population of your town and the intensity of existing centers. For my own town of 110,000 people, for example, which averages approximately three-and-a-half miles wide, the area around the downtown that should be up-zoned — that is, have its building heights and density increased — should be about three-quarters of a mile in diameter. The areas around the smaller neighborhood centers should be upzoned for only about two blocks from their centers (four blocks in diameter), give or take about a half-block. Middle-sized areas should be up-zoned for about three or four blocks from their centers (six to eight blocks in diameter). The eventual total area of land covered with development, both thin and intense, depends on these decisions, too. As a starting point, half to three-quarters of the land area should be returned to nature or agriculture. This can be reassessed later. If you take the time to re-draw the map several times, it will start making sense and become more self-evident.

3. Adjust the circular zones and draw them in relation to nature corridors and nature areas. Decide on the best locations for nature corridors and agricultural areas and draw them in on a third map.

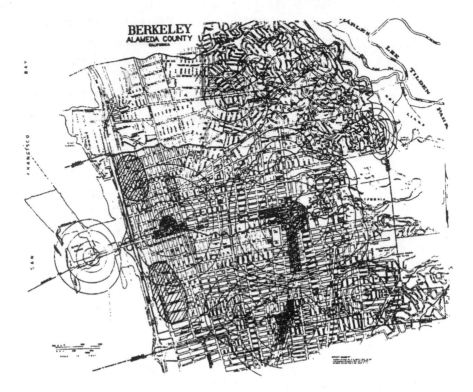

Ecocity zoning map (#2), indicating potential areas for higher density and diversity and for removal of car-dependent development.

You are now prepared to adjust the concentric circles to create nature corridors and to lay out areas for creek restoration and other special purposes. Some of the concentric circles around the downtown, major centers and neighborhood centers will overlap, cutting off potential connections between restoration areas. You will need to compress their edges so that the nature corridors can be established. The circles will thus become somewhat flattened on the sides closest to other circles. The restoration areas between the circles with somewhat flattened sides, together with other natural and agricultural areas suggested by studying Map #1, including creeks and ridge lines, indicate the location of the future nature corridors connecting future natural zones. Creeks become another kind of nature corridor that can penetrate right into the middle of

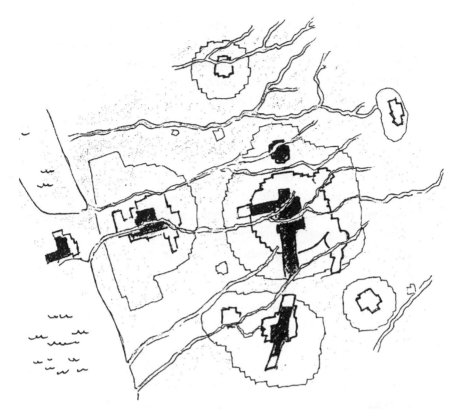

As an ecocity zoning map evolves over many years, it can illustrate the transformation of a city toward centers linked by transit and bicycles with natural watercourses restored and auto dependence virtually eliminated.

a center. Creek setbacks — the distance between buildings and other structures and the creek itself — should be wide in areas far from the centers and narrower in the centers, where land is of very high social and economic value, but creeks should not be buried.

4. Show the limits of discontinuous boulevards and the location of railroad right-of-ways. Since urban development naturally concentrates around transit hubs and along transit corridors, draw in higher intensity development areas along boulevards that connect centers. But, somewhere near the limit of or just outside of the centers, make boulevard development discontinuous — that is, identify the entrance to the center right there. After major land use shifts in the course of many decades, the boulevard turns into a

country road at this point, and there is the potential to do something interesting, even spectacular, here. Call these places "gates to the city" or, if defined by large structures, "ramparts." Not just architecture, but big trees could mark these entrances, too.

As the boulevard-become-country road enters the zone of highest priority for restoration or crosses any special nature corridor, it should rise up on a causeway-like structure or, preferably, plunge underground so that people and natural species can cross without undue disturbance of one another. Railroads should do this, and bicycle and foot paths, too. You can take advantage of hills, even very low ones, and valleys for burrowing under or rising over nature corridors.

Railroad right of ways should be featured on the map and, if not active, saved for future rail lines or changed into bicycle paths. They should not be built on. Once sold off, this land becomes extremely expensive and difficult to reassemble. Show all these features on Map # 3, your ecocity zoning map.

5. Prepare sample vertical cross sections. To make clear the three-dimensionality of ecocity zoning, Map #3 should be supplemented with drawings representing vertical slices through buildings and landscapes, which illustrate various arrangements of uses, ones on top of, as well as adjacent to, one another. Features such as rooftop cafes, bridges, elevators and terracing, and the relationships of buildings to sun and views can be illustrated in this way to help explain the options for using the third dimension imaginatively and for ecological benefit. These images can be drawn in the margins of Map #3 or on a separate sheet.

6. Provide keys for the maps.

7. Add scenario maps. To illustrate changes into the future you might draw up several other maps representing different stages in the ecocity's development. (Maps #4, #5, and so on.)

Developing these maps is a challenge, but it is worth it. Doing it yourself will appear to take the initiative from the planners, citizens and developers. Once you've drawn a map, people will rage against your presumption in not having consulted them first, but if you don't draw one they will have no idea what you are talking about. Presenting two or three

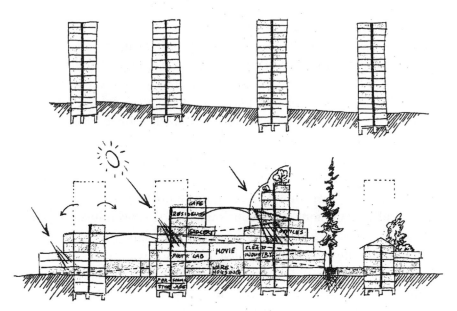

Ecocity cross-section. Modernist towers are contrasted with highly mixed-use buildings with elevated street systems, bridges, basement warehousing, and the like.

versions will help to maintain flexibility of vision and possibly help invite their ideas. Someone has to exercise some imagination here and take some responsibility. When it comes to maps representing possible scenarios, many people will say they are unrealistic. They are not; they are simply long range.

I am convinced that the entire ecocity map-making project has to be thought through publicly if it is ever to be adopted by the citizens of any city and serve as more than a fantasy exercise. Map #3 provides guidance. Map #4 begins to interpret that guidance, featuring keyhole and off-center parks and plazas providing urban views of nature and quiet public spaces off main streets. "Lone-wolf buildings," big ones standing in restoration zones that don't make sense in the centers scheme of things but have special economic or historic importance should be saved. When they are relatively far from the centers, their uses may be changed to ones demanding less commuting. They may become very compact ecovillages, or be remodeled to become parts of very small arcologies. Transformed into factories that are incompatible with residential and social uses, lone-wolf buildings could appropriately stand separate from city centers, collecting workers daily with pleasant country bicycle rides where once there were one-story ranch houses, for example. Or a lone-wolf building's very existence could modify the ecocity zoning map. It could become the hub of a new neighborhood center, perhaps a small artist colony with a coffeehouse to which people could take the streetcar on a Saturday afternoon to watch the sunset.

A usable ecocity zoning map in our hands provides broad outlines and a considerable number of details. It is essentially a "zoning overlay," not the actual official zoning of a city. Its unofficialness is what makes it what I call "shadow zoning," an allusion to the "shadow ministers" of parties out of power in, for example, Australia's parliamentary government. Like shadow ministers, ecocity zoning maps stand ready to take over when there is a failure of confidence, in our case, in present zoning. Its rationale is impeccable, and it takes everyone in the Great Majority into consideration, including citizens of the future, animals and plants. It does not have to wait for the future, either. It can function immediately upon completion. The ecocity zoning map is not as crisp, hard edged or directive as the actual zoning map, though it could be used to modify the existing one. Nor is it the "soft planning" of a regional metaphor like Frank and Deborah Popper's Buffalo Commons. It's somewhere in the middle, empowering the building in the physical world of something from the imagination.

The ecocity zoning map is an "overlay" in the sense that it can be imagined as superimposed on the existing map. It can then be used for influencing existing zoning and pushing its interpretation in ecologically-healthy directions, encouraging more diversity and density in one place and restoration of natural habitat and agriculture in another, and delineating ways to withdraw from automobile dominance everywhere.

The map can be used as a guide for activists. Many environmental organizations oppose, support or comment on development projects in their cities and counties. Ecological zoning maps clarify what should be supported and what should be opposed. As these maps are utilized, their legitimacy increases, and the chances of rebuilding cities for pedestrians instead of cars increases proportionally. For example, Ecocity Builders produced such a map for Berkeley and distributed it to city council members, developers and environmental groups to let them know whether we will support or oppose particular projects and why. It makes for a very fair game board, and we use it and invite others to use it when development issues arise.

Changing land uses in a major way may not yet be a traditional tactic for most environmentalists, transit boosters, creek fans, urban gardeners, energy conservers, bicyclists and the disabled, but these activists will all find that ecocity zoning provides a context for changes beneficial to their projects and positions. The opportunity for the creation of a powerful coalition awaits their recognition of this potential. If they use the map and support its application, their work can become synergistically reinforcing, accelerating the effectiveness of all their various kinds of actions. This is one of the most powerful aspects of ecocity zoning — that it clarifies what changes fit the whole, benefits all the groups striving for a healthier community, and avoids the pitfalls of placing a good development in a bad place.

Ecocity zoning maps help advance us beyond simplistic categorical thinking toward whole-systems thinking. For example, supporters of greenbelt initiatives who attempt to stop sprawl by placing land on the fringes in legally-protected farms or nature areas call for infill development — filling in any vacant space available within existing cities with development. But if we are to restore nature in places where sprawl is now located, some vacant spaces should not be filled in. Buying a vacant lot for restoration of nature or agriculture is far cheaper than buying a lot with a building on it for the same purpose and demolishing the building. Vacant land in or near existing centers should, in contrast, be filled in with appropriate development, in some cases with intensely-utilized, big buildings. Ecocity zoning maps tell us where both open space preservation and infill development are best located and where unfill — removal of buildings, driveways, walls and culverts — should happen, too.

The ecocity zoning map can be a guide for developers and owner-builders as well as environmentalists and appropriate-technologists. Some developers would like to contribute to ecological health but don't how. Ecological zoning maps can help them make decisions as to where particular projects may be helpful and, again, let them know in advance whether the map's supporters will be working for or against the approvals they are seeking from the city. The ecocity zoning map can also let everyone know how the city's zoning code needs to change if ecologically-healthy and imaginative projects are to be built. Often the zoning and incentives are against such projects, but if enough people realize this the zoning and incentives can be changed.

Thus the ecocity zoning map can be a guide for policy makers and legislators, too. These maps begin to establish the framework for a new landscape of ecological laws and regulations — step three of our four steps to an ecology of the economy — as well as, eventually, the actual physical city itself. They provide an idea around which imaginative legislators can design incentives, disincentives, changed tax structures and codes, and some day — hopefully sooner than later — official ecocity zoning. The ecocity zoning map puts a land-use/infrastructure foundation under legislators' healthiest ambitions. If they want to be the builders of a civilization designed for the twenty-first century and beyond, ecocity zoning is indispensable.

At first, ecocity zoning maps will not be enforceable descriptions of how a city should be developed, but they start from what actually exists, and therefore are partially implemented already. Even car cities, after all, do exhibit an almost natural expression of the basic access by proximity principle in their cores, and malls struggle to re-create the magnetism that the automobile has diminished by physical distance. These would-be pedestrian centers are engines of economic prosperity that can be tuned up for high economic and cultural performance.

It is very likely, then, that some town and city governments will eventually hire planning firms or knowledgeable local organizations to draw up ecocity zoning maps. Early on, though, we will likely see such firms, organizations, or even teams of urban design students producing ecocity zoning maps without the assistance of governments — their work being paid for by organization membership dues, foundation grants, or by professionals, activists or students themselves. So far, to the best of my knowledge, Ecocity Builders in Berkeley and Urban Ecology Australia in Adelaide are the only such organizations to have produced these maps. Some people may produce ecocity zoning maps just for the fun of it. Maybe Sim City, the video game, could be redesigned for real relevance and applicability. If the maps are good and pass the test of reasonable local scrutiny, city councils may just endorse them as overlays to help guide zoning changes.

In the meantime, we will see small pieces of the puzzle fall into place from very different places. State legislatures, for example, may write mixed-use, car-free condos and apartments into their housing incentives and require that such developments be located in or near existing transit centers in order to qualify for certain state benefits. City governments may raise the height limit in one or several of their towns' future walkable centers without yet making a commitment to creek restoration, or — much better — retain existing height limits but allow much taller buildings if the developers utilize ecological features in their buildings and purchase transferred development rights. A developer may decide not to develop at a particular location, even thought the city zoning would allow it, because the ecocity zoning map indicates it should not be developed and people who understand the map will oppose the project. A downtown businessperson may decide to build a multi-story residential addition over his or her store because of the logic behind the ecocity zoning map — that the added population means more customers.

It will take a long time to reshape any city with an ecocity zoning map. Major changes in land use and infrastructure are expensive, and it is in their nature to require time. Improvement can, however, be expected immediately, and we can begin moving resolutely, step-by-step in the right direction.

The ecocity zoning map is an offering — a kind of illustrated discussion paper — rather than the product of an all inclusive public process. Simply calling a forum together and asking people how they would like to see their city changed will barely inch in this direction unless someone works persistently to insert ecocity principles into the discussion. Ecocity mapping is complex and novel enough that it will have to come from people who have been thinking about it for some time. One cannot expect healthy results by asking a random sampling how to proceed with a surgical operation. A surgeon is needed. The city's body is in need of ecocity doctors to get the urban anatomy back together after a terrible accident — a car accident. If there is respect for ecological city design knowledge, the citizen in the street and the ecocity expert can eventually work together. After the pioneers have taken the risks to get the ball rolling, an open political process can amend and adopt it.

Probably the ultimate card up the sleeve of ecocity zoning map makers is that the map is based on important information that present zoning fails to consider. With an ecocity zoning map in hand, supplemented by descriptive explanations, it does not matter if anyone supports you, initially. What you are saying makes sense. All ideas and built realities start somewhere as a tiny seed. In this case you have the logic of the human body's needs and dimensions, and the logic of ecology on your side. You have good information about resources that conventional zoning has yet to deal with, and your map is based on the spatial and ecological realities and the fabric of your town.

You can simply say, "I support this kind of project in this part of town and oppose this kind of project in this other part of town because these changes are needed to create a pedestrian, low-energy, ecologically-healthy city." You are in the world of development and city building like the intelligent consumer in the marketplace, and like that consumer you are in an extraordinarily powerful position. Just as the consumer armed with information on destructive companies and a list of green products can boycott or purchase new realities out of or into existence, the citizen equipped with an ecocity zoning map can change the fabric of society. Starting in small but real ways immediately, by supporting or withholding support from particular projects and from products and services offered there, the ecocity zoning map works.

A final important point about the ecocity zoning map: You don't have to wait for regional government. You can act now and act effectively. Many thoughtful people promote the connection of land uses and transportation, encouraging higher density near transit and greenbelts. So far so good, but many of the best of them believe we can be only marginally effective until we create regional governments like Metro in Portland, Oregon, governments larger than the city and often embracing several cities and even counties. The idea is to gain the authority and power to rationalize transit, combine conflicting bus lines and commuter rail systems, coordinate schedules, devise greenbelts for whole regions and select areas for future development. It's true that today's many separate municipal and county governments create regional chaos in this regard, but we don't have to imagine that only through regional government can we be effective. In fact, the ecocity zoning strategy is safer, because the intended specific results do not necessarily follow from setting up a regional government, which is almost as likely as state government to support new freeways and acquiesce to pressure from sprawl developers and car-dependent drivers.

Planning a recent visit to Sacramento to see a friend and visit two government offices, I thought it would be fun to take the train. When I called the people I was planning to meet I discovered that they were scattered all over the big flat town and I would not be able to visit all of them in the same day unless I went by car. Sprawl at the other end of the intercity trip made the use of the train and local transit impossible within what should have been a reasonable period of time. If Sacramento had been well along in the transitions created by an ecocity zoning map — finding its centers and shifting people to those centers so that its own transit system could work efficiently — I could have made the trip by train. What we do in the city we live in to make transit work with land uses will enable people from far away to visit without bringing their cars. Thus, if we act for ecocity zoning we start to solve the regional problem locally — while reinforcing what the regional government should do when and if it is created.

TRANSFER OF DEVELOPMENT RIGHTS

Transfer of Development Rights (TDR) is a real estate transaction tool established in zoning ordinances that makes it possible to buy and transfer the rights to develop from one piece of property to another. Most commonly TDR is used to protect farm or natural land from development or save historic buildings. If the owners of real estate can sell their land for development, but there is good reason not to develop there, some governments have written ordinances that make it possible for developers to buy those rights and "sever" them from the deeds. The people selling the development rights get the money, but are prohibited from developing the property from then on, and the developer is allowed to shift those development rights elsewhere and build more than would otherwise be allowed by the local government. Using TDR, hundreds of thousands of acres of land and hundreds of buildings have been preserved in the United States that otherwise would have been developed, in the case of open land, or demolished and replaced with more development, in the case of buildings.

Double TDRs are twice as good. They are a particular kind of TDR that removes the existing buildings, driveways, walls or other improvements at the "sending site" (the location where the rights are purchased) as a condition of the developer being able to build more elsewhere at the "receiving site" (the location where the development rights are exercised and new development is built). South Lake Tahoe's ordinance permitted the removal of sixty houses causing polluting runoff into the lake, and the transfer of development rights to elsewhere in the area. Sixty housing units is a lot of housing, but in Berkeley a single new apartment called the Gaia Building, eight-stories high, houses as many people as those sixty South Lake Tahoe houses and all on one sixth of a downtown city block. Sixty low-density properties in Berkeley translates into twenty blocks of creek daylighting and ten community gardens. Density can do a lot in the right place and at the same time pay for the restoration of a great deal of open space, complete with creeks, ridge lines, farms, parks and playing fields — whatever the community wants.

When shifting density away from car dependent areas toward pedestrian/transit centers, it's important to create far more mixed-use building where the development takes place. The overall objective is to bring most people within walking or bicycling distance or a short transit ride of the places they need to be for a full range of their lives' important activities. For occasional pleasure trips, cultural and social involvements at greater distance, and relatively short commuting to jobs, they can use transit, but long distance commuting is intrinsically a bad idea. Therefore development rights should be shifted so that if commerce, jobs, education, and so on, are near the centers but not much housing, more housing is created. That's often called "balanced development."

In addition, it's important to create the density in a way that is pleasurable and ecologically-healthy. This book is replete with visions of terraces and rooftops buzzing with life. I am convinced that the meaning of the beautiful, fun, money-making larger building in the right place, with spectacular views to the local bioregion and associated natural features such as a restored waterways, would be lost on no one. The fears that those projects arouse in distant neighborhoods would evaporate in the face of such successes. TDRs can help build such projects and at the same time restore open space benefiting the whole city.

The Double TDR functions because the developer is given a bonus in density when he or she pays for the transferred rights. One unit in a sending site might, for example, get the developer five in his or her new building — which is good for those who need housing — and if built in the right place, greatly reduces commuting. It's important to hold standard height limits relatively low at the sites where the rights to build can be exercised, thus creating the incentive to trade upward to tall buildings as ecological building features are added. For example, a city might decide to limit buildings to five stories in its downtown, but allow three more stories if TDRs are purchased in a particular quantity, another three stories if features such as bridges between buildings, terracing, public space on the sixth floor, promenades, mini-parks, or solar greenhouses are included. Each city would have its own formula depending on climate, sun angles, history and hardiness of its population.

It should be clarified that the Double TDR is a standard free market exchange — it requires a willing seller and willing buyer. The idea is not condemnation, eminent domain and forced market value compensation. Instead, by design of the ordinances involved, the deal is attractive for all parties. If the development is in the right place, of course, transit and bicycling works better, energy is conserved and local businesses thrive. The ecocity zoning map is the key tool for directing where the development rights should come from and go. A sense of the proportions of restoration and development can be developed by thinking through the relationships indicated on the map.

To encourage the transfers that open up nature while building the city in the right place and with the right mix, I propose restoration tax credits. Developers would apply for credits by demonstrating that the project proposed is in the right area, will add density and diversity there, and will remove development to restore a creek, create a greenway, expand a community garden, or consolidate an interrupted railroad right-of-way. Any real estate within a hundred feet of the centerline of a creek in outer zones, sixty feet in middle zones, and thirty feet in inner zones, could be defined as an eligible sending site for development credits, and developers removing improvements there could total their expenses in purchasing the property, removing the improvements, and restoring the creek as restoration project expenses, and be awarded tax credit certificates by the state and/or federal government. Developers with large tax bills might decide to use the tax credits to reduce them. Others might sell the tax credit certificates to a company that wanted them right away. Anyone who bought the tax credits would be helping the restoration project. Because the restoration would now be ensured, the developer could be awarded building permits for the restoration site work, and approvals for the added height, density and fancy features of ecological development at the project construction site. This is essentially how preservation tax credits work for development projects protecting historic architecture. It's time that waterways, hills, trees and soils were considered as valuable as historic architecture and as worthy of restoration.

Here, then, with Double TDRs and restoration tax credits, we have a means for significantly reshaping cities. In many, including my own, there are constant complaints that there is not enough open space, not enough parks, and not enough money to buy more land for them and pay for maintenance. But with Double TDRs we have a mechanism for creating open space and parks while providing new housing and creating a larger tax base from the new higher density development.

It might be mentioned that the wider the setbacks for creeks the less maintenance work and expense per acre, because creeks then have enough room to meander back and forth a bit, causing nobody any problem — just eroding one way for a few years, then the other, and back. The whole idea is to let them be as natural as possible. If the corridor is wide enough there can be a buffer zone of minimally managed landscape with perhaps a bicycle and pedestrian path or urban orchards of the sort we created at our restoration project on Codornices Creek, and the creek itself and its banks can be almost completely wild. TDRs and restoration tax credits make it feasible to purchase and maintain enough land to restore major natural and civic open space. In Berkeley, at the rate we are progressing, it will take over 5,000 years to open up our buried creek system. These real estate tools working with ecocity zoning maps can speed that up many times over.

Rick Pruetz, who wrote the book on TDRs,[90] says that a revolving fund is helpful for rolling back sprawl development through Double TDRs. Any nonprofit or municipality can create such a fund to buy land and sell development rights so that they can be shifted to other parts of town and call it a Double TDR Bank. Funds can be gathered from contributions from individuals, foundations, businesses, governments or any combination of these and the nest egg turns into land and buildings at the time of purchase. The building or buildings are then removed and nature, agriculture or other open space is restored. At the time the developer buys the development rights for use elsewhere, the fund is recapitalized (gets the developer's money) and the land can be maintained or deeded over to the city, a land trust, community group or some other steward. This puts the bank in a position to buy more real estate for further transformation of the urban structure and further restoration. If major foundations or big donors to civic or environmental causes catch on to the potential, the fund might grow quickly and some truly magnificent projects might transpire.

We could think of this revolving fund as a "should-be open space acquisition fund." It would buy real estate where buildings are in the wrong place with regard to automobile dependence, floods, efficient urban structure, and so on. Municipal, state or federal governments could set up or contribute to such a fund and eventually come out money ahead. They would save money by reducing highway construction, and city government would make more money in taxes from the new development. The developer who buys the transferable development rights will make more money, too, by being able to build more. The private individuals needing workplaces and housing will get just that, and in a place served well by transit and full of cultural benefits. And, in the most general terms, people and nature will thrive in an urban environment that is ever healthier and more vital.

THE ECOLOGICAL GENERAL PLAN

Cities get their broad directives for zoning from a General or Master Plan. This document expresses the intended tenor of relations between citizens and their built and natural environments and is one of the most important instruments in shaping cities for decades at a time. The zoning ordinance, which has the force of law, is based on the General Plan and is supposed to be consistent with it, though politics does produce inconsistencies as people and their leaders change their minds over the years. In its broadest definition, the General Plan is a framework for public decision-making. It is made up of different elements — land use, transportation, public safety, open space, citizen participation, and so on. General plans and the zoning codes based upon them lay out a vision for the city and policy directives for actualizing that vision. The zoning ordinance gets precise about the details, down to specifying punishments for violations of the ordinance.

Citizens wanting to build and maintain an ecologically-healthy city would do well to make sure that their vision is explicitly stated in the introductory comments to their city's General Plan. Then the document should follow through by spelling out policies and actions throughout. General plans draw general guidelines, but can also get quite specific about what should go on in particular locations. One could argue that General Plans calling for the health and safety of its people would provide a policy context for ordinances that would build an ecologically-healthy city. But, unfortunately, much contained in General Plans, as in the zoning codes, gets in the way, such as calling for low height limits near transit, which makes it impossible for transit to function efficiently, or calling for large quantities of parking for new buildings that guarantee a glut of cars.

In Berkeley, for example, there are "eco" elements in the General Plan, but some of the most important pieces are missing. Berkeley has excellent recycling and a styrofoam ban. Other policies that are at least somewhat encouraged in the city's General Plan include moderate but significant support for bicycle parking, bicycle paths and bike lanes on streets; green building policies for non-toxic, energy conserving and recycled building materials; encouragement for at least one block of pedestrian street; encouragement for traffic calming on residential streets such as the Slow Street; and encouragement for creek daylighting and community gardening. But the degree of support in all these cases could be much stronger and a long list of different policies would be required to qualify the plan for something heading towards an ecocity General Plan.

In summer of 2000, Ecocity Builders Treasurer Kirstin Miller and Berkeley Planning Staff member Andrew Thomas suggested that concerned community members compile a limited list of crucial policies we thought would nudge the General Plan toward becoming a real ecocity General Plan. We would call them collectively the "Ecocity Amendment," and try to convince the City Council to adopt them into the General Plan. We decided that there were four policies that had a fairly good chance to be adopted: encouraging centers-oriented development, establishing TDRs, supporting ecological demonstration projects, and laying out some funding mechanisms for the other three policies. We could argue these policies' positive contributions and gather support. At the time of this writing over seventy organizations support them, which means we actually have a good chance of seeing the Ecocity Amendment soon become part of the revised Berkeley General Plan.

At the time we wrote the four policies, we had recently seen "progressive" city council members vote against car-free housing, so we left that policy off our list thinking it might reduce the chances of acceptance of the package. But a pleasant surprise: a planning commissioner appointed by one of the car-free housing council opponents became a champion of car-free housing, and the idea is now encouraged in the draft plan submitted to the council by the commission.

But more is required if we are to have a solid ecocity General Plan. We need to methodically shift away from automobile-dictated development patterns and say so explicitly in the plan. There should be a policy to methodically reduce parking — a good model is Copenhagen which is cutting back about 2 percent per year — while encouraging bikes and transit and, especially, while taking care to shift land uses toward balanced development. Any new parking built should be temporary replacement for parking lost due to other changes in city infrastructure, and it should be easily convertible to other uses. Low ceilings and sloped floors must be avoided so that other uses can be easily accommodated in remodeling for housing, shops, day care and nursery schools or other uses. Of course, any ecocity General Plan worthy of the name would have to adopt an ecocity zoning map, and a major step would be the establishment of an Office of Ecological Development, which we will look at shortly as part of an "International Ecological Rebuilding Program."

With an ecological General Plan in place a city would have the written mandate to shape policies to manipulate the city's land use infrastructure and create the physical reality of an ecocity over two to five decades. Not for the impatient, but substantial benefits would start accumulating with the pursuit of such ecocity policies, says Jaime Lerner, within two years.

ROLL BACK SPRAWL

Tools to roll back sprawl development exist. With strong interest on the part of legislators, we can strengthen them considerably, craft a few more, and make it profitable to implement and replicate them. With Jaime Lerner-like appeals to the people, we can create a culture of acceptance with its own imagination to shape the many unique places in this coun-

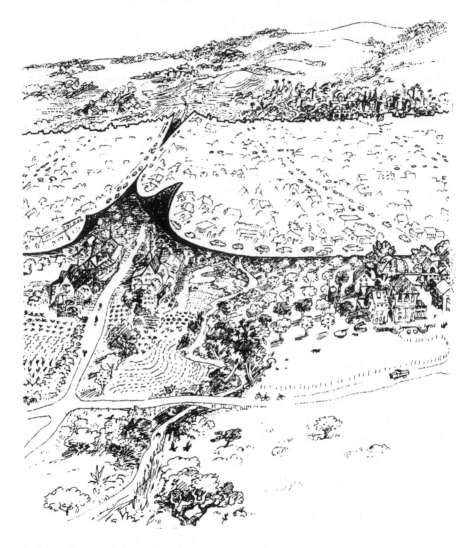

Roll back sprawl. Low-density, car-dependent development replaced by natural and agricultural landscape, small hamlets, neighborhood centers and ecological cities.

try — in all countries. Millions of people lament the loss of better times and the better towns that went along with them. Here's a way to get them back and at the same time build better cores for our cities in ways that actually address the future. The strategy of a Roll Back Sprawl campaign is simply to identify means to remove sprawl and shift development toward centers. Double TDRs, supportive zoning, city government commitments to purchase real estate with car-dependent uses and remove those uses, foundation and investor support for the transition — all these can be facilitated and accelerated by such a campaign. It's first order of business should simply be to let people know such changes are possible, that tools exist and we already know they can work well.

I spent several months in 1999 researching not just the possibilities for a campaign against sprawl, but the means to reverse its spread, to roll it back toward pedestrian/transit centers. I found that of the several larger environmental organizations I talked with none wanted to join such a campaign unless other major organizations or foundations got on board first. "Start it by yourself or with someone else," they said, "and if you succeed we'll likely join you." We had too little money to do more than lay out a credible strategy and what it could accomplish.

The Sierra Club, which runs a campaign called "Challenge to Sprawl," was satisfied with action far short of working systematically to remove sprawl development and was unclear on the concept of ecological whole systems. Most Sierra Club members seemed to think they needed their cars to get out into the wilderness. Once we could use trains, horses and bikes — and if we design the right way, we still can. Sierra Club's campaign against sprawl supports infill development along corridors up to about four stories, but is fearful of talking about higher density centers, convinced that higher density than that is politically unpopular. I question their assumption since millions of people in the United States work and/or live above four stories, but more importantly, there is a theoretical problem with filling up corridors with four-story development. It hardens the arteries and makes it much more difficult to restore natural zones and corridors. It preserves the vision of cities surrounding little islands of "park," and prevents the possibility of cities as islands in nature. Centers-oriented development is many times superior to thickening the arteries of the city, even though that would help transit in a fairly major way. Centers-oriented development would help transit even more and allow for the resurgence of nature.

As we spread the word about ecocity design and planning and continue to refine tools for rolling back sprawl, the day may soon come when a Roll Back Sprawl campaign will make so much sense as to be easily organized. I am convinced that it could be among our most important tools for creating ecocities and building a healthy future. With the sort of demonstration projects I've been describing, people could begin to put two and two together. If the possibilities offered by reshaping our cities with these restoration/development tools can capture the attention of creative people and tweak their sense of the possible, an explosion of little paradises could ripple, then roll in waves across the continents. The land yearns to breathe free, and real community longs for expression — a Roll Back Sprawl campaign is the means.

THE INTERNATIONAL ECOLOGICAL REBUILDING PROGRAM

We have now looked at several new tools designed specifically for ecocity building, but where is the institutional support for all of this? Where is the scheme, plan or program in which the ecocity zoning map would work and Double TDRs would be designed, passed as legislation and applied through everyday administrative practices? Perhaps ecological rebuilding could come about chaotically — a little here, a little there, in a pattern not too different from today's groping forward — but I doubt it. In a crisis like the one enveloping the biosphere today, it would be helpful if we had a concerted effort to build as if we thought building had something to do with ecological health. If we set the goal of bringing society into balance with nature — and set out to develop a methodology for achieving that goal — we would have a context in which the transformation would have a far better chance of success. But we have not yet made such an effort.

Why don't the governments of the world have ecological development departments? Are they not supposed to be working for the common good? Haven't there been enough experiences in the EPAs of the world, enough environmental conferences, for people to have caught on to the necessity of a major rebuilding? There are serious international efforts to cut CO_2 emissions, but where is the work going on to create a treaty on city development and restoration that would solve the problem? The governments of New Zealand and the Netherlands are leading the way with their own national "green plans," but they are not focusing on the built habitat as centrally as they should be — and are not quite so presumptuous as to call for a genuine rebuilding of our Western technological civilization.

If there were a scheme for rebuilding civilization, its name would be something like the International Ecological Rebuilding Program. Al Gore had a similar idea when he wrote his book *Earth in the Balance*. He developed the idea in some detail, addressing major reduction of pollution, restoration of nature where possible, and an organized effort to promote technologies that conserve resources. "Human civilization is now so complex and diverse, so sprawling and massive," he said, "that it is difficult to see how we can respond in a coordinated, collective way to the global environmental crisis. But circumstances are forcing just such a response; if we cannot embrace the preservation of the earth as our new organizing principle, the very survival of our civilization will be in doubt."

He says that, "There are no precedents for the kind of global response now required," but he does point to the Marshall Plan, which organized much of the rebuilding of Europe after World War II. He credits that plan with enormous success and proposes naming a new initiative after it, a Global Marshall Plan that would have five major goals: (1) population stabilization; (2) developing and sharing appropriate technologies; (3) new global "eco-nomics," meaning ecological economics; (4) a new generation of treaties and agreements to accomplish ecologically-healthy ends; and (5) a new global environmental consensus.

His chapter "Developing and Sharing Appropriate Technologies" is as close to confronting the built civilization as he will bring us. Under the subheading "Building Technology," he calls for passive solar design and greater energy efficiency in buildings. In other places he speaks of the benefits of decentralized electricity generation and expresses some surprise that wind electric energy is economically viable and promising for larger scale applications in many locations. He speaks of "emphasizing attractive and efficient forms of mass transportation." He even makes one of the most stunning statements against automobiles I have ever seen: "We now know that their cumulative impact on the global environment is posing a mortal threat to the security of every nation that is more deadly than that of any military enemy we are ever again likely to confront."[91]

His Global Marshall Plan, however, says almost nothing of that created object in which most of us live, that invention for maximizing exchange and minimizing transportation that Jane Jacobs describes as the chief engine of industrial and cultural production and consumption, that thing that can be designed and physically rearranged to reduce demand radically and, therefore, add to energy efficiency like nothing else: the built community. The city simply does not appear, much less serve as the foundation of the plan, but it could and should.

In 1991 I tried my own hand at an outline for an International Ecological Rebuilding Program and took it with me to the Second International Ecocity Conference in Adelaide, Australia, the next year. There it was amended and adopted, if not yet adopted by nation-states or the United Nations. Its main points are as follows:

1. We must declare an emergency in human and environmental affairs and create programs specifically for ecological rebuilding in every country and in the United Nations. "The emergency is not temporary. We are entering a period of permanent emergency, and we will cling to the edge of this precipice until we fall off or until we solve the problem."

2. Energy policies must be linked to ecological development. "We need to recognize that energy powers something, and mostly it is the city, town and village — the built human habitat." The ecologically-healthy structure of the city is the foundation for energy conservation and should be item number one in any energy strategy.

3. Because living systems cannot function well when they are effectively cut up into isolated chunks, we should establish departments of ecological development on the national, state and local level. The United States and other countries have Environmental Protection Agencies empowered to enforce environmental regulations for prevention and amelioration of pollution, but these agencies don't build. There are, however, housing agencies and other departments that do build, using their own construction corps or directing grants, loans and contracts to builders. We need governmental departments or agencies that coordinate ecological objectives with actual construction. It is important to see that building right in the first place is at the root of environmental protection, and the ecological development department would be charged with just that. Under it there would be research wings, such as the National Renewable Energy Laboratory and an Ecocity Research Institute, that would assist projects from small integral-neighborhood scale up to whole new-town projects like Arcosanti.

Departments of ecological development should "initiate massive spending programs to develop renewable energy technologies and ecological community building as two coordinated facets of the same overall effort." They should "transform defense programs and companies into builders of elements of ecocities and associated technologies and products, and reward pioneering companies in these fields with profitable contracts. They should make federal, state and local moneys available to ecocity projects as loans, grants and research and development contracts." They could provide assistance and oversight to other governmental branches as well, so that the left hand would know what the right was doing in relation to ecological building and ecological policy in general. They could even build their own experimental projects. Whereas environmental protection agencies function appropriately on the federal and state level, there should be departments of ecological development on the municipal level as well.

4. We need ecological rezoning, complete with the mapping method with which we are now familiar.

5. We need programs to restore wildlife habitat and farmlands, withdrawing from tracts as large as the proposed Buffalo Commons and as small as narrow creek and wildlife corridors in cities.

6. We need economic restructuring — phased, steadily-increasing taxes on pollution and energy waste over time. A land tax could be designed to shift society toward ecocity development patterns. Taxes per square foot of developed usable floor space should be descending toward the centers, while taxes toward the fringes in automobile dependent areas should be rising (except for natural and agricultural land, which should pay no taxes in the city at all). Such taxing can work as powerfully as outright zoning change, and so can the restoration tax credits described earlier.

7. We need not only to develop foot, bicycle and public transportation, we need to put transportation into the land use context. Politicians and everyday citizens can use imaginative leadership and planning to allocate city, state and national funds to alternative modes of access, a practice that was started with the Intermodal Surface Transportation Efficiency Act. Building diversity at close proximity is the most effective route to the same end as efficient

transportation: access. Therefore we need Departments of Access and Transportation on the federal and state levels that could still deal with conventional transportation strategies, but emphasize providing access through ecological urban and architectural design.

8. End automobile subsidies. We can start with a steadily increasing gasoline tax and a tax on second cars, then add a tax on all cars, then higher taxes on all of them, and finally some way of charging drivers for the smog damage to crops (money to be transferred to farmers) and damage to people with lung cancer and emphysema (money to the victims) in proportion to the percentage of pollution car drivers contribute to the atmosphere. Insurance companies could pay these victims and pass the cost along in higher automobile insurance rates. As a pedestrian advocate in my neighborhood suggests, we could require drivers to pay pedestrians for time wasted at traffic lights — hours every month — by redistributing part of the car taxes as tax rebates to non-drivers. It takes only a sense of fairness and justice and the public will to act upon it.

9. We need to develop strong educational programs for the ecological rebuilding effort. No one should be abandoned in the transition. Retraining workers and retooling industry to produce and operate ecocities is the plan.

THE ECOCITY ORGANIZATION

The ecocity organization is a rather everyday type of association of people working together, chipping in dues, running fund raisers, doing mailings, hosting events, promoting what they feel improves life, and so on, but with an extraordinary mission. It's an organization designed specifically for exploring theory, experimenting, learning, teaching and building ecocities. I know of very few organizations that are explicitly just that: Ecocity Builders, Urban Ecology Australia, Urban Ecology China, Ecocity Cleveland and the Cosanti Foundation. If we included ecovillages, then the Global Ecovillage Network out of Denmark would also qualify.

There are many organizations that protect one aspect of the environment or another, and a fair number that provide expertise to community groups on energy conservation and recycling. There are professional associations like the Congress for the New Urbanism that have theories on urban design and work to promote their ideas tending in an ecocity direction while benefiting their architect and planner members. There are public transport and greenbelt advocates, bicycle clubs and bicycle-promoting organizations, anti-car organizations, "road ripping" and dam removing organizations, anti-oil industry groups, wilderness protectors and river and creek restorationists, community gardening associations, and permaculture groups whose design principles are essentially the same as ecocitology's. There are academic institutions like Jeff Kenworthy and Peter Newman's Institute for Science and Technology Policy at Murdoch University in Perth, Australia that study the structure and functioning of cities and advocate for pedestrians, bicycles and transit over automobile land use infrastructure. There are city governments like Vancouver's and Curitiba's that are writing and executing policy while building features that help them convert their cities in an ecocity direction. They run in-house ecocity organizations, such as the planning department of Vancouver and Curitiba's IPPUC.

But we need a clear, specific focus on basic principles — a scientific approach that may not yet be a popular preoccupation, but that simply looks for the truth about the relationship of the physical community to ecology and evolution. We also need to involve millions of people, and therefore we need organizations in every city. We need organizations that try to put all the pieces together. Rusong Wang, host of the Fifth International Ecocity Conference to be held in 2002 in Shenzhen, China, and president of Urban Ecology China has proposed an International Ecocity Society which would promulgate ecocities and consult on ecocity development around the world. To join in the real action in Vancouver or Curitiba, you'll have to be hired onto the government team. But you can also join one of the ecocity non-profits (usually called Non-Governmental Organizations, or NGOs) or start your own organization for similar purposes. With your supportive thought, work, time and money these organizations could do more than practically any other conceivable tool to transform our cities.

Arcology Circle, as it was turning into Urban Ecology around 1980, was probably the first real ecocity organization. It was not only exploring the theory and practice of the three-dimensional pedestrian city, but applying the ideas to existing cities. After all those years, all those miniscule budgets wrung from a few hardy and faithful souls and a small number of unusual foundations willing to take a risk on a new idea, it is evident that our work is a genuine struggle. Some people congratulate us on doing exactly what has to be done, but decline to join or help because we will do it anyway.

I've thought long and hard about why so few become involved in ecocity organizations and why most foundations decline to help us while telling us we are doing great pioneering work. Now I think I know the answer. We point the finger at ourselves, and only a few are strong enough to face that truth. It's one thing to blame distant corporations, globalization, the loggers and industrial farmers, the greedy shareholders, power-hungry executives and vote-grasping politicians. It's quite another thing to see that we may all have to change and, not only that, but build something that has never been before. The ecocity organization requires three rare things of its members: willingness to confront our complicity, a great deal of creative imagination, and hope in the face of depressing facts. A very small band of supporters from a diversity of perspectives is all we have had for more than twenty-five years. But the point of greatest resistance, in typical paradigm-shift theory, is also the place where we may well have the real breakthrough. Nobody said that this would be easy.

10
Toward Strategies for Success

Whatever strategies we are using to build our society aren't working very well. We need ones that work significantly better, strategies that can build ecologically-healthy cities that further creative and compassionate human evolution. I'll be talking about strategy in some detail here. First, though, partly by way of summary, some general guidance for people who want to change things:

1. Follow the builder's sequence, starting with the land use foundations of the city, then build up the details, the ecocity features, upon that foundation.
2. Pursue the four steps to an ecology of the economy — the ecocity zoning map, the list of technologies, businesses and jobs for building and maintaining the ecocity, the incentives, and the people to animate it and get it built.
3. Move steadily and as vigorously as possible away from sprawl and toward the pedestrian compact city. Add to the pedestrian compact city appropriate technology and biodiversity and you have the ecocity. Wherever people have been satisfied with small steps, failing to see them as early steps in a long journey, progress has soon been overwhelmed by cars and sprawl. If we start with one car-free building, we have to move on toward more of them. One

car-free street needs to beget another faster than car streets increase in number, length and area. Being proud of your city's one solar greenhouse, one block of opened creek, one park with a fruit tree, is being proud of going nowhere fast. Symbolism has its place, but mainstreaming ecologically-healthy functioning is what we need.

4. Take small steps as needed — planting fruit trees on the curbside, helping with thorough recycling, or collecting signatures on an open-space initiative — but move on to bigger things when you can: arranging work and home close together, giving up driving, becoming committed to an ecocity organization. You don't have to wait for enlightened regional government to have a profound effect. The Ecocity Zoning Map shows us that so much room has been set aside for cars that density shifts within the city can liberate hundreds of acres of land even in small cities. Just use the map to see where to open up the landscape and where to reposition the displaced uses.

5. Use whatever tools you feel comfortable with and no others. Make commitments you can keep and those only. People who overextend themselves for causes and community work often burn out and then quit, resentful because of their exhaustion and perceived lack of appreciation on the part of others. Substantial change is difficult to accomplish, and every individual is in an excellent position to see his or her own efforts and in a poor position to see the full efforts of others. Of course we all, from our limited perspective, know that we work harder than others recognize, so to avoid burnout it is important to pace ourselves. Many people volunteer to do more than they can deliver, and when they fall short they are sometimes so embarrassed that they never come back. Pace your promises as well as your efforts. We need you with us for the long haul.

6. Be flexible about changes. Take the time to consider the connections that make up a holistic view. Ecology is whole-systems thinking, and it's complex enough that understanding usually comes slowly. The passage of time gives us the opportunity to think about benefits and costs. If your house would be best removed for a creek restoration, look at the positive side of selling and moving

Colin Davis enjoys the banks of a daylighted creek in Berkeley. Previously this stretch of Codornices Creek was under a parking lot.

closer to a center and having your old environment become a wonderful place for wildlife to return and for children to learn. This effort to build ecologically-healthy cities is new. We are learning on the way. We will make mistakes — but not as many as we would if we were not making the effort. Therefore practice flexibility, forgiveness and perseverance — and expect improvement.

There are a number of actions that any of us can take, either alone or in a group. In the "alone" category are these: voting and spreading the word by talking with friends and acquaintances; learning more — using the bibliography here and in other books on related subjects to follow your interests, or using keywords on the worldwide web; conserving and recycling; avoiding toxics and buying, boycotting and investing accordingly; and helping restoration projects by dropping in on their activities.

In the "group" category are these: joining and supporting an ecocity-building organization; supporting good transit and delivery services (especially pedal power), proximity policies such as hiring and renting locally, ecocity design for conservation, recycling, building soils and building biodiversity and car-free buildings; recruiting people to participate in the above through education and direction; and moving to have the International Ecological Rebuilding Program adopted and implemented by governments or supporting such a move.

It's important to choose the level of commitment that best suits you. Know your starting level and work into a higher commitment level if it is in your nature. The first level is joining a group and learning more, volunteering in a modest way. The second level is making lifestyle changes to fit the pattern. The third level is becoming more deeply involved in major projects, perhaps helping to develop or use the tools for ecocity building described in this book. The fourth level is becoming professionally involved and an activist for ecocity policies and projects at the same time — as an architect, planner, builder, journalist or educator.

Though professionals are supposed to serve their clients (architects and carpenters serving developers and homeowners, for example) or elected officials (city planning and management staff members serving city councils) they influence outcomes by bringing professional insights to their employers. They can always remind everyone concerned of what they think is best for the community, and ecocity ideas and actions are good for the community and environment. If the compromise that would be required is just too much, professionals can in many cases refuse to take the job. That action is often dramatic and has real educational potential. The fifth level is working for an ecocity-building organization, lending your skills to helping it succeed, forming one with other people, or becoming a genuine ecocity developer gathering investment capital, hiring ecocity designers and building contractors, and actually creating important parts of the evolving ecocity.

BACK TO BASICS: STRATEGY FOR CURITIBA

When it comes to ecocity successes, it's hard to beat Jaime Lerner. Though his triumphs in Curitiba are many, two loom over all the others. First, by resolving the land use issues at the foundation of the physical city, he made possible the successes of transit and left room for the restoration of waterways, the expansion of public open space, tree planting and very efficient recycling. At the same time, he set up a system so efficient that money was saved to provide Curitiba's remarkable human services. He knew how to prioritize. He got the builder's sequence right. Second, he recognized that his fellow citizens were absolutely essential in achieving ecocity design goals, and he told them so. Step-by-step, from that basis up, he proved that various pieces of the ecocity worked well, and the citizens' trust grew.

Lerner didn't postpone anything. "The starting is very important. If you wait until you have all the answers," he said, "you will never start."[92] Thus he dispensed with excuses and launched into major changes for Curitiba almost the minute he became mayor. His administration quickly created institutional support for the new ideas and thus strengthened community ecocity memory. "Being enthusiastic is not enough," he said. "They [the people and especially the children] have to have knowledge."[93] And so his administration founded the Institute for Urban Research and Planning of Curitiba (IPPUC), and the Open University for the Environment. Lerner and all the imaginative people working with him got it right.

But as good as it gets in regard to ecocity-building, all is not well in Curitiba. In an interview at the Fourth International Ecocity Conference, Lerner began to hint that the time for a reevaluation was at hand. "You have to always have the way to combine, to propose a better offer, a better alternative. From time to time, you can lose two points in the game, but as soon as you realize this — and this is very important — always maintain a high quality of public transport, so the people use it in their normal itineraries." Then he seemed to equivocate somewhat. "I'm not against the car. I'm against using the car too much. That's the problem. You shouldn't need the car for normal itineraries."

Later he added, "You have to take risks, because you cannot have all the answers. But fortunately, planning is a process that you can always correct. So, that's why you don't have to wait. You don't have to be perfect first."[94] But the car is being used more and more by people there, even for "normal itineraries" as we learned dodging them to save our lives while visiting Curitiba for the Fourth International Ecocity Conference. Twenty-seven blocks of pedestrian streets and five major dedicated routes for busses, but much of the rest is another story. As our conference videographer Tim Alley, who had made a film on Curitiba just four years earlier, noted, re-visiting an Italian restaurant in Curitiba in April of 2000 was a shock. It had been in a quiet and very pleasant part of town, but in the intervening years the area had become clogged in nervous, fuming traffic. The conference convener, Clovis Ultramari, complained to me about the traffic, too.

What had happened, I think, is this: As the city's five high-density arms reached farther out into the countryside, diverging ever more from one another, the area of land between the arms grew much faster than the area of the arms themselves. In other words, at some point in the city's recent history the low-density, much more automobile-dependent development between those arms began growing proportionally faster. Furthermore, the twenty-seven blocks of pedestrian streets have grown slowly compared to the hundreds of blocks of streets for cars. Both the ratio of transit-oriented land use to car-oriented land use and the ratio of pedestrian-oriented land use to car-oriented land use had been declining.

At the same time, with the bus system working so well from the early 1970s through the early 1990s, the city prospered. Low-income people in particular could save money on low-cost transit, and when they could afford it, many started buying cars. Some of them moved to the low density areas, and others looked for high density housing with parking structures built in. Alfredo Vicente de Castro Trindade, the city's environmental planning manager, told me that the cars had suddenly appeared in one stunning month in 1994. "Hard though it is to believe, the Brazilian currency, the *real*, was re-evaluated, and suddenly people who were making three hundred dollars per month were making eight hundred dollars in purchasing power. So, naturally, after riding the bus for years, many people decided to buy cars.

"In one month car ownership went up here by an amazing 20 percent, and it has continued to go up since then." Most disturbing of all, three new automobile factories have been built in Curitiba in the past five years — Renault, Peugot and Chrysler. Volvo has been in town making both cars and busses for decades. Industrial planners in Curitiba are working with Amory Lovins on designs for manufacture of the energy-efficient "hyper" car that Lovins has been promoting. For Curitiba to make such a large commitment to cars is something like a health food company's going into tobacco in a big way. Why not bicycle and streetcar factories and equipment for solar power manufacturing rather than cars? Why not organic farming equipment and healthy fiber products, even everyday competitive electronic products rather than cars? "When you are talking about 5,000 good-paying jobs at a time," Trinidade responded, "a car factory can really help the economy."

Back to the basics again. If flat sprawl works with cars and linear higher-density corridors work well with transit, then three-dimensional high-density centers, if articulated with open space, work well for pedestrians. Transit is certainly better for the planet than cars, but it is still far more energy-consuming, polluting and pushy than people on foot. Well-designed pedestrian cities are by far the best way to go. Curitiba put most of its eggs in the transit-corridors basket; many of its highest-density centers and pedestrian streets were approached as a kind of beautiful civic flourish. Two apparent assumptions have been problematic in Curitiba: that cars really aren't too bad if you resist the temptation to use them overmuch, and that pedestrian centers are special in the sense of "rare" as well as special in the sense of "important."

Pedestrian centers are the solution and the beauty of conquering environmental problems. They should be valued so highly that they become common. Every city center, even every neighborhood center, should have a car-free area as soon as possible. Curitiba's great pedestrian streets and parks should be the model for most of that city's future development. In fact, whole, car-free cities are possible in infinite variety. It is truly bizarre that the planet has been capable of generating only one, but Venice proves that hundreds of them are possible, each with its own spectacular features, cozy recesses and "grand canals" in endless variety.

In my trips to Curitiba I fell in love with this picture: tall buildings — sometimes modern, sometimes colonial or Art Nouveau or almost baroque— rising up behind the big epiphyte-covered trees and palms of the parks, and, viewed from the Telecommunications Tower, a green and rolling landscape with craggy distant mountains capped with streaming clouds in the east. An idea for Curitiba in particular, but applicable elsewhere, came from that. Why not, along the transit corridors and just a block or two to one side, create centers that become new pedestrian town centers — encouraging taller buildings there and, rising up in their midst, elevated parks and plazas, say, five or ten stories in the air, with views between the buildings toward the coastal mountains or along one of the city's rivers? These would be keyhole plazas and parks lifted high into the views. They would seem to float in the sky, or give the impression of being on the top of hills. Underneath them would be warehousing and other uses that don't have much need of natural lighting. There are six stories of parking under the San Francisco park called Union Square. Union Square is a roof garden on top of a six-story building placed in a six-story hole in the ground. Take the same idea, raise it up and make it for warehousing something other than cars. Curitiba could do it.

As new streets are built like ramps between buildings, leading "uphill" to the new parks, storefronts that used to be at street level will be lit by skylights and artificial light under the level of new sloping pedestrian streets. At the same time, valuable new commercial window space and floor space will be created on the second, third and fourth floors as the street rises toward the park. The new sloping street might be partially a staircase, something like the Spanish Steps in Rome, with landings and terraces at the edges of buildings defining a new set of vital areas in front of doors and display windows. Essentially we would be trading valuable ground-level store fronts for new ones on the sloping street. There would also be new space in the taller new buildings, much of it enhanced in value by the busy pedestrian street with its sculpted terraces and the elevated park with its great views.

In this context, transfers of development rights could function three-dimensionally: trade outward and upward from the darker zones to the new sunny spaces in the sloping canyons and around the rooftop parks. These could be called "3-D TDRs." The total development value of the new "hill" with park and taller buildings would be extraordinary, and would make possible not just the storage space at arm's reach, but high-density pedestrian environments and the newly created public parks and plazas. Teamed with more conventional Double TDRs, natural and agricultural lands could be restored by the new, more dense building and in sufficient quantity to actually make a dent on sprawl. As Jaime Lerner says, "Fortunately, planning is a process that you can always correct." Given Curitiba's capability for ecological imagination and leadership, it might be among the first cities to begin removing large areas of low-density development, not to build just a few pedestrian centers, but to move a whole city toward pedestrian/ecological design.

I suggested to Maria di Rocio Quandt, information officer for IPPUC, that Curitiba might want to create high-density pedestrian areas with elevated public parks in a few centers. In fact, she reported, IPPUC was beginning to explore expanding some of the community centers on the transit corridors called "Citizen Streets" into higher-density, real town centers in a similar way, though they were not planning strictly pedestrian zones as part of them. Elevating parks and plazas for views would be a new idea for their tool box. Curitiba and other cities should consider a strategy that says, "We will build pedestrian infrastructure at a proportionally faster rate than we build for the car." Then see what happens. Paradise, I predict.

Additional pedestrian streets could be located largely around new public squares and involve not just the squares, but a block or two surrounding them in new centers. This would not be too disruptive of the automobile infrastructure being steadily replaced. Add in a closed street or two at an old square every so often, and requiring the designers of new developments everywhere to provide 50 percent more pedestrian blocks than automobile blocks, and encouraging innovation in the third dimension would produce some very imaginative solutions.

If, for example, the city's leaders decided to reduce the number of new car streets added per year, with the same gradual increase in population new development would become more vertical. And if development rights were transferred, money would be generated for open space restoration where existing roads had been overbuilt, also shifting the pedestrian street-to-car street ratio in the right direction. What if new development were so vertical that rooftop pedestrian streets bridging over ground level streets from block to block were created to help meet the quotas? What if population stabilized as it has in most European countries? In Brazil the rural areas have been largely emptied of small farmers, and so we can imagine a gradual population shift back toward the country and toward complex organic farming centered on ecovillages and ecotowns taking pressure off the cities. Meanwhile, a shifting toward a situation of growing predominance of the pedestrian would steadily and, perhaps, fairly rapidly move toward solving the problem of car glut. This pattern could take Curitiba to its next level of ecocity leadership, from the primarily transit city featuring a good complement of pedestrian areas to the primarily pedestrian city with assistance from transit — and this just as it was sliding off into automobile dependence.

Another piece of a strategy for Curitiba would be to identify some small neighborhood centers as satellites of the larger Citizen Street centers. These smaller centers would be between the five, high-density arms of the city and agricultural ecovillages would be located there. Double TDRs could reinforce those centers through staged removal of automobile-dependent development around them and between the five transit corridor arms. These new pedestrian ecovillages would be focal places for another kind of new pedestrian environment structurally very similar to the traditional village.

The new Citizen Street centers could become places for commercial pedestrian projects similar to those of the architect John Jerde. Canal City in Hakata, Japan, created around an artificial branch of a natural local waterway, is the largest private construction project in Japanese history. Jerde's gargantuan, enclosed Mall of America in Minneapolis, Minnesota, with its 1.2 miles of skylights and 4.5 miles of looping walkway through the interior, might at first glance be puzzling in a book on ecocities — consider the parking lot! But a look at what's going on there suggests profound ecological possibilities. These projects are intensely pedestrian and very three-dimensional. That they are unabashedly, aggressively commercial makes them not so different from the central city markets throughout history. The Grand Bazaar in Istanbul is a spectacular ancient version, if only on a single level. Such markets have been, and still are, vital economic and social foundations for cities, crass though they may seem to those of refined aristocratic or escapist environmentalist tastes. They work.

Where they require a geological-scale parking desert to function, giant pedestrian malls like Jerde's Fashion Island in Newport Beach, California, constitute a contradiction and, in fact, an assault on nature. But where, as in his Horton Plaza in San Diego, California, they are part of the urban fabric and enhance the diversity of human life in a center, they are part of the wave of healthy possible futures. Tens of thousands of people live close enough to walk, bike or bus to Horton Plaza, with its pleasurable environment of pedestrian streets and multilevel structures with many bridges creating the kind of adult jungle gym I've mentioned in these pages. Much of Jerde's work can serve as precedent and idea source for three-dimensional pedestrian areas at all population levels, and as a kind of node of DNA in the living protoplasm of the city, containing enough "genetic" information to precipitate change throughout the whole city and in its progeny cities into the future. There is powerful urban change potential here.

Jon Jerde says that he was profoundly influenced by Paolo Soleri. Jerde arrived at Soleri's workshop in Paradise Valley in 1959 and was amazed by his drawings. He asked if he might stay a couple of days and, he says, "ended up sleeping under Paolo's drafting table for three nights, poring over his drawings and notebooks until 2:00 AM." Until very recently, however, he was designing a crucial component of the basic, three-dimensional structure Soleri had proposed as an arcology while letting the existing urban infrastructure take care of access to it. Now he's thinking through ways he might be able to connect his work with Soleri's.

If Curitiba is not too lost in the recent, automobile-induced trance that its transit-assisted prosperity has helped produce, it could be a prime candidate for Jerde-type commercial centers finessed toward the biodiverse and the technologically "appropriate." Such centers could be integrally connected to the Citizen Street core areas, or the central business district itself could be reshaped with three-dimensionality that creates taller buildings and elevated parks. Underground space there would provide commercial and private storage for businesses and residents in the downtown. Jerde's bridges could link many old and new buildings alike. Mid-block passageways already exist in considerable number in Curitiba. There could be more.

Ken Yeang of Kuala Lumpur, Malaysia, has recently been designing "bioclimatic" skyscrapers — typically, towers with movable windscreens and sunshades, some of which circulate around the outside of the tower on fixed tracks, regulated according to daily conditions, to let in or keep out breezes and sunshine. One of his smaller buildings — three-stories high — is shaded under a hovering sunscreen that looks something like a pair of pointed pillows tethered by steel cables between the ground and high tech crane towers. These things cast cool shadows in a hot climate, letting the breezes slide on pleasantly through, saving the building enormous sums in air conditioning. When I met Paolo Soleri in 1965, he spoke about urban "garments," and introduced me to a micro version immediately. Stretched over his semi-outdoor drawing table was a modest canvas awning on poles, perhaps twenty feet long. Maybe Jerde slept there.

In that sweltering climate Soleri would occasionally take a hot hose from under the Arizona sun and sprinkle the canvas awning over his drafting table, the water getting cooler as it snaked out from underground and sprinkled over the cloth. The evaporation and shade cooled the drafting room, the moist canvas giving off a pleasant fresh air. On a larger scale, marketplaces around the hot regions of the world shade the stands and stalls, vegetables, fish, customers and dusty traders under canvases similar to Soleri's. Ken Yeang blows them up to shade whole buildings. For cities, I advocate this idea writ large: billowing horizontal clouds of cloth over whole sections of cities in the hottest climates, with thin steel cables and towers carrying them up into the daytime skies and electric winches reeling them in when the sun settles near the horizon. The cloth could be tapered in thickness, reinforced toward the edges of higher stress or cut into checkerboard or strip patterns to let dappled shade and sunshine fall into the activity below. I've always marveled at the great billows of dark netting at construction sites draped over scaffolding ten, twenty, fifty stories high to catch falling construction debris. Federico Fellini celebrated the windy billowing and rippling of large cloth shrouds in the movie *8½*.

It may seem excessive, expensive, experimental to a fault to suggest creating such immense city garments, but they could save copious amounts of energy, producing comfortable environments and at a cost that would be nothing compared with that of a new freeway interchange. In what way, in fact, are innovations such as urban garments and in-city basement warehousing, large-building solar greenhouses and publicly accessible high places "impractical"? A few thousand years ago our grandparents a few dozen times removed were rowing big ships through the Mediterranean, or up and down the Tigris and Euphrates. Then someone had the idea of catching the wind by lashing cloth into giant sheets, and a whole new age of utility and exploration erupted into reality. Maybe it was a woman who, hanging out the laundry one day, said to her husband, the captain who directed the drum beat for the rowing crew, that if the clothesline pole were made bigger and attached to the boat and a big piece of cloth provided, the rowers could take it easy for a while and practice for their next war or read some cuneiform. Who knows? But at that point, raising fabric to the gods of the wind created a new world. Moreover, given its absolutely incredible historic leverage, such creative innovation is the cheapest investment on this planet.

Yeang's buildings are situated in hot climates. I'm not aware of what he might do in terms of capturing and storing heat in cooler climes, but similar thinking with regard to taller buildings in these areas could be promising, too. This is the "climatic" part of his architecture. The "bio" features of his skyscrapers include continuous gardens circulating around and up the building from one terrace to another, and "skycourts" cut into the twenty-, thirty- or forty-story structures. The continuous ascending terraces are like three-dimensional nature corridors, with insects and lizards, birds and tree frogs. The skycourts become small neighborhood parks of a sort, but at the edge you might look up or down at ten or thirty more stories of building, and then to the sky or the ground. They are like the celestial garden terraces in the Andes, *a la* Machu Picchu, but carved into modern buildings. These vertical greenbelts and parks work in concert with the climate-tempering structures to help refresh and cool the air and support the biology and appropriate technology. All these become integral to one another.

In Curitiba or other cities willing and able to experiment with larger projects, Jerde's commercial centers and new clusters of buildings and open spaces could use Yeang's ideas to temper the extremes of climate. Yeang says that his buildings are more expensive to build in the first place, but consume far less energy, and in a few years are far less expensive overall, with both construction and maintenance calculated. My suspicion is that covering public spaces with canvas awnings would save enormous energy and financial investment. If the strategy were used to block unpleasant winds between buildings with transparent movable wind screens operated by the municipality as cities currently maintain streets, this, too, would create pleasant environments while saving energy. In the pedestrian city of the future, moveable devices for moderating temperatures would probably run on less energy than the street signal lights required in a car city of the same population, saving the city millions of dollars.

Pulling these elements together from Curitiba's land uses and the refinements of architects like Jerde and Yeang is a complex undertaking, to say the least. But is it very much more complex than cities already are? Or is it any larger an investment than much of the infrastructure we are already used to, such as freeways, automobile factories, petroleum cracking plants, subway systems, and the like? Even today's large buildings are formidably complex, with their elevator systems, grand lobbies, machinery for climate maintenance and electronic hook ups. Would it be that much more difficult to include ecological design?

Talking about Curitiba is not talking about a typical city growing out into rural territory, but since the strategy of the Curitiba planners is off to a successful start, we can outline what they've done there and add suggestions based on ecocity principles. This could give us an overall strategy that might make good sense. We can describe this strategy in terms of the Four Steps to an Ecology of the Economy: map, list, incentives, people.

Curitiba started with the layout of the city ecologically considered — the map. it was not so much pedestrian-centers-oriented as transit-arms-oriented, however, and to progress from where Curitiba is now its planners need to find centers on the high-density arms and focus yet more density and diversity there while creating progressively more pedestrian areas in these centers and the downtown city center. We don't have to talk Curitiba into using TDRs. They adapted the idea from their American sister city, Orlando, Florida, in the mid-1990s. Following this pattern the arms could eventually break into semi-separate pedestrian neighborhoods linked to the downtown and other centers by transit and bicycles. Transformations in this direction are likely to lead to a healthier city to the degree to which the whole city moves toward pedestrian infrastructure and independence from cars.

Probably one of the best incremental approaches would be to start with car-free apartment buildings and one or two car-free streets, and then promote a little natural restoration and the more complex mixed-use buildings with appropriate technology for the centers. Curitiba was strong on the mapping and step four, people, but weak on step two, the list. The planners tended to encourage whatever industry seemed available for financial prosperity, including even the manufacture of automobiles. This may change, but it will probably be a long time before that problem can be corrected, that is, until the car factories are replaced with factories for ecocity products and services. Along with that change, incentives will have to be coordinated, too.

STRATEGY FOR BUILT-OUT CITIES

Ideas for Curitiba apply well to any growing city in an open area, but a similar arrangement of pedestrian land uses and infrastructure can be created for an existing "built-out" town by transferring density within the city limits. In both cases the strategy for creating an ecocity is a steady and methodical moving away from automobile and toward human infrastructure — and also away from "auto" as in "mechanical," and "reactive," and toward the reasoning and intuitive capacities of the human mind.

The "built-out" city, hemmed in by other cities, greenbelts or unfillable waters, is typical in our large metropolitan areas these days, but if it is built-out, it is very seldom "built-up," arranged on the principle of access by proximity. It lacks, as Michael David Lipkan called it, "proximity power." Instead it utilizes gasoline power.

Dealing with the built-out city, in fact, is the real action for ecocities. First, if cities are sprawled out two-dimensionally, shrinking back to smaller footprints is called for immediately. In fact, because we have spent a hundred years building cities for cars, the vast majority of cities are built-out in the most important sense of the term. Second, we are in an overpopulated world, and cities shouldn't expand in population unless there is even more influx from the countryside and the villages. Third, if organic agriculture, permaculture and intensely-managed, ecologically-informed farming of any style make sense, then the population shift should be generally away from further urbanization, or at least largely toward the building of towns and villages associated with this sort of agriculture, along with forest management, eco-tourism and study.

One approach, as we have seen in the case of Curitiba, is to start anywhere you can in a particular city with car-free streets and systematically expand from there, building pedestrian infrastructure more quickly than auto infrastructure. If your town can go directly to a car-free street or district, you need not wait for the car-free apartments or condos. A building with an interior garage can be remodeled to replace the garage with better uses as units shift out of the typical lease agreement and over to a car-free agreement, thus making more housing or a wider variety of services available to the residents of the area. In Berkeley, unfortunately, as we have seen, the city council majority rejected car-free housing, and its excuses for doing so are typical in some ways, unique in others. Politicians perceived their constituents were not well acquainted with ecocity planning ideas and information, and they lacked the energy or courage to assume responsibility for educating the public on the subject. We hope to change this situation and are working on new car-free-building initiatives. But it all takes time and patience, and time is running out for the biosphere.

The Berkeley developer Patrick Kennedy has had a similar experience. Kennedy has built four residential buildings, each with shops at street level, in downtown Berkeley. Neighborhood activists and architectural conservatives have opposed him, arguing for low height limits, and he has countered by rounding up and bringing to hearings all the low-income, disabled, minority people and environmentalists that he has benefited so that he can win his next approval and build his next building. He was amenable to including ecological design features in what he called the Gaia Building, and adopted several from Ecocity Builders. I sketched out solar-oriented terracing with rooftop gardens and trellises and he incorporated them into his design. Then the city's zoning adjustments board and design review committee simply took the model of the building off its base and reversed it one hundred and eighty degrees so that there would be slightly less shade on the street to the north. They had no interest at all in solar energy for the building, rooftop biodiversity and views to the bioregion. They also cut the top floor off, reducing the building's esthetic value and its housing potential, despite the fact that the city's most active regional rail station was only half a block away. This was exactly the place where it made the most sense in Berkeley to build considerable housing. Nevertheless, the Gaia Building was completed, and instantly historic — the first building in the city to bring life up to its terrace and rooftop in the form of trees, gardens, trumpetvines on trellises and people enjoying tremendous views of the Bay Area.

Once people buy into a neighborhood, they generally want to keep it as it is or gradually improve its financial and aesthetic value. Housing and work space for others who need it should be put somewhere else, they argue, not in my back yard — the NIMBY syndrome. In most cities this freezes a low-density pattern that causes further low-density development on the fringe, fueling sprawl development. In Berkeley this attitude also extends into the town centers as a kind of low-density doctrine of aesthetics. Some people who live so far from downtown that they can't see it and seldom even visit it use their political clout to keep people out of the city. They vigorously oppose taller buildings of any design or any purpose. They sometimes bolster their moral position by saying the world is overpopulated and we shouldn't encourage that situation here. Their exclusionary policies are softened by rent control, which has worked fairly well in the short term to keep rents low, but has worked even better at freezing housing construction and keeping people out, and, in the long run, driving prices up dramatically and ultimately contradicting rent control.

Because those favoring a low-density Berkeley have been so successful, there is an enormous imbalance between housing and jobs. From 1970 to 2000, the citywide population dropped almost 14,000, from 116,532 to 102,743. Meanwhile, fueling an enormous imbalance of land uses and all the commuting, street-clogging, energy waste and pollution that goes with it, the city created space for approximate 19,000 new jobs.[95] In one period of fifteen years the city lost 10,000 people and gained 10,000 cars. But, of course, a smaller number of richer people were replacing a larger number of poorer people as housing prices escalated.

I'm not sure how to get around this situation other than identifying it for what it is and continuing to put out positive alternatives. We can hope that the public will think a little more deeply. Everyone is slowly beginning to learn something. At some point we should cross the political threshold and finally get majority support for ecocities.

The Heart of the City Project

For twenty-five years I worked with others of similar mind trying to transform a city into an ecocity, adding one project to another and supporting everything that might help. I didn't have a real system or an awareness that a particular sequence of efforts might further the cause. I had no real strategy and never confronted serious land use changes at the foundation, mostly because I never conceived projects at a scale where the need for them was clearly evident. By 1997 I began to face the fact that very little was adding up. I was beginning to comprehend the larger forces working against ecocity efforts locally and, it seemed, almost everywhere else. I also noticed that there wasn't much coherence in the details we ecocity advocates were trying to weave together in our various projects. The ecocity features weren't together physically, so putting them together in the mind was a stretch. If we could literally put them together and meaningfully connect them in one place, a special place visited by many people — if they collectively looked like an ecocity — we might finally be able to communicate about the whole integral pattern of parts.

We had very particular ideas in mind for the city of Berkeley. Ecocity Builders proposed to restore Strawberry Creek downtown, create a public plaza and pedestrian street or two, and add considerable new housing there, right next to the main transit station, in a set of taller-than-usual buildings with ecocity features. If, in addition, these ecocity features were conspicuously linked together with busy footbridges, if they were spectacular in their regalia of solar greenhouse glass, covered with people on the rooftops under colorful umbrellas, and obviously a celebration of nature, then maybe people would begin to grasp the ecocity concept. In fact, it would be hard not to notice it, not to be intrigued and inspired by it. It would be profitable for local businesses, a destination for tourists curious about the future, and something to photograph to show to friends back home and buy postcards of to send around the world. It would be a "postcard breakthrough." With a single glance at an image as small as a postcard, the observer would say, "Ah-hah! So this is what ecocities are all about!" It would be a downtown integral neighborhood, a big one, with nature and regional transit. Like a strand of DNA it could replicate mixed-use, bio-rich, urban tissue throughout the anatomy of the city and spawn ecocity projects elsewhere by example.

Most cities have quite a few functions already established in their downtowns: jobs, housing, shops, transit, entertainment, food. Typically, though, as in Berkeley, housing is very limited, and ecological architectural features are non-existent. If you simply supply the missing pieces, however, presto! You have what might be called a "Heart of the City" project. Downtown Berkeley is the perfect place for this. The transit station is located on the corner of Shattuck Avenue and Center Street just a block from the University of California campus. Eight thousand people walk here every school day from the station to campus and back. Thousands of other people see this corner as the center of town. Along this route to campus there is a one-story Bank of America building that would look completely at home in suburbia. There's a parking lot for the bank and next to that a printing press building owned by the university, displaying a blank wall to passing pedestrians. The university, the bank and the city of Berkeley all seem to see this urban design problem as a bit of an embarrassment.

We suggested building housing, opening the creek, creating a public

Rooftop cafe with views of nature and city life in a proposed Heart of the City Project.

plaza and pedestrian street, connecting buildings with bridges, putting in public rooftop cafes and gardens, and firing up the project with the power of the sun in solar greenhouses cascading down from the heights to the lower floors. Others found the idea intriguing, and forty small businesses and nonprofit organizations joined a coalition to explore the idea further. We arranged for half a dozen architects to contribute drawings of possible variations on the theme. We also organized a conference with speakers from six countries focused on city center plazas and works of water restoration and celebration.

Realizing that we were facing height limits too low to allow a Heart of the City Project with relevance for an urban future, we began working on amending the Berkeley General Plan to allow taller buildings, if they included ecocity features and helped finance the opening of creeks and the expansion of community gardens and public parks. Years earlier we had begun to think that we needed major land use changes to accommodate creek restoration in the city. Now we realized from another angle how important modification of the city's land use ordinances would be if we were to be able to create ecologically-healthy rearrangements of the city. We simply had to change zoning for our Heart of the City Project to be possible.

We knew that the General Plan needed to provide means to remove development from areas farthest from the transit centers and shift density toward those centers. The Heart of the City Project area should, then, be a place where more density should be built, while buildings in car-dependent areas should be removed. It was natural to imagine Heart of the City projects as receiving sites for Double TDRs, and so we developed language specifically calling for ecological demonstration projects, and recommended that the land use element of the General Plan include a policy encouraging the use of the TDRs.

Sometime in 1999, Harrison Fraker, who had moved from St. Paul and his involvement in the Phalen Village project to Berkeley to become Dean of Environmental Design at the University of California, suggested that our project was lacking something. What he had in mind was liberating the buried Strawberry Creek from downtown all the way to San Francisco Bay and building a bicycling, walking and jogging path nearby that would connect with the San Francisco Bay Trail. This Strawberry Creek Greenway could also connect with an existing greenway named after the local Ohlone Indians that comes partially into town from the north, and could be extended to Strawberry Creek and on to Oakland to the south. An excellent idea. A heart needs a vascular system and here it was, both water- and human-powered, linking the heart of the city to the whole region.

In terms of strategy, this begins to look like a reasonable outline:

1. Find your centers and create Heart of the City Projects by filling in the missing pieces.
2. Create a "vascular system" of bicycle and foot paths, as well as transit, from that heart to the other nearby major centers and to the most appreciated natural features in your area.
3. Now, looking at the whole living system, make an ecocity zoning map to help put in order and connect the functions of all of the rest of the city, much of it properly returned to agriculture and nature.

The second part of this ecocity strategy would be utilization of such tools for transfer of density and financing of the shift as Double TDRs.

Should local governments be opposed to restoring waterways and opening up agricultural landscapes in areas dependent on cars, then state governments concerned about the collective detriment of car cities and the positive benefits of ecological cities could pass TDR legislation that would read something like this: "Any person owning improved property within fifty feet of the historic centerline of a buried or open creek may sell the development rights of his or her property to a developer for demolition of improvements and restoration of open space on the sending site, and for transfer of those rights to any site within three blocks of a regional rail transit station or intersection of four or more bus lines."

City governments could buy up properties and sell the development rights to developers for this purpose themselves, creating a publicly managed revolving fund or TDR bank for more such projects. Nonprofits could also buy up such land and sell the development rights, thus creating their own revolving funds for restoring land and waters, or they could become developers of ecological projects themselves. Ecocity Builders is looking into setting up an Ecocity Conservancy Trust for exactly this purpose. If all goes well, we will collect contributions from people, foundations, businesses and government programs to buy houses along the Strawberry Creek culvert, demolish the buildings and carefully recycle the building materials, open up the creek and either manage the property or donate it to the city to manage. When we sell the development rights to a developer, we will be ready to use our revolving fund all over again, buy more land, remove more buildings, and thus consolidate the land for opening the waters.

The same trust can be used to expand community gardens and parks. Similarly, when houses in poor condition come up for sale in car-dependent areas, they could be bought and demolished, leaving an empty space between two other houses. The land itself could be sold to one or both of the neighbors, donated to the city as a mini-park or community garden, or retained by the Ecocity Conservancy Trust. Open spaces between houses are not what we are used to, but they could become beautiful places in the neighborhood, a source of food, education, camaraderie or simply visual rest. And the cars that used to park in the driveway there and on the street would be gone. The neighborhood would be quieter by two to six people, while in a transit center two to six times as many people would be provided with housing at walkable distances to practically anything

279

urban people might want. These open spaces could expand with time, becoming new parks and agricultural areas and eventually joining up with creek and ridge line restorations, profoundly reshaping the city into a healthy urban anatomy.

All the tools you have read about here, all the projects, can come into play once a city decides it wants to pursue ecocity building. Basically this is what happened in Curitiba, though a number of the tools offered in this book would be new to that city, too. For the strategy to work, we will need to reverse the transportation hierarchy that we currently see in cities to place pedestrians first, and we will need to build the kind of interlinked buildings and public spaces and natural features that become the built expression of the principle of access by proximity. Environmentalists, who already know why, and developers, who know how to build and have a good idea why with regard to the services their buildings provide, can and must be allies in this effort.

Another strategy would be the International Ecological Rebuilding Program suggested earlier, the ecocity-building equivalent of Al Gore's Global Marshall Plan. Yet another approach would be to challenge a government or large corporation to build experimental ecocities. China, for example, having no fear of density, a very centralized government and large capitalist corporations, might like to build three experimental cities of 100,000 people each — large enough to really teach us about the basic form and function of particular urban arrangements. These would have to be located in rural areas, but on convenient rail routes to other cities, to function well within the present larger economy. One city would be strictly for pedestrians only, very dense and rigorously respecting local bioregional conditions, designed for solar access and technology, organic farming, and so on. No cars, no transit, not even bicycles. The second city would be for pedestrians and bicycles. No cars or transit. The third city would be for pedestrians served by both bicycles and transit, but no cars.

Thinking about how to build these three experimental cities and then following through would be an important and useful exercise. Since cities are whole, living systems, creations of integral organs or parts, strategies starting from any one part of the whole, if cognizant of the dynamics of the whole, could work equally well. This is good news, because it means that we are all, with our different perspectives, talents and training, in a position to be effective in the ecocity building enterprise.

BUILDING A CULTURE OF ACCEPTANCE

Jaime Lerner knew that Curitiba needed a culture of acceptance for the ecocity and he went about creating it. When he put on the uniform of the garbage collector and thus redefined the job as recycler, he became an ordinary citizen engaged in building the ecocity. Everywhere in the world the culture of acceptance will grow as demonstration projects increase in number, as one incentive after another is passed into law, and as education gets through to ever more people. Good examples and policies will build up and capture the imagination. At some point the imagination of whole cities will kick into gear. We'll get over the threshold of sufficient votes to pass important policies and launch projects, and the latent energy of the whole community will release a cascade of creativity.

To build this culture of acceptance, the strategies I advocate will have to meet more conventional "better ideas" halfway. Thus we can admire and emulate the cities building metropolitan light rail and regional, medium-weight rail systems around the world, the European cities creating and expanding car-free areas in their ancient cores, the bicycle-promoting cities of Europe and the developers of traffic calming streets. When cities calmly reject the next big parking structure, we should celebrate. These decisions should get national urban design prizes until they are so common the local papers don't notice them any more. The New Urbanists take pains to conventionalize their transit villages and even write model ordinances and codes to make their replication faster, the approach even more conventional. And as more and more creek restoration projects, greenbelt laws and slow-growth initiatives pass, as more natural areas are preserved, we should be happy about it but keep on working until these things are much more common than they are today.

One would hope that the really fundamental experiments like Arcosanti and the ecovillages around the world would become common, too. The same could be said for solar and wind energy technology, "green" architecture, recycling, non-toxic cleaning products, and for regulations to achieve those ends — fines for polluting, higher car registration and gasoline taxes, and the like. But as we support we can't let our guard down. A billion Chinese are craving cars and almost as many Indians, and Americans want their cars bigger than ever. This is why it is so important to embrace not only the "conventional" improvements, but the truly basic changes potential in the use of the tools in these pages, from the land use foundation up, from the ecocity zoning map to the rooftop garden cafe. This is why I'm proposing that we acknowledge that we need strategies to reorganize our thoughts, roll back sprawl and reorganize the city and the whole civilization it supports.

ART AND IMAGINATION

Can we create afresh our natural and built environments, even ourselves, as we look out onto a hopeful future? Can we, with the strength of our conscience hitched to our reason, make peace between ourselves and our world, pounding the swords of the city on the attack into the plowshares of the city building soils and biodiversity? Can we learn to live that way, into a future of ecological health and human creativity and compassion? If we can, we will inevitably build the ecocity. Our home, our garden, our wildness and nature's wilderness will all spring into full bloom. The ecocity itself will not be Venice or Curitiba, Shaban or a New Mexico pueblo. Those precursors are valuable lighthouses to the future, but some new permutation is anchored in a sense of our own times and the needs of a profoundly different future.

Building ecocities will be a new version of the ancient art of city building in which we are, collectively, the artist. Each ecocity will be different. The art of city building and the art of living will be combined in this effort, and like all arts, this will be a struggle that promises pain and pleasure, failure and undreamed-of reward. Everything depends on our selection of the field of action, the choice as to what game board we are going to construct, what stage for our performance, which physical community we build. Are we going to continue dismembering our communities and scattering them to the winds? Are we going to continue to pretend that nature is primarily a repository of exploitable resources with no inherent value or rights of its own? Or are we going to set out to make of ourselves and our creations a reflection of our best inner selves, and a celebration of the Earth by whose graces we live?

We have barely begun the ecocity experiment, but concerned citizens can create little pieces of it immediately, giving us all insights into life on the other side of that Ecozoic divide, and perhaps inspiring us to shift to a healthy way of living. Ultimately we might just build environments that will keep the artist alive in all of us so that we can all live in conscious, co-creative coevolution with each other, nature and our homes. There is no easy way, no sure way, and each solution will also cause new problems, but there is magic down the path that we have yet to choose, that we have every opportunity to create, the path through ecocities.

Notes

1 Philip Shabekoff, *Earth Rising: American Environmentalism in the 21st Century*, Washington DC: Island Press, 2000. p.178.

2 Thomas Berry, "The Ecozoic Age," a lecture delivered to the E.F. Schumacher Society, 1991.

3 Paul and Anne Ehrlich, *Healing the Planet*, Menlo Park: Addison-Wesley Publishing Company, 1991.

4 Kenneth Schneider, *On the Nature of Cities*, San Francisco: Jossey-Bass Publishers, 1979.

5 Bernard Rudofsky, *Architecture Without Architects*, Albuquerque: University of New Mexico Press, 1987.

6 Vakhtang Davitaia, From his presentation at the INTERARCH Conference, Sofia, Bulgaria, 1992.

7 Thomas Berry, "The Ecozoic Era," lecture before the E.F. Schumacher Society, Great Barrington, MA, Oct. 19, 1991.

8 Brian Swimme and Thomas Berry, *The Universe Story*, San Francisco: Harper San Francisco, 1992

9 Paolo Soleri, *Arcology: The City in the Image of Man*, Boston: MIT Press, 1969, p. 31.

10 David Quammen, *The Song of the Dodo*, New York: Simon and Schuster/Touchstone, 1999.

11 Ibid., p.117.

12 Mathis Mackernagle and William Rees, *Our Ecological Footprint*, Gabriola Island, British Columbia: New Society Publishers, 1998.

13 Peter Newman and Jeff Kenworthy, *Sustainability and Cities: Overcoming Automobile Dependence*, Washington DC: Island Press, 1998.

14 James Miller, *Living Systems*, New York: McGraw Hill, 1978, p.162, 191. I thank Fritjof Capra for calling Miller's book to my atttention.

15 Ian McHarg, *Design with Nature*, Garden City: Doubleday/Natural History Press, 1969, p. 5.

16 Malcolm Margolin, *Earth Manual: Working Wild Land Without Taming It*, Berkeley: Heyday Books, 1975.

17 Kirkpatrick Sale, *The Conquest of Paradise*, New York: Knopf, 1990; David E. Stannard, *American Holocaust: Columbus and the Conquest of the New World*, New York: Oxford University Press, 1992.

18 Sale, *The Conquest of Paradise*, pp 75, 76.

19 Sale, ibid. p. 85.
20 Sale, ibid. p. 85
21 Stannard, *American Holocaust,* p. 18.
22 Ibid.
23 Ibid.
24 Ibid., p 25.
25 Vernon Masayesva, "Conference Report, The First International Ecological City Conference," Christopher Canfield, ed., Berkeley: Urban Ecology, p. 28.
26 Jane Jacobs, *Cities and the Wealth of Nations,* New York: Vintage Books, 1984, p. 29.
27 Lewis Mumford, *The City in History,* New York: Harcourt, Brace and World, 1961, p. 35.
28 Jane Jacobs, *Cities and the Wealth of Nations,* p.42.
29 Lewis Mumford, *The City in History,* p. 7.
30 Jonathan Rabin, *Bad Land: An American Romance,* New York: Pantheon, 1996. p. 60.
31 Deborah Epstein Popper and Frank J. Popper, "The Great Plains: From Dust to Dust," Planning Magazine, December 1987, p. 572.
32 Deborah Epstein Popper and Frank J. Popper, "The Great Plains: From Dust to Dust," *Planning* Magazine, December 1987, p. 572.
33 Deborah and Frank Popper, "Can We Reinvent the Frontier?", *This World* Magazine, November 3, 1991, *San Francicso Chronicle/Examiner.* p. 16.
34 John Reader, *The Rise of Life,* New York: Alfred A. Knopf, 1986, p. 18.
35 Brian Swimme and Thomas Berry, *The Universe Story,* San Francisco: Harper Collins, 1992, p. 175.
36 Lewis Mumford, *The City in History,* p. 106.
37 Lewis Mumford, ibid., p. 28.
38 Lewis Mumford, ibid., p. 19.
39 Jules Henry, *Culture Against Man,* New York: Random House, 1963.
40 Sybl Moholy-Nagy, *Matrix of Man:* An Illustrated History of Urban Environment, New York: Praeger, 1969, p. 41.
41 Riane Eisler, *The Chalice and the Blade,* Cambridge: Harper and Row, 1987. p. 34.
42 Eisler, ibid.
43 Christopher Tunnard and Henry Hope Reed, *American Skyline: The Growth and Form of Our Cities and Towns,* New York: New American Library, 1953, p. 122. Many of the facts in this section are gathered from this source and Mumford, *The City in History.*
44 Tunnard and Reed, *American Skyline,* p. 125
45 Jonathan Kwitny, "The Great Transportation Conspiracy: How Big Business Destroyed Mass Transit," *Harper's* Magazine, February, 1981.
46 Kirkpatrick Sale, *The Conquest of Paradise,* New York: Knopf, 1990, p.79.
47 Kenneth Schneider, *On the Nature of Cities,* San Francisco: Jossey-Bass, 1979, p. 255.

48   Ebenezar Howard, *Garden Cities of Tomorrow*, ed. F. J. Osborn, London: Faber and Faber, 1951 (1902).

49   Lewis Mumford, *The City in History*, p. 522

50   Council on Environmental Quality, Department of Housing and Urban Development, Environmental Protection Agency, *The Cost of Sprawl*, Washington, DC: U. S. Government Printing Office, 1974.

51   E. F. Schumacher, *Small is Beautiful: Economics As If People Mattered*, London: Blond and Briggs, 1973.

52   Thomas Kuhn, *The Structure of Scientific Revolutions*, Chicago: University of Chicago Press, 1962, second edition, enlarged, 1970.

53   Fritjof Capra, *The Tao of Physics*, Wildwood House, Bungay: The Chaucer Press, 1975.

54   Bill Mollison, *Permaculture: A Practical Guide for a Sustainable Future*, Island Press, Washington DC, 1990, p. ix.

55   Declan Kennedy, "Permaculture Workshop: Urban and Rural Approaches to Community in Balance with Nature," *Conference Report of the First International Ecocity Conference*, Berkeley: Urban Ecology, 1990, p. 23.

56   Peter Calthorpe, "Transforming Suburbia," from *The First International Ecocity Conference Report*, Berkeley: Urban Ecology, 1990, p. 36.

57   "The Charter of the New Urbanism," pamphlet by the Congress of the New Urbanism, 1994.

58   Roberta Brandes Gratz and Norman Mintz, *Cities Back from the Edge: New Life for Downtown*, New York: Wiley, 1998.

59   Brandes and Mintz, *Back from the Edge*, p. 3.

60   Michael Kepp, "Curitiba's Creative Solutions: Learning from Lerner," *Choices: The Human Development Magazine*, November 1992 p. 24.

61   Margolis, "A Third World City that Works," *Choices*, p. 43.

62   Larry Beasley, "Vancouver, British Columbia: New Urban Neighbourhoods in Old Urban Ways," paper distributed at the "Urbanism: New and Other" conference, University of California, Berkeley, February 25, 2000.

63   Richard S. Levine, "Sustainable Development," in *Conference Report of the First International Ecocity Conference*, Berkeley: Urban Ecology 1990, p. 24.

64   Ivan Illich, *Energy and Equity*, New York: Harper and Row, 1974, p. 12.

65   A 1993 study by Runzheimer International Ltd., Runzheimer Park, Rochester, WI 53167-0009. Website: www.runzheimer.com.

66   John Witelegg, "Do Something Outrageous: Drive a Car Today," *Manchester Guardian*, August 3, 1993.

67   *Utne Reader*, September/October 1993, p. 57.

68   Matthew L. Wald, *New York Times*, March 16, 1994, p. 1.

69   Reuters, "Auto Industry is No. 1 Priority, Says Trade Negotiator," *San Francisco Chronicle*, March 6, 1992.

70   Marshall Berman, quoted by David Engwicht, *Towards an Eco-City: Calming the Traffic*, Sydney: Envirobook, Sydney, 1992, p. 75.

71 Peter Newman, "The Truth About Cars and Freeways," in *Conference Report of the First International Ecocity Conference,* Berkeley: Urban Ecology,1990, p. 43.

72 Dashka Slater, "Working on the Railroad," *The Express,* February 26, 1993, p.11.

73 Ed Ayres, "Breaking Away," *World Watch,* January 1, 1993, p. 10.

74 V. Setty Pendakur, "Bicycles: World Class Vehicles," in *Conference Report of the First International Ecocity Conference,* P. 43

75 Pendakur, ibid.

76 Ayres, "Breaking Away," p. 18.

77 Michael David Lipkan, in a letter to the editor, *Permaculture Activist,* 1993.

78 Bernard Rudolfsky, *Streets for People: a Primer for Americans,* Garden City: Anchor Press/Doubleday, 1969, p. 69.

79 From Torstenson and Buss interviews by Richard Register, February 1999.

80 Joel Crawford, *Car Free Cities,* Utrecht: Utrecht International, 2000.

81 James Kunstler, *The Geography of Nowhere,* New York: Simon and Schuster, 1993.

82 Peter van Dresser, *A Landscape for Humans,* Santa Fe: The Lightning Tree, 1972.

83 Anne Whiston Spirn, *The Granite Garden,* New York: Basic Books, 1984.

84 Stewart Brand, *How Buildings Learn,* New York: Viking, 1994.

85 Richard Register, *Ecocity Berkeley: Building Cities for a Healthy Future,* Berkeley: North Atlantic Books, 1987, p. 35.

86 Hazel Henderson, *Building a Win-Win World,* San Francisco: Berrett-Kohler, 1996, p.58.

87 Joan Bokaer, "Rebuilding Our Cities in Balance with Nature: A Proposal," Ithaca: EcoVillage at Ithaca, 1996, p.4.

88 Bokaer, ibid., p. 4.

89 Michael Parenti, *History as Mystery,* San Francisco: City Lights Books, 1999, p. 2.

90 Rick Pruetz, *Saved by Development: Preserving Environmental Areas, Farmland and Historic Landmarks with Transfer of Development Rights,* Marina del Rey: Ardje Press, 1998.

91 Al Gore, *Earth in the Balance,* Boston: Houghton Mifflin, 1992, p.325.

92 Jaime Lerner, "A Shared Course," video by Tim Alley, Berkeley, 1996.

93 Jaime Lerner, interview by Kirstin Miller, *Ecocity Builder Mini-Bulletin,* April 2000.

94 Jaime Lerner, ibid.

95 Berkeley Planning Commission and Berkeley Planning Staff, Berkeley Draft General Plan, version going from the Planning Commission to the City Council, July, 2001, Berkeley: City of Berkeley, 2001, p. 9.

Index

About the Author

Richard Register is an internationally-recognized urban design specialist and activist. He is the founder and President of Ecocity Builders, a non-govenrmental organization dedicated to environmentally-responsible urban development through public education and consulting with governments and planners. In 1990, Mr. Register initiated what has become a key component of the ecocity movement, the International Ecocity Conference, which has been held every two years since, on five different continents, attracting more than 2,000 participants. Mr. Register's consulting and educational activities have taken him to nineteen countries, including South Africa, Senegal, Brazil, Chile, Australia, China, India, Nepal, Finland and Austria. He also addresses audiences widely in the U.S. and has served as a public consultant on such issues as military base conversion and open space design. Mr. Register is the author of *Another Beginning* (Treehouse, 1987), *Ecocity Berkeley: Building Cities for a Healthy Future* (North Atlantic, 1987), and the editor of *Village Wisdom, Future Cities* (Ecocity Builders, 1997). He lives in Berkeley, California.

Inquiries regarding the work of Ecocity Builders and the International Ecocity Conferences may be addressed to: Ecocity Builders, 1678 Shattuck Avenue #66, Berkeley, California, 94709, or emailed to ecocity@igc.org.